Everyday
Justice

D1378317

Date Due

Contents

Figures

Tables

Preface

We judge each other every day. Wrongdoing and accountability for it are facts of human existence. But when we first set out to study the processes by which people are deemed responsible and punished for wrongdoing, we never imagined that the consequence would be a book comparing the United States and Japan.

In 1976, we began planning a survey of Detroit to ascertain how ordinary citizens judge wrongdoing in various settings. By happy accident, Hamilton got into a conversation about the project with Robert Cole, then the director of the Center for Japanese Studies at the University of Michigan. He asked the fateful question: "Why don't you replicate it in Japan?" Through Cole's contacts, we were able to build a collaborative relationship with a group of Japanese scholars who were also interested in studying how people judge wrongdoing. This book is our version—or vision—of the surveys of Detroit, Yokohama, and Kanazawa that resulted.

Acknowledgments

First, we owe a major intellectual debt to Robert Cole, for without his intervention the project would not have become a cross-cultural exploration of the judgment of wrongdoing.

This book is a companion piece to a Japanese volume, *Sekinin to Batsu no Ishiki-kozo* (The cognitive structure of responsibility and punishment), published in Tokyo in 1986. That book, edited by Zensuke Ishimura, Kazuhiko Tokoro, and Haruo Nishimura, is the Japanese-language report of our joint venture. The Japanese volume is primarily a scientific report of our surveys and of additional research done by its editors and the other members of the Japanese research team (Yoko Hosoi, Nozomu Matsubara, and Nobuho Tomita). This book, in contrast, ranges farther from the data in an attempt to present a model of the relation between individual and society in two cultures. If it contains egregious errors in its image of Japan, these are our errors, not those of our Japanese colleagues.

In this collaboration, we have benefited especially from the help of Kazuhiko Tokoro, professor of law at Rikkyo University in Tokyo. He has graciously read and commented on an earlier version of the manuscript and has on numerous occasions provided us with bibliographic advice. In particular, he has helped us to address the problem that our view of Japanese law and society may be colored by the fact that we do not read Japanese. He and other scholars of Japanese law and society, both American and Japanese, have been sources of information about Japanese-language publications. In this regard, special thanks go to Professors Frank Upham of Boston College Law School, Setsuo Miyazawa of Kobe University, and Takeo Tanase of Kyoto University for their books and articles that bring Japanese research findings to English-speaking audiences.

We also wish to thank the students of the University of Michigan's 1977 Detroit Area Study and its director, Robert Groves, for their role in the creation and execution of the U.S. survey. A number of individuals over the years have assisted in the data analysis report here. Among them, we are particularly grateful to Richard Hogan, Mark Vaitkus, and John Boies, who served as research assistants or consultants while graduate students at Michigan. Research assistant Kiseon Chung at the University of Maryland did a superb job of proofreading the manuscript and preparing the index.

We also received help from a number of people in our efforts to translate the study's concepts and content into Japanese. At Michigan, Carol Yorkievitz and Richard Beardsley translated during our initial meetings with Japanese scholars. Shunichi Kato advised us on the initial translation of the Detroit survey instrument. Naoko Komyo served as translator for two crucial meetings in which we reviewed the Detroit data, evaluated the Yokohama study, and planned the Kanazawa survey; she also identified the minor translation problems in the Yokohama instrument that were subsequently corrected in Kanazawa (see chapter 5). Later, Masami Iburi translated the open-ended Yokohama punishment items discussed in chapter 7. Hamilton would also like to thank a number of individuals who have attempted to teach her the words, concepts, and culture of Japan: Mutsuko Endo-Simon, who patiently provided formal instruction in Japanese at the University of Michigan, and Hiroshi Akoh, John Campbell, Mark Fruin, Kanae Miura, Takemi Nagamura, and Kazuko Tsurumi, most of whom she met in Tokyo and all of whom know far more about Japan than she ever will. In Tokyo, we both owe a debt of gratitude to the International House of Japan. Since 1978, it has provided us a place to stay, to think, and to meet both Japanese and American scholars who are studying Japan.

A number of people helped shape the final manuscript. We wish to thank those scholars of law, Japan, and social psychology who were not part of the research project but who were generous with their time in reading earlier drafts of part or all of the manuscript: John Braithwaite, John Campbell, William Hadden, Robert Kidder, James Lincoln, Frank Munger, Mark Ramseyer, Morris Rosenberg, and Stanley Presser. We are particularly grateful to two of the reviewers for Yale University Press: both an initial anonymous reviewer whose comments inspired a number of revisions and a final reviewer, Neil Vidmar, who liked what resulted. At Yale University Press, we were fortunate to have a wonderful copy editor, Jeff Cook, and manuscript editor, Laura Dooley; heartfelt thanks to editor Gladys Topkis for believing in the first draft enough to encourage us to submit a second.

A number of agencies and institutions supported this research. On the American side, primary support came from the National Science Foundation, Law and Social Science Program (grant no. SOC-77-242918). Seed monies were also provided by the Social Science Research Council and the University of Michigan, and travel money for one meeting with the Japanese group was supplied by the Ford Foundation. In addition, Hamilton received a Social Science Research Council grant to make two extended visits to Japan in 1980 and 1981. In Japan, the investigators were supported by grants from the Nihon Gakujutsu Shinkokai (Japan Society for the Promotion of Science) and Mombusho (Ministry of Education). Sanders received support during the writing of this book from the University of Houston Law Foundation. Without the encouragement of these agencies, this book would not have been possible.

PART ONE   Structure and Culture

_____

1

The Problem of Responsibility

People the world over seek justice when they or their loved ones have been wronged or harmed. To obtain justice we have to establish who is responsible for what happened, and then we want punishment for the offender, restitution for the injured, or both. But cultures and individuals differ in the grounds for seeking justice—the reasons we think someone else is responsible for what has gone wrong.

Empirically, this is a book about responsibility and sanctions, about what makes wrongdoing wrong and what should be done about it. Images of the offender—the *responsible actor*—vary dramatically across and within cultures as a function of the social ties and obligations between actor and victim. Theoretically, the book treats responsibility and sanction as core aspects of *legal culture*. By legal culture we mean the attitudes, values, and opinions held with regard to law, the legal system, and the process of holding someone accountable (L. Friedman, 1977). This includes values and attitudes about whether to take disputes to law, how to conceptualize a dispute, how disputes are to be settled, and even how to view the actor who is held responsible.

When the judgments of other individuals differ from our own, we often decide that these others are peculiar. When nations differ, the citizens of each are tempted to attribute the difference to the strange "culture" or "customs" of the other. Both explanations basically relabel the phenomenon without showing what its origins are. Although this book will pay a great deal of attention to cultural differences in responsibility and other aspects of legal culture, our perspective is fundamentally social structural. We search for concrete social facts that can account for "cultural" differences. We do so on two levels, attempting to suggest a social structural basis for how individuals *or* nations may come to differ in their judgments of wrongdoing.

A recent issue in sociological theory concerns the relation between explanation at the level of individual interactions and explanation at the level of larger units, including the nation-state. This relation has been termed the micro-macro link (Alexander, Giesen, Munch, & Smelser, 1987). Although there are many useful ways to distinguish micro and macro phenomena,[1] our approach is perhaps most similar to Blau's (1987) distinction: "Microsociology analyzes the underlying social processes that engender relations between persons. The focus is on social interaction and communications, and important concepts are reciprocity, significant symbols, obligations, exchange, and dependence. Macrosociology analyzes the structure of different positions in a population and their constraints on social relations. The focus is on the external limitations of the social environment on people's relations, and important concepts are differentiation, institutions, inequality, heterogeneity, and crosscutting circles" (pp. 71–72).

Micro-macro distinctions are particularly useful when examining legal phenomena. Law, at least in complex societies, is a set of organizational structures (courts) and rules of behavior (laws) that impinge on and shape behavior; at the same time, it is a set of case-by-case interactions and judgments that involve obligations, exchange, and dependency. Moreover, legal judgments are a window into a culture's perceptions of what it is to be an actor in that culture. As Coleman (1986) notes: "All case law is based inherently on a theory of action. For example, modern Western law, both continental law and English common law, is based on the conception of purposeful individuals with rights and interests, who are responsible for their actions" (p. 1313). The same may be said of non-Western law. Legal culture reflects a theory of responsibility for one's actions. In turn, legal culture reflects on the larger culture of which it is a part.

This book involves both a microsociology and a macrosociology of responsibility and punishment. Explaining judgments concerning particular acts of wrongdoing is a problem in microsociology; explaining the aggregate judgments (or actions) of whole social units, such as nations, is a problem in macrosociology. The relationship between micro and macro processes is one of both articulation and causal direction. For example, although in a common law system a macrolevel body of rules is constructed in part through a process of examining the microlevel activities and judgments in individual cases, the final body of rules is not simply some additive function of the outcome of the cases (Coleman, 1990; Whippler & Lindenberg, 1987). Furthermore, causal relationships go in both directions: if micro actions maintain or alter macrolevel rules and institutions, these macro social arrangements in turn shape the nature of micro actions and judgments.

Given this perspective, a preliminary note about the data reported in this book is in order. Our data come from the responses of individuals to vignettes describing acts of wrongdoing.[2] The unit of analysis is the individual. Theoretically, however, we do not believe that individual judgments are solely or inevitably a reflection of micro processes. As Alexander et al. (1987) note, the "equation of micro with individual is extremely misleading, as, indeed, is the attempt to find any specific size correlation with the micro/macro difference" (p. 290). At a microlevel, different social relationships between and obligations of the parties involved in a dispute lead to different judgments of responsibility and punishment. However, judgments are also shaped by the overall structure of relationships in society. At the macrolevel, we will argue that differences in the distribution of relationships of different types shape perceptions of what it is to be an actor in general and a *responsible* actor in particular; in turn, these perceptions can help explain observed differences in the pattern of Japanese and American judgments and ultimately in Japanese and American legal systems.

These two societies are especially important ones for social scientists to understand. Discussions of their differences with respect to how law is conceived of, resorted to, or ignored frequently degenerate into stereotypes about a lawless and litigious United States versus a mysteriously harmonious Japan. The following stories appear to fit these common stereotypes.

Conflict and Harmony

On August 2, 1985, a Delta Air Lines jumbo jet crashed in Dallas, killing 137 people. The lawyers gathered soon thereafter: "Survivor Esther Ledford, 37, having endured the impact, the flames, and a 15- or 20-foot fall from her seat to the ground, was in bed at 7:30 a.m. when her husband, Roger, turned away two representatives of the airline's insurance carrier who wanted to see her. They left their cards . . . offered to pay her bills and urged that he call them" (Sawyer, 1985, p. A14).

Indeed, lawyers for both sides descended upon the survivors so quickly and aggressively that the Dallas County district attorney's office and the State Bar of Texas investigated. The litigation over the following years was characterized by bitter accusations of behavior that was at best unseemly, if not immoral:

> In a case tried in Dallas, Fort Lauderdale resident Katheren Ann Reynolds claimed her marriage to Paul Reynolds, who died in the crash, was "idyllic and made in heaven" . . .
>
> Delta attorney Frank Finn said the investigation indicated the claims were "fairy tales." He produced testimony that Reynolds used cocaine, had a drinking problem and had not filed a tax return since 1980. . . .

Katheren Reynolds' attorney . . . said the investigation of Reynolds amounted to a "shakedown." Investigators made surveillance films and sent a letter to a neighbor saying, "Call us so we don't have to subpoena you." . . .

Bob Montgomery, attorney for the parents of Scott Ageloff, 29, who died in the crash, objected when Delta lawyers said they might introduce evidence that Ageloff was allegedly a homosexual and thereby increased his risk of exposure to the fatal disease AIDS. Delta lawyers said that might have affected Ageloff's future earning capacity and life expectancy. ("Crash Survivors," 1986)

The actions of those who acted for Delta seemed designed to intensify resentment and animosity against the airline. From their point of view, of course, these same actions were taken to limit the company's damages in a court of law.

Ten days after the Delta crash, a Japan Air Lines jumbo jet crashed into Mt. Ogura on the island of Honshu. The subsequent actions of JAL reveal a very different attitude toward responsibility:

The president of Japan Air Lines faced the relatives of victims of the world's worst single plane disaster and bowed low and long.

He turned to a wall covered with wooden tablets bearing the victims' names. He bowed again. Then, in a voice that sometimes quavered, Yasumoto Takagi asked for forgiveness and accepted responsibility.

The ceremony . . . marked the final memorial service sponsored by the airline for the 520 people who died in the Japan Air Lines crash on Aug. 12.

For Mr. Takagi and his employees, the service marked the culmination of a two-month exercise in accountability. . . . In the days after the accident, when family members had to travel to a small mountain village to identify the bodies, airline staff stayed with them, paying all expenses, bringing them food, drink, and clean clothes. Even after most of the bodies were identified, the airline assigned two staff members to each family to attend to needs as varied as arranging for funerals or blocking obtrusive reporters.

JAL set up a scholarship fund to pay for the education of children who lost parents in the crash. It spent $1.5 million on . . . elaborate memorial services. The airline dispatched executives to every victim's funeral, although some were turned away. And Mr. Takagi has pledged to resign soon as a gesture of responsibility. (Chira, 1985)

Mr. Takagi kept his pledge to resign, consistent with Japanese ideas about who is responsible for what, and with what consequences.

These stories are near-perfect examples of the stereotypes many of us hold about law and justice in the United States and Japan. But the stereotypes are overstated. The litigiousness of Americans or the harmoniousness of Japanese arises from the nature of the social relationships of the people involved—the textures of their lives. As relationships change, so too may the process of resolving disputes. Consider the controversy surrounding the construction of Narita Airport outside Tokyo: "The first confrontations occurred in 1967; between 1971 and 1977 pitched battles were fought at various interludes. The farmers and militants built forts, towers, underground bunkers and tunnels to obstruct the clearing of land, the leveling of houses, the obliteration of grave sites, and the construction of roads and facilities. Major violence ended in 1978 with a final large-scale confrontation. Just as the first stage of the airport was about to open, militants stormed the control tower, cut the main cables, and destroyed valuable electronic equipment" (Apter & Sawa, 1984, pp. 80–81).

The events at Narita serve to illustrate two important points about social conflict in Japan. First, for all its social harmony, Japan is not immune to instances of extreme upheaval and violence. Second, the intensity of these instances is probably related to the cultural insistence on harmony.

Just as nasty conflict is not an American monopoly, neither is profound reverence for harmony a Japanese monopoly. Consider the view held by the Baptists of a small Southern town, here called Hopewell: "Ted and Eileen, a local couple, had not been married for more than a year or two but were considering a separation. . . . One night as they were driving home, they were caught in a tornado—not uncommon in the early spring—and were paralyzed with fear. As the winds abated, they realized that they were clinging to each other. . . . Their survival without injury led them both to decide that Jesus had been the author of the storm and that he had brought them through it so that they could realize their love for him and each other . . . the things they had been arguing about were not important" (Greenhouse, 1986, p. 45).

In the religious beliefs of Ted and Eileen and others like them, notions of legal conflict and even of rules themselves are subordinated to a vision of harmony.[3] "Baptists do not conceptualize or discuss conflict in terms of cases or rules but in terms of salvation. Cases and the adversary model of conflict are entirely extraneous to this idea. The difference between harmony and conflict is not one between the sanctity and violation of rules and their lapse, or even the Bible's exhortations, but simply the difference between salvation and damnation. . . . The only valid remedy, in the Baptists' eyes, is salvation" (Greenhouse, 1986, p. 118). In such a setting the importance of Romans 13:19—"Avenge not yourselves . . . I will repay, saith the Lord"—is hardly surprising (Greenhouse, 1986, p. 109).

The same American society that produced Delta Air Line's lawyers also produced Hopewell's Baptists; the same Japanese society that taught Mr. Takagi to accept responsibility without hesitation also chronicles a long history of peasant uprisings that inspired the members of the Narita movement in their struggle against the government. Cultures are not all of a piece. In part, they flow from and incorporate varying social structural realities. The reality of a Dallas lawyer is not that of a small-town Baptist housewife, nor is the reality of a Japanese executive that of a radical student or militant farmer. This book examines responsibility and justice within and across cultures by stressing the impact of the structure of social relationships.

Dimensions of Social Life

Social relationships can be thought of in terms of two fundamental dimensions: vertical and horizontal ties to others. We will refer to the vertical dimension as *hierarchy* and to the horizontal dimension as *solidarity*.[4] Various linguistic, legal, and sociological sources suggest that hierarchy is a key dimension of social life (e.g., Blau, 1964; Brown, 1965; Dahrendorf, 1959; Green, 1930; Weber, 1947). Some role relationships are normally thought of as relationships between equals while others are between superordinate and subordinate; hierarchy refers to variation in authority or standing between the parties. Formal hierarchy may be counteracted by economic resources or other power, and it should not be confused with such power. For example, a buyer may be powerless when a seller gains a monopoly, yet society does not make a structural distinction between buyers and sellers; one role is not considered dominant over the other, nor is one participant considered responsible for the actions of the other. The same can be said about friends and about co-workers of equal rank. Such dyads differ from employer-employee, teacher-student, and parent-child dyads. Typical positions on the hierarchy dimension are those of authority (superior-subordinate relations) versus equality (equal-equal relations).

Relationships also vary in the extent of solidarity between the parties. High solidarity refers to strong ties of personal closeness and identification, embodies long-standing and enduring connections, and taps the multiple and noncommensurate ways in which individuals may relate to one another.

Table 1.1   Social Scientific Distinctions: Closeness of Social Ties

Theorist	Distinction	
I. Dynamic trends		
Gluckman (1967)	Multiplex	Simplex
Nader (1969)	Multiplex	Simplex
Maine (1963)	Status	Contract
Tonnies (1957)	Gemeinschaft	Gesellschaft
Durkheim (1933)	Mechanical solidarity	Organic solidarity
Parsons (1951)	Ascribed	Achieved
	Particularistic	Universal
	Diffuse	Specific
II. Distinctions within modern society		
Cooley (1909)	Primary group	Secondary group
Blau (1964)	Intrinsic exchange	Extrinsic exchange
	Integrative institution	Distributive institution
Clark and Mills (1979)	Communal	Exchange

Highly solidary ties are extensive, permanent, unalterable, and individually unique. The parties share a collective identity (e.g., family) based on the bond of their relationship. In low-solidarity relationships the ties are more limited, temporary, voluntary, and interchangeable; they exhibit an absence of closeness between autonomous individuals; and they involve unidimensional and closely monitored exchanges. Extreme examples of low-solidarity ties are interactions between strangers who have no connection outside of an accident, crime, or other unfortunate event.

Many social scientists have argued that solidarity—or something very like it—is a key dimension of social life. In some fields, theorists have drawn distinctions that are intended or generally interpreted to be *developmental:* Societies or social groups progress from one pole to another in the course of becoming an industrial, market, or modern society. In legal anthropology, as table 1.1 indicates, an important distinction has been drawn between *multiplex* and *simplex* relations (Gluckman, 1967; Nader, 1969). Multiplexity connotes standing in multiple roles vis-à-vis the other party, as in working for one's uncle, the grocer. In jurisprudence there is Henry Maine's (1906/1963) distinction between *status* and *contract* as bases of social order. Status connotes permanent, irrevocable ties between persons who are not conceived of as separate "entities," as in feudal society. Contract connotes the modern legal individual, who stands separate from others and can form—or break—legal bonds with them. And in sociology, a host of relevant distinctions have been drawn: Tonnies' (1887/1957) *Gemeinschaft* (community) versus *Gesell-*

schaft (society); Durkheim's (1893/1933) *mechanical* versus *organic* solidarity, referring to the division of labor; and Parsons' (1951) *ascribed, particularistic,* and *diffuse* relations versus *achieved, universalistic,* and *specific* relations.

A second, more social psychological, group of distinctions typically refers to variations in relationships within a modern society. Thus, Cooley (1909/1962) distinguished between *primary groups,* such as family, and *secondary groups,* such as voluntary associations (see table 1.1). In psychology, recent research has contrasted *communal* and *exchange* relations (Clark & Mills, 1979; Clark, Quellette, Powell, & Milberg, 1987; Mills & Clark, 1982; see also Aron, Aron, Tudor, & Nelson, 1991). In communal relations the parties have a commonality of interest, while in exchange relations the parties are individuals negotiating for personal benefit. Similarly, Blau's (1964) social psychological distinction between *intrinsic* and *extrinsic* exchange involves relations in which the partner has inherent value versus those in which the partner is incidental to an ulterior gain. Unlike the dynamic trends in societal development, shifts in these exchanges are frequently from low solidarity (extrinsic exchange) to high solidarity (intrinsic exchange)—as when, for example, one gets to know the postal worker or the grocer learns one's name. Paralleling these personal exchanges, Blau (1964) also contrasts institutions as *integrative* (e.g., family) versus *distributive* (e.g., economic institutions of production). Integrative institutions emphasize intrinsic exchange; distributive institutions, extrinsic exchange.

Overall, these social scientific distinctions involving hierarchy and solidarity capture much of the content of the relations we wish to consider. However, the allocation of responsibility rests on the existence of third parties: other people whose explicit or implicit expectations help to define the obligations of the actors. Thus in order to be an authority you need a subordinate, but you also need some other person or persons who define you as the authority; similarly, with regard to the dimension of solidarity, marriage partners are defined as such by the state as well as by their personal decision. Our dimensions of hierarchy and solidarity are intended to capture not only relationships between people but also the social enforcement of responsibility by others viewing the dyad.

Together hierarchy and solidarity create a typology of relationships (see fig. 1.1). Each quadrant in figure 1.1 represents a particular social relationship that characterizes a combination of hierarchy and solidarity. The four ideal types of social relations represented in this two-dimensional typology are meant to serve as exemplars of the combinations in question. These social roles should not be seen as discrete categories, nor should sharp distinctions between the quadrants be inferred.[5]

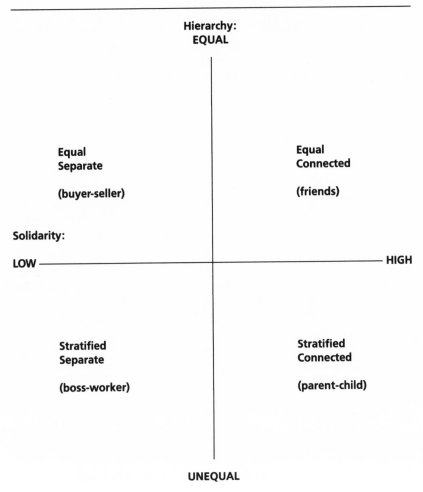

Figure 1.1   Dimensions of Social Relationships

These ways of relating to other persons can be thought of in several ways. Within any society, some roles more closely correspond to a particular quadrant of the figure than others. Buyer-seller, friend-friend, boss-worker, and parent-child are each dyads that appear to fall naturally in one of the four quadrants, and each exemplifies a different relationship type. Buyer and seller, or friend and friend, are each at least formally equal, but they differ in the closeness that can typically be presumed for their relationship. Similarly, although boss-worker and parent-child dyads are both asymmetrical, characterized by authority and subordination, the solidarity of the bond between parent and child can be presumed to be far greater. Between societies, differences can also be observed in the characteristic form or forms of social relationships. In societies such as Japan, people spend more of their time in— and more often think in terms of—relationships characterized by stratification and interconnection. In contrast, Americans spend more of their time in relationships of equality and separation.

Human Action and Responsibility

Responsibility and punishment, the core concepts of this book, are central issues in the life of groups and individuals. Decisions about these issues permeate social interaction. They determine fines, jail terms, and death sentences; they lie behind lost jobs, docked wages, and attached bank accounts; they lead to school suspensions, lost privileges, and paddled bottoms. To clarify the factors that people use in judging responsibility and determining sanction is to clarify how they understand the moral rules of their society. From our perspective, why and how we blame others is organically linked to what we decide to do about it; punishment presupposes responsibility. Together, the attribution of responsibility and the imposition of sanctions are at the heart of a society's legal culture.

Determining responsibility is a complex matter. Which events are defined as occasions when it may be appropriate to assign responsibility to someone? What factors are considered in judging whether a person is responsible and whether that person should be sanctioned? Do these factors vary with the type of situation or outcome? Do they vary with the personal attributes of the actor being judged or of the individual doing the judging? Are cultural differences part of decisions about responsibility? Our purpose is to outline a general theoretical perspective concerning responsibility allocation that builds on the model of social structure outlined above. In part II we relate this perspective to data on responsibility allocation in the United States and Japan.

A theory of responsibility requires a theory of causation and a theory of human action. The causal question is usually a component of the question of responsibility: In what sense must a person's behavior be the cause of an event in order for the person to be responsible for the event? The concept of causation has been problematic, however, at least since Hume. For simplicity, our own research concentrates on exploring wrongdoing in which causation is not an issue.[6]

Next come questions of action. What does it mean to be a human actor? Which of our behaviors deserve the label "actions"? Although there are many views on these issues, it is widely agreed among philosophers that "intentional action is the highest level of behavior undertaken by persons. It is the kind of activity for which persons are primarily legally and morally responsible" (Brand, 1984, p. 32; see also Davis, 1979; Hornsby, 1980; Shaver, 1985). At the other end of the spectrum are behaviors that are commonly thought not to be "our actions" at all, such as fainting or experiencing a seizure. These actions are not intentional, nor are they preventable: we are not the *agents* of these behaviors. Between these two extremes are things we did not intend but which, nevertheless, are under our control in the sense that we could have avoided them. Many accidents are not "unavoidable"; they are at least partly the product of our actions, and they are outcomes that could have been avoided in some sense. For example, many automobile accidents are the result of a person's carelessness or negligence; if the person had been more attentive or more careful, had the person exercised more prudence or foresight, the accident could have been avoided.

Within these broad categories are many nuances to human actions that further describe what we do and what we could have done. The adjectives and adverbs of performance modify our actions into a thousand shades of meaning. We do things thoughtfully or flippantly. We are clumsy or precise in our actions. We are childlike or mature in our judgments about what to do. We are "merely" thoughtless or we are evil in our purposes (Feinberg, 1970).

Meanings of Responsibility

The term *responsibility* is used in many ways that often engender confusion. Legal scholars and psychologists have attempted to distinguish differences in the use of the term. One of the more important explorations of the meaning of responsibility is that of H. L. A. Hart (1968):

> As captain of the ship, X was responsible for the safety of his passengers and crew. But on his last voyage he got drunk every night and was responsible for the loss of the ship with all aboard. It was rumored that he was insane, but the doctors considered that he was responsible for his actions. Throughout the voyage he behaved quite irresponsibly, and various incidents in his career showed that he was not a responsible person. He always maintained that the exceptional winter storms were responsible for the loss of the ship, but in the legal proceedings brought against him he was found criminally responsible for his negligent conduct, and in separate civil proceedings he was held legally responsible for the loss of life and property. He is still alive and he is morally responsible for the deaths of many women and children. (p. 211)

In this passage *responsibility* takes on at least four meanings, according to Hart. Together, these meanings can constitute a model for the attribution of responsibility. Therefore it is important to review each in some detail. Although responsibility can be an issue in the administration of rewards—positive sanctions—this discussion will examine only negative behaviors and outcomes because of the book's focus on wrongdoing.

CAUSATION. At times the word *responsible* is used as a synonym for *cause*. To be responsible for something is to have caused it, as in "My father's death is responsible for my grief" or "The winter storms are responsible for the loss of the ship." Although this usage is not particularly helpful because it does not distinguish human acts from other possible causes, it does remind us that attribution of responsibility almost always includes a purely causal element. Generally people are not responsible for things with which they have no causal relationship. Thus Shultz and Schleifer (1983) argue that at the very least "a judgment of moral responsibility presupposes one of causation" (p. 59). But the nature of the required causal relationship can be difficult to define. Causal relationships can become so attenuated through time and space that they are no longer thought to be sufficiently strong to support an attribution of responsibility. The acts of others may intervene between the individual's conduct and the outcome. Multiple acts, each in itself sufficient, may join together to produce an untoward event. The result of some behavior may be so bizarre or unforeseeable that we are reluctant to hold someone responsible. For these and other reasons the causal question can become quite complex in formal legal systems (Hart & Honoré, 1959). At a minimum, however, in most cases where responsibility is assigned there must be, in the language of tort law, a "cause in fact" relationship between the individual's behavior and the consequence. The behavior must be a necessary part of a minimal set of conditions sufficient to produce the consequence (Mackie, 1965).

CAPACITY. To be "responsible for one's actions" is to have the capacity to respond. The legally insane and minor children are often thought to lack the capacity to be criminally responsible. Incapacity, however, is relative to the activity under question. Young children may not be capable of violating the criminal law, as they are presumed to be unable to form the necessary "guilty mind" or intent (*mens rea*), but they are routinely held responsible for wrongdoing by their parents.

ROLE OBLIGATION. The meaning of responsibility can vary according to whether expectations of performance are fulfilled or violated. A "responsible" citizen or worker is one who fulfills expectations. But a person who fails to perform some task satisfactorily is considered "responsible" in a negative sense and is liable to be punished. Because the tasks people are required to perform are tied to the roles they occupy, Hart (1968) calls this type of responsibility "role responsibility." Thus responsibility is connected to the rules and obligations attached to tasks and roles. The broadest role is that of an emancipated member of a society; hence obligations even attach to the unavoidable condition of personhood. Some obligations are a matter of personal civility, convention, or etiquette; others are better described as moral norms; still others are backed by the sanctions of criminal or civil law.

Specific roles incur obligations that modify and magnify the general obligations of personhood (Hamilton, 1978b, 1986). Thus Hart notes that "as the captain of the ship, X was responsible for the safety of his passengers and crew." Hart's definition of the captain's responsibility is couched in the most general and expansive terms. Within this overall obligation are numerous specific obligations, such as remaining sober on the job. The ways in which obligations attach to roles can be understood in terms of hierarchy and solidarity; relationships of authority over others and relationships in which close ties can be presumed each engender responsibility on the basis of role.

Looking first at the dimension of hierarchy, higher-status roles typically involve obligations that are more numerous and more generalized. Occupants of these roles are responsible for a set of diffuse obligations to act. In Hart's story, the captain is "responsible for" the entire ship, including supervisory responsibilities over many other individuals. Actors in lower-status roles do not usually have these diffuse obligations. Their responsibility is tied to more specific rules and obligations. Overall there are fewer, and narrower, expectations for such roles.

The existence of role-based responsibility provides an important exception to the requirement of a "cause in fact" relationship between person and deed. Vicarious responsibility of a legal or moral nature may be assigned to an individual because of a relationship to another who has produced some untoward consequence. Responsibility on this basis is most richly developed as a formal part of law in the military context, where superiors can be held responsible for the actions of their subordinates (Hamilton, 1978a, 1986; Kelman & Hamilton, 1989). Even in the civilian realm, employers are generally civilly responsible for the torts of their employees under the doctrine of *respondeat superior* ("let the superior answer"). That is, liability may be based on the existence of the role relationship as well as on the employer's actual behavior with respect to role obligations in the relationship.

Solidarity—the closeness of ties—also helps to produce the presumption of obligations toward the other party. Outside of workplace relationships, parent-child ties are a main arena for appeals to role responsibility. In dealing with their children, parents are authorities as well as closely tied parties. A parent may be responsible for the tort of a child, either solely because of the role relationship—pure vicarious liability—or because of some failure to supervise or control the child. For example, Texas, like many American states, statutorily creates pure parental vicarious liability with the following language: "A parent or other person who has the duty of control and reasonable discipline of a child is liable for any property damage proximately caused by . . . (2) The willful and malicious conduct of a child who is at least 12 years of age but under 18 years of age" [Texas Family Code 33.01 (Vernon, 1986)]. Note that Texas holds parents liable only for property damage, and only for malicious behavior of children of a certain age. Moreover, there is a cap of fifteen thousand dollars for liability. Under most situations vicarious liability is rarely and narrowly applied in American law.

Failure to adequately supervise is also grounds for liability. Thus, for example, parents may be guilty of "negligent entrustment" by giving a minor child access to the family car if they know that the child is a very dangerous driver. In this sense the parents are not vicariously responsible, but rather are responsible for their own activities. Nevertheless, the activities are negligent only because the parents had special obligations with respect to their child, their property (the automobile), or both. A person has no general obligation to take steps to prevent a neighbor's child, who is also known to be a bad driver, from gaining access to the neighbor's family car.

LEGAL AND MORAL LIABILITY. When a person is accused of failing to perform some task adequately, he or she may be called upon to explain what happened—to provide an answer for the allegation of wrongdoing. When the captain claimed that storms were responsible for the loss of the ship, he was attempting to answer the allegation that he was responsible for the loss of his ship. Hart (1968) notes that etymologically, the core meaning of *responsibility* seems to involve the notion of having "to answer" (as in the Latin *repondere,* to answer).

When a person has a general capacity to follow rules and has apparently failed to satisfy a general norm or specific rule of role behavior, the person may be called upon to answer as to why he or she failed to follow the norm. An inadequate answer means the person is liable for sanctions. Until we hear the answer, we usually do not know whether or how much to blame someone for some act of wrongdoing. The existence of an answering process indicates that responsibility is a social phenomenon, a relationship between people.

Answers may be more or less successful. There are different types of answers that, if successful, will excuse or mitigate a finding of responsibility. On the other hand, a person who is unable to provide a satisfactory answer may be held liable and subjected to sanctions. Thus *liability,* whether explicitly legal or entirely moral, is Hart's final category of nuances of the meaning of responsibility.

Types of Answers

The existence of answers reveals the relationship among the obligations of roles, human action, and the nature of responsibility. Perhaps the most frequent answer to criminal charges, *denial* ("I didn't do it"), is relatively uninteresting conceptually. It is another way of raising the question of causal relationship by severing the connection between the accused and the untoward event.

A second answer might be given by a parent alleged to be responsible for the behavior of another family's child; a reasonable answer under those circumstances is what lawyers call a *demurrer.* This answer essentially says "so what?" It is a plea that says "yes, I did what you say, but there is no rule making me responsible for that action"—or, in blunt terms, "Don't blame me, that's not my job." A demurrer asserts that for this role, under these circumstances, there is no duty to behave in a certain way. The proper response of the ship's cook to the loss of the ship is a demurrer.

Similar to demurrers are *collateral defenses* that challenge the right of someone to enforce a rule. "What's it to you?" does not necessarily deny that a norm has been violated, but it does deny that the speaker must answer to this particular accuser.

Legal *justifications* go one step beyond demurrers. Where a demurrer says "it wasn't my job to do otherwise," a justification says "hey, I was doing exactly what I was supposed to do, or more." In short, a justification is an assertion that what one did was the right thing to do. In military law, for example, receiving superior orders is treated as a legal justification for one's action; to follow orders is what the soldier is normally supposed to do. In civilian or military contexts, justification is sometimes based upon an appeal to some "higher law," principle, or rule. Various forms of civil disobedience, conscientious objection, and religious sanctuary are usually accompanied by justifications rather than excuses. The legal system recognizes some justifications. For example, shooting a person who is committing a major felony is usually a justifiable homicide. (See Tedeschi & Reiss, 1981, for a typology of justifications.)

If demurrers, collateral defenses, and justifications indicate ways in which responsibility is tied to roles, *excuses* indicate how responsibility is connected to concepts of human action. Excuses are a type of what Erving Goffman (1971) calls "remedial work" designed "to change the meaning that otherwise might be given to an act, transforming what could be seen as offensive into what can be seen as acceptable" (p. 109). As J. L. Austin (1961) notes, an excuse admits that what happened was not a good thing to have done, but "that it is not quite fair or correct to say *baldly* 'X did A'" (p. 2). Excuses come in many varieties, and many taxonomies might be applied in understanding them (e.g., Bies, 1987; Schonbach, 1980, 1985; Scott & Lyman, 1968; Semin & Manstead, 1983; Shaver, 1985; Sykes & Matza, 1957; Tedeschi & Reiss, 1981).

Most excuses speak to the two distinguishing elements of human action: agency and purpose. If, as Francis Raab (1968) has suggested, there are two criteria for full moral responsibility, that the "agent did what he did intentionally and that he could have helped doing what he did" (p. 702), excuses indicate ways in which our actions were not fully intentional (motivational excuses) or were in some relevant way inescapable under the circumstances (situational excuses), or both. In Hart's story, the captain's claim that storms were responsible is a situational excuse that says, essentially, that given the seriousness of the storms there was nothing the captain could have done.[7] What was intended (whether the act was done "on purpose") and what one was capable of doing (whether the act was avoidable) are key ingredients in responsibility.

Some rules of behavior are such that certain excuses will not work to exculpate the actor. As Heider (1958) and other social psychologists have noted, and as even a casual examination of legal systems demonstrates, it is possible to speak of types or levels of responsibility that allow for different excuses. For example, lack of intention will excuse one from a first-degree murder charge, but not from a manslaughter charge. Lack of negligence will normally excuse us from responsibility for traffic accidents, but not for manufacturing a defective product. Even within legal categories the variety of excusing conditions is quite complex, and similar excuses may meet with different responses (Lempert & Sanders, 1986; Packer, 1968).

These points from philosophy and jurisprudence yield the conclusion that responsibility is contingent upon at least two factors: what the person did, and what the person was obliged to do. General obligations may apply to anyone in any situation; social roles also impose further, more specific obligations. These specific obligations are at the core of our conception of differences within and between legal cultures; in terms of dimensions of social life, they follow both from the person's hierarchical position and from closeness of social ties.

The combination of what a person did and what he or she was obliged to do defines what it is to be a *responsible actor*. At the macrosociological level, structural and cultural differences between Japan and the United States produce different understandings of the responsible actor; at the micro-sociological level, differences in role relationships within cultures lead to differences in perceptions of wrongdoers and to differences in responsibility allocation. According to the perspective outlined above, two fundamental dimensions of social relations—the hierarchy and solidarity of relation-ships—govern variations in judgment of wrongdoing that occur both within cultures and across cultures.[8] The variations across cultures occur because of differences in the characteristic social ties that people experience, not be-cause of some mysterious cultural force that leads them to see right and wrong differently.

The further development of this view of responsibility is closely tied to the empirical research reported here. The research is based on predictions about how responsibility judgments should vary within and between Japan and the United States based on the nature of social ties and the content of deeds. In the United States a person tends to be perceived by self and others as an *individual* actor whose identity and sense of self stand apart from the commu-nity, while in Japan a person is perceived by self and others as a *contextual* actor whose identity is, in substantial part, defined by social relationships. Greater emphasis on role obligations is consistent with a contextual or network view of perpetrators; greater emphasis on deeds is consistent with seeing individuals as isolated entities. In turn, the response to responsibil-ity—the possible punishment—that is consistent with a contextual view is to restore the role relations. The response to responsibility that is consistent with the individualistic view is to isolate the perpetrator.

Conclusions

To ask questions about topics like responsibility is to ask questions about how we understand human action itself. Such an investigation covers—or invades—the territory of a number of disciplines. We have noted that the model has both a microsociological and a macrosociological level. In addi-tion, the substantive themes represent the interests of social psychology, law, and Japanese studies. From a social psychological standpoint, the investiga-tion is one of attribution processes and, to some extent, conceptions of the self in a legal context. From a legal standpoint, it can be seen as a cross-cultural investigation of the micro and macro components of legal culture. From the standpoint of Japanese studies, this work may help to highlight similarities and differences between Japanese and American legal culture and society. The result, we hope, will be meaningful and applicable across an array of disciplines.

The argument of the book forms a set of concentric circles. At the core, and at the most empirical level, it demonstrates certain things about the nature of responsibility and the allocation of punishment. At a middle, theoretical level, it links these findings to a general conception of cultural trends in the United States and Japan. A parsimonious account of individual, microlevel judgments of wrongdoing and of societal, macrolevel differences in judgments can be found in the nature and distribution of social ties along the dimensions of solidarity and hierarchy. Finally, at the most general level of their moral and social implications, we use these findings to address some stubborn problems: What are the prospects for legal change? Who is my equal? Who is a stranger? And what legal or moral difference should it make?

2

Social Structure and Legal Structure: A Comparative View

Judgments of responsibility and conceptions of the wrongdoer grow out of the ways people behave toward each other. Therefore they depend on the nature of relationships in a society. At the macrolevel, the distribution of types of relationship differs systematically between Japan and the United States. In our terms, Japanese relationships seem both more highly solidary and more hierarchical than those of Americans. The *combination* of hierarchy and solidarity characterizes much of Japanese society.

Why compare the United States and Japan? The United States and Japan are similar in key respects. They share a high level of economic development. Both are industrialized and they constitute the world's two largest economies. Moreover, they are both capitalist economies. But Japan appears to differ substantially from the United States in attitudes toward responsibility and its outcomes. For example, the United States and Japan differ in how citizens typically assess and respond to misdeeds. Both the differences and the similarities are important for comparative purposes.

Urbanization, a concomitant of highly developed economies, is an especially pertinent issue for studies that include crime and other wrongdoing, as crime is often blamed on the process of urbanization or the crowding that results. Japan and the United States are highly urbanized. But Japan's population density is much higher; its population is roughly one-half that of the United States and is crowded into an area about the size of California (Bayley, 1976). Nonetheless Japan's crime rate is much lower than that of the United States. Levels of economic development and urbanization, therefore, are not competing explanations for differences in responsibility rules used to judge wrongdoing.

Comparable literacy rates are a prerequisite for a study of this type; it is difficult to compare the operation of law, and of rules that determine when law may be called upon, if one society is literate and the other is not. Japan and the United States have comparable literacy rates, although currently a higher proportion of Americans are illiterate (Kozol, 1985; see also Comber & Keeves, 1973; Husen, 1967; Stevenson, Lee, & Stigler, 1986).

A nation's history of experience with violence and aggression may be relevant to the adjudication of wrongdoing. American history, for example, has often been characterized as unusually violent and lawless. But as Bayley (1976) has stressed:

> Americans often explain criminality in terms of their history, especially the frontier tradition of individual self-assertion, violence, rough-hewn justice, and handguns. Americans accept the recently-coined aphorism that violence is as American as apple pie; they believe that their unique tradition underlies contemporary lawlessness. Yet Japan's history has also been marked by blood. . . . Political assassinations, for instance, have been much more common there than in the United States. Martial arts have always played a large role in popular culture. Japanese glorify the sword-wielding samurai every bit as much as Americans do the straight-shooting cowboy. Violent samurai dramas saturate Japanese television as monotonously as westerns do American television. Japan made a virtue at one time of unquestioning loyalty to the Emperor and, by extension, to military discipline. It has openly fought to create an overseas empire and has committed acts of brutal oppression. If Japanese social relations are tranquil today, it is not because their national experience is a tale for children. (pp. 10–11)

Japan even had a "wild West"—Hokkaido—where a substantial proportion of the native Ainu population were killed during the latter half of the nineteenth century (H. Kato, 1979).

Finally, the nature of a nation's legal system may itself shape citizens' handling of wrongdoing and dispute. Although there are substantial differences between the American and Japanese legal systems, there are also important similarities when viewed in a broad cross-cultural context. Japanese law prior to its modernization during the Meiji Restoration was certainly at a far remove from contemporaneous American law (Henderson, 1965), but Japan began incorporating elements of modern legal systems more than a century ago, primarily from Germany and France. Other elements of law were modernized during the American occupation of Japan. Japanese citizens may use law differently, or with a different frequency, from Americans. But the law they work within is a modern body of doctrine borrowed in substantial part from the West, doctrine that does not establish unfamiliar concepts or rules and does not proceed from substantially different definitions of responsibility.

Furthermore, certain often-cited contrasts between the legal professions in Japan and the United States are to some extent overstated. Japan has very few lawyers compared to the United States, but there are many quasi-legal actors who perform routine legal functions. When all such individuals are counted, the per capita number of legal actors in Japan is not strikingly different from that in Western Europe. The number of Japanese lawyers is small per capita (approximately one per 9,400, compared to one per 370 in the United States, one per 1,400 in the United Kingdom, and one per 3,400 in France). However, the ratio falls to one per 1,070 when licensed non-lawyer legal specialists (including 41,000 tax agents, 31,000 administrative scriveners, and 15,000 judicial scriveners) are counted. This is still low by American standards, but if anything a bit high by European standards (Hattori & Henderson, 1985, sec. 2.09).

Thus a number of features of the legal system of Japan overlap or resemble, or were even modeled after, the legal system of the United States. As Upham (1989, p. 879) puts it: "No other legal culture is at once so similar in its economic and political context and so different in origin and history from our own."

Dimensions of Social Structure

Social life can always be analyzed according to its vertical and horizontal aspects: hierarchy and solidarity. If we do not stand as equals in a relationship, then it follows that one party has the authority or power and the other party is the subordinate. If we are not close to a given person, then we stand in some sort of distant relationship, or we are strangers. The broad characteristics of Japanese social life can be characterized as follows: Japanese relationships tend to be hierarchical; they tend to be highly solidary; and as a result relationships that are simultaneously hierarchical and solidary have long been typical of Japanese social networks. Below we consider social structural and macrolevel evidence for each of these points.

Hierarchy

The hierarchical element in Japanese life is obvious to the American who watches two Japanese greet each other by bowing or reads about the emperor system. The American nation was founded by known historical figures in revolt against a parent government. The Japanese nation traces itself to the goddess of the sun, and the emperor—her putative descendant—is one link in what is claimed as the longest unbroken royal lineage in the world.

The fulfillment of obligation, a longstanding value among Japanese, was a major theme used by the elite in the process of modernization (e.g., Fruin, 1980). One's ultimate obligation, called *on,* is the indebtedness of subordinate to superior for the superior's benevolence in bestowing resources on the subordinate.[1] In principle, *on* can never be completely repaid. The prototype relationship generating *on* is that between parent and child; historically, this concept of indebtedness to one's superior was part of the ideology of the feudal hierarchy. From the late 1880s until the end of World War II the Japanese government attempted to extend the boundaries of *on* to include, first and foremost, the emperor as the father of his country. This effort was linked to the transformation of Shinto, the indigenous pantheistic Japanese religion, into the state religion, with the emperor at its head (Tsurumi, 1979a). The result was *kokutai,* the ideology of Japan as a patriarchal state. The defeated Japanese nation was thus doubly shocked after World War II to hear the voice of Emperor Hirohito for the first time in a radio broadcast and then to hear the content of his message: that he was renouncing the claim of divinity.

A divine monarchy seems part of a rather distant past for the Japan of the 1990s—even if the distance is less than a half-century—but hierarchical relations still permeate modern Japan. This hierarchical reality occasionally stands in contrast to the egalitarian Constitution of 1947 imposed on Japan by The United States.

Among the most famous social scientific treatments of Japanese hierarchy is the work of anthropologist Chie Nakane (1970). Nakane calls Japan a vertical society. Her central theoretical concepts for understanding the vertical web of relations are the contrast between *frame,* the geographical or institutional setting, and *attributes,* characteristics carried by the individual: "Groups may be identified by applying . . . two criteria: one is based on the individual's common *attribute,* the other on situational position in a given *frame. . . . Frame* may be a locality, an institution, or a particular relationship which binds a set of individuals into one group: in all cases it indicates a criterion which sets a boundary and gives a common basis to a set of individuals who are located or involved in it" (p. 1). Thus an individual's assertion "I am a welder" is an assertion that an attribute is possessed by a discrete social unit. In contrast, the assertion "I work at Ford" places the individual in a social and geographic frame. Of course, the welder works at places like Ford Motor Company, just as places like Ford employ people to do particular jobs. Attribute and frame coexist and coclassify individuals at any given time and place.

Nakane stresses the extent to which Japanese life, especially the workplace, is organized around the principle of frame rather than attribute. For example, unions form within companies rather than across companies. Western commentators have long noted the relative weakness of a labor movement in which employees and supervisors each belong to, say, the Mitsubishi union (e.g., Cole, 1971, 1979). The American labor movement, with its broad industry-wide organizations among production-line workers (e.g., the United Auto Workers), stands in striking contrast. One reason for these differences is Japanese firms' tendency to offer workers permanent employment, in contrast to American firms' willingness to lay off and fire workers; commitment to an institution is weakened by the prospect of being ejected from it. In Nakane's terms, then, American workers are organized on the basis of attributes they can carry with them rather than the frames they may be leaving. Attribute-based organization lends itself to equality; frame-based organization, to hierarchy.

Solidarity

The employment policies of major Japanese firms are not purely a matter of hierarchy. Television presentations of workers singing "hail to thee, o Mitsubishi" at the start of work suggest to an American viewer both an uncomfortably high level of conformity and an unusual level of feeling toward one's workplace. Employees in the Matsushita Company (manufacturer of Panasonic, Quasar, and other products) sing together each morning:

> For the building of a new Japan
> Let's put our strength and mind together.
> Doing our best to promote production,
> Sending our goods to the people of the world.
> Endlessly and continuously,
> Like water gushing from a fountain.
> Grow industry, grow, grow, grow!
> Harmony and sincerity!
> Matsushita Electricity! (Hsu, 1983, pp. 364–365)

It is important to understand, however, that solidarity per se is neither conformity nor warmth; it is a structural interconnectedness of relationships. Solidarity may foster conformity and may be accompanied by emotion, but it need not involve either of these elements. Closeness can be a cool rational calculation just as it can be a warm emotion.

A number of writers suggest that one source of Japanese solidarity is the wet-field rice farming typical of Japanese agriculture throughout recorded history (e.g., Befu, 1971). Farmers could and did grow crops other than rice, but rice farming was more productive, and rice was "the basic unit of economic exchange, measure of wealth, and symbol of political power" (Befu, 1971, p. 69). Rice farming depends on irrigation, which in turn requires coordinated action by and cooperation among a series of individuals and families. Over the long term, a farmer could expect to deal—and cooperate—repeatedly with the same set of other farmers. Failure to coordinate actions could mean drastic consequences for oneself, one's family, and one's village.

It is not surprising, then, that economically oriented accounts of Japanese farming life can make cooperation appear to be plain self-interest. Consider, for example, one "rational actor" account of the context in which collective economic decisions are made in a Japanese village:

> One way of reducing defection is to embed each transaction in a never-ending series of similar transactions among the same participants and exclude those who defect from agreements from future transactions. With this method, however, the rate of exchange obtaining in any transaction is not determined in the decision-making process at each turn but is fixed across the entire series and applied and interpreted to fit the objective circumstances of the issue under consideration. The interdependence and continuity of the exchange relation creates a corresponding sensitivity to the underlying exchange relation itself and a sensitivity to the long-term effects of collective decisions on the exchange relation. (Marshall, 1984, p. 4)

Even if an isolated utility-maximizing individual were to be placed in each Japanese rice paddy, it is not rational *in this context* to behave so as to isolate oneself or to maximize immediate personal gain.[2] A farmer need not be a sentimentalist to seek the "collective good."

In the village context, solidarity was traditionally promoted between equals and unequals alike. Tsurumi (1979b) describes three variants of hierarchical obligation: the traditional village patterns of leadership and dependency that predated feudalism; the official feudal relationships, which sometimes conflicted with the former; and, after 1868, the more modern governmental units of the Meiji Restoration, signaling the end of feudalism. Multiple opportunities to generate solidarity among equals also existed. Growing up in a village, a Japanese youth joined various *kumi*, peer groups for youth of different ages. Adults in turn could belong to a bewildering variety of *ko*, or interest groups, where most of the crucial decisions involving village affairs were worked out informally, often accompanied by food, drink, and merry-making. Solidarity—interconnectedness—often builds emotional bonds, although it does not require them.

Like the exchange among rice-growing villagers, the employment relationship in modern Japan also depends on long-term ties. This goes well beyond "permanent employment" practices. The prototypical Japanese firm is a synthesis of bureaucracy and paternalism that has been given a number of names including welfare corporatism (Dore, 1973) and Theory Z (Ouchi, 1981). According to Hill (1981, p. 53), welfare corporatism encompasses permanent employment, tall job hierarchies and many work units, job rotation and enlargement, informal employee participation in decision making, socialization into a strong organizational culture accompanied by rituals and ceremonies, and the provision of a variety of family, housing, educational, and health benefits. As a result of these structures and practices, the firm exerts a degree of paternalistic control over both the work life and the nonwork life of employees (see, e.g., Rohlen, 1974). Supervisors may legitimately be expected to advise their subordinates on a host of matters, as when supervisors help workers find marriage partners.

Not only are workers closely tied to the firm, they are closely tied to one another. Ties among co-workers as well as among near superiors and subordinates are more enduring and more complex than is likely in an American counterpart firm. In a recent comparative study of Japanese and American workplaces Lincoln and Kalleberg (1990) found that Japanese employees form stronger social bonds: "They appear to have more frequent relations with their supervisors, both on and off the job. They are more likely to develop close friendships with their workmates and to see them after work. They are more likely to perceive their jobs as requiring interaction and coordination with others, and they are much more likely to participate in shop-floor small group activities such as quality circles" (p. 114).

An important example of Japanese employee relationships is *tsukiai*, the practice of informal socialization after work among employees. It is both pleasurable and obligatory, and may take up several hours of after-work time nearly every day. It is, in many respects, a modern version of village *ko* meetings. Food and drink abound; decisions are informally discussed; and any hierarchical distinctions within the group are dropped or at least discouraged. The husbands and fathers who practice *tsukiai* are, not surprisingly, known as "weekend guests" at their homes; a children's nickname for fathers of this type is "Sunday friend," referring to the one day on which *tsukiai* is *not* practiced (R. J. Smith, 1983; White, 1987).

American workers now employed by Japanese firms in the United States often report, to describe their work experience, that the workplace has a "family atmosphere" or that it "feels like family" (R. J. Smith, 1983, p. 61). The aspects of industrial organization outlined above amount to an employment relationship that is literally more like family relationships than is typically true in the United States. Enduring, frequent exchanges of emotional as well as monetary coin occur in such settings. Wrongdoing, harm done, or even rubbing someone the wrong way have altogether different consequences if you neither seek nor are likely to find a way out of the relationship—if the worker next to you, or your superior or subordinate, is as inexorably likely to be present tomorrow as the uncle who starts fights at every reunion. In such relatively solidary settings, members of the group seek to find ways to alleviate tension, to prevent breaches, and to restore good will when breaches have been unavoidable.

It is important not to exaggerate the prevalence or importance of patterns in Japanese social life that appear exotic to Americans. For example, as Atsumi (1979) points out, it would be a misconception to think that *tsukiai* makes workers into close personal friends; theirs is an employment relationship. Feeling "like family" is not necessarily the same as being family. Nevertheless, given the fundamental importance of the employment relationship in all industrial societies, the relatively multiplex and enduring Japanese work relations may be thought of as tilting the entire corpus of potential societal relationships in a solidary direction. To the degree that basic cultural values are shaped by the dominant type of social relationship in a society, Japanese perceptions of the person should reflect individuals embedded in networks rather than individualized actors who can, or wish to, stand alone.

Ie and Social Organization

At the historical core of Japanese social structure is the organization of the family. Patterns of family life have changed very slowly, and the values that undergirded family organization have been imported to other institutions, either spontaneously or through indoctrination (Hamaguchi, 1985; Murakami, 1985; R. J. Smith, 1985).

Japan's historical form of family organization is called *ie*. Until the 1947 Constitution the *ie* was the fundamental legal and social unit. The contrast between the Western individual in a family and the Japanese *ie* exemplifies the issue of cultural variation in organizational forms. In Japanese family life *ie* refers to the descendant group to which an individual belongs. The *ie* continues backward and forward in time, and the living family members are but a representation of the underlying lineal genealogy. The historical *ie* concept included the family property and occupation and defined the family status position: "The *ie* . . . was far more important than the individuals who were at any one time living members of it, and it was seen as natural that the individual personalities of family members should be ignored and sacrificed if necessary for the good of the whole" (Fukutake, 1982, p. 28).

The *ie* traditionally was supported by two customary elements of family organization. First, the family unit was a multigenerational structure in which "the axial relationship . . . was not the marital relationship but the parent-child relationship. . . . [P]atriarchal authority constituted the basic building unit of Japanese society" (Fukutake, 1982, p. 25). Second, the eldest son had first claim to the family property under a system of primogeniture, thus ensuring the stability of the property and business of the *ie*.[3] The Meiji Civil Code formalized this method of inheritance and made it the law throughout Japan (Fukutake, 1982, p. 26). Postwar reforms gave all children equal right to inherit, but Hendry (1986) reports that a single successor is chosen to inherit most of the land.

Many observers have seen *ie* as an organizing principle for much of Japanese society beyond the family. As noted above, traditional village social organization has been perceived as more hierarchical and more interdependent than is typical in the West, and membership in organizations in urban neighborhoods was by household, not by individual. Many have argued that other secondary organizations also reflect family structure. Hsu (1975), for example, argues that the quintessential secondary organization is the *iemoto*, an organization consisting of a master of some skill and his disciples. The *iemoto* pattern also exists in organizations not called by that name. The principle of solidarity of the *iemoto* is what Hsu (1975) calls the kin-tract: "the fixed and unalterable hierarchical arrangement voluntarily entered into among a group of human beings who follow a common code of behavior under a common ideology for a set of common objectives. . . . It is partly based on the kinship model so that once fixed, the hierarchical relationships tend to be permanent, and partly based on the contract model, since the decision for entering and occasionally for quitting a particular grouping rests with the individual" (p. 62). According to Hsu, most Japanese organizations, including Japanese firms, are *iemoto*-like in their organization.

The parallel between firm and family must be understood in light of the fact that even the traditional family *ie* was as much a corporate group, an economic unit, as it was a bloodline. Membership in an *ie* was to some extent determined by who contributed to the economic welfare of the group. Movement into and out of the *ie* was considerably more fluid than was true for "family" in many countries; adoption was commonly used to keep the *ie* going. In Nakane's terms, the *ie's* fluidity of membership and its economic base make it more of a frame for activities than an attribute attached to individuals. Thus the Japanese household is both a descent group and a corporate group (Fruin, 1980). This is especially true of *dozoku*, a large lineage or clan composed of several *ie*, with a main household and a number of branch households where descent from the main house is traced through males (Befu, 1971). In important respects it is valid to consider the traditional Japanese family to be like a firm, just as many modern observers see the Japanese firm to be "like family" (Fruin, 1980). In both institutions the dominant tie is one of kin-tract.[4]

Modern Japanese at Work

Since the end of World War II, and perhaps earlier, the legal and biolog-ical-genealogical basis for the firm as family has eroded. The *ie* is no longer a legal entity, and large corporations are no longer held by a single *dozoku* (Fruin, 1980), but the concept remains important. Fruin, who is generally critical of the idea of firm-as-family, notes that small businesses are still frequently family affairs. Even within large enterprises, "Japanese display a cultural preference for affective as well as instrumental work commitment which large firms are more easily able to take advantage of through their considerable emphasis on corporate welfare and paternalism" (p. 447).

Perhaps the two most distinctive features of Japanese employment reflec-ting *ie*-like structures, especially in larger firms, are permanent employment and seniority-based wage and promotion systems (Cole, 1972; Eisuke, 1984; Lincoln & Kalleberg, 1990; Lincoln & McBride, 1987). Permanent employ-ment is in some respects more an ideology than a social structural reality. The ideal, which may be realized by only 30 to 40 percent of the work force, is a lifelong tie between the individual and the firm (Hashimoto & Raisian, 1985). Permanent employment is more common in large firms and those that dominate their sectors than among smaller and more marginal firms. How-ever, this feature should be understood not merely as a contractual provision that is sometimes breached but as a pervasive norm influencing the treat-ment of regular employees (Cole, 1972).[5]

Wages in Japan are based more on seniority and special life circumstances (e.g., marital status or the birth of a child) than on job attributes and man-agerial rank (Kalleberg & Lincoln, 1988; Koike, 1983). This *nenko* (seniority-based) system, like permanent employment, ties individuals to the firm while at the same time reducing the gap between white- and blue-collar workers (Dore, 1973). It also maintains hierarchical patterns existing when each individual enters the firm.

Japanese firms have fewer occupational specialties than American firms. The relatively weaker influence of occupational roles limits within-group differences and facilitates group-centeredness. Individuals tend to rotate through a number of jobs and enjoy more generalist careers (Lincoln & Kalleberg, 1990; Ouchi & Johnson, 1978; Sasaki, 1981). As Lincoln and McBride (1987) note, "A common characterization is that Americans pursue careers within occupations that cut across firms, while the opposite pattern holds in Japan" (p. 297). In order to accommodate lifetime employment and careers within firms, Japanese hierarchies tend to be taller than those in the United States. Job ladders are longer, creating more opportunities for upward mobility within the firm. Employees are linked to one another in chains of superior-subordinate relationships (Lincoln & Kalleberg, 1990). Nakane (1970) argues that when Japanese join a group they focus on the frame—the institutional ladder—to which they wish to belong rather than on the common attributes of the members. Vertical rather than horizontal networks dominate within the group.

It would be a mistake to conclude that community among equals must be sacrificed in order to achieve vertical integration. Indeed, the opposite is more nearly true. The vertical society coexists with relatively close horizontal integration. *Tsukiai* is one practice that, like the traditional *ko* groups within the village, breaks down hierarchy and builds solidarity. And this dinner-and-drinking after work is but one of a host of activities that Japanese co-workers carry on together. Fukutake (1982) notes that "as social groups become functionally differentiated with modernization, people begin to develop multiple membership in different groups. Hence conflicts of loyalty arise. . . . When [Japanese] workers who owe loyalty to their workplace form recreational groups, instead of seeking people of similar interests wherever they may be found, they are likely to make up a group from within the firm. Group memberships are concentrated within a key group" (p. 55). Japanese firms are, to use Lincoln and Kalleberg's (1990) term, commitment-maximizing organizations.

The next section considers parallels between the microsociology of individual decisions about wrongdoing—insofar as these decisions depend on types of social relationships—and the macrosociology of societal variation in how wrongdoing is judged—insofar as this variation rests on the preponderance, the relative weight, of social relationships of different types.

Legal Structure

A legal system shapes and is shaped by the society in which it operates. In modern societies, groups usually use legal means when they wish to introduce change. On the other hand, the legal system is a central institution of social control, maintaining the existing order until diverted to new ends. The structure of a legal system is multifaceted. It includes but is not limited to legal organization per se, such as the number, level, and jurisdiction of the various courts. It also includes the costs of engaging the system and the relationship of the system to other institutions and rule systems. The following discussion focuses on dispute processing structures. The dispute processing options available to disputants in Japan and in the United States reflect and preserve differences in the structure of relationships in the two societies. Japanese legal structures tend to reflect and support high-solidarity relationships while American structures tend to reflect low-solidarity ones. But there are similarities as well as differences in the social and legal structures of Japan and the United States. Within each society, as social relationships vary so, too, do forms of dispute processing.

Dispute Processing Rules

The central contrast between the Japanese and American legal systems is that the Japanese legal system "reinstitutionalizes" rules differently from the American legal system (Bohannan, 1965). From Bohannan's perspective, this reinstitutionalization results in a "double institutionalization" of customary rules.[6] That is, customs are enforced in the first instance by the resources of the institution in which they are originally lodged. Each family enforces family rules, workplaces enforce workplace rules, and so on. Laws serve as generalized guarantors of the rules already existing in various societal institutions. In that sense, legal rules are rules that are doubly institutionalized. Taking this perspective, it would appear that historically, customs in Japan have been less likely to be reinstitutionalized as generalized legal rules. As R. J. Smith (1983) notes : "By and large the [Tokugawa legal] system did allocate to representatives of groups both complete authority and total responsibility for the performance and conduct of group members, based squarely on the principles of vicarious liability and collective responsibility. . . . Domain law was never intended to deal with civil disputes in the village, which was expected to see to it that its residents behaved according to local custom and were properly cared for if in need" (p. 38).

Masao Maruyama (1974) comments on the nature of the resulting legal order: "The right to establish and administer the law was allocated broadly to each status level. . . . To characterize this aspect of the feudal society in a phrase, we might call it a hierarchic structure of immanent values. The values of the total social system are diffused and embedded in each closed social sphere. As a result, each of these social spheres plays an indispensable part in the preservation of the total structure" (pp. 243–244). In such a system, the local social relationship is relatively more important in the overall system of social control.

As important as the number of reinstitutionalized rules, however they might be counted, is the way in which rules are reinstitutionalized. How are rules applied and enforced when claimants turn to law? This is largely a matter of procedure. We use the term *procedure* in a broad sense to describe the set of rules establishing the terms and conditions under which people can use law. Procedures define the way in which a legal system ties claimants to the law and to one another when they turn to law.

Two basic procedural distinctions are useful in understanding differences in the way Japanese and Americans reinstitutionalize rules: *adjudicative* versus *non-adjudicative* proceedings and, to a lesser extent, *inquisitorial* versus *adversarial* proceedings (see Lind & Tyler, 1988). In formal adjudication a third party (usually a judge) has the power to decide the case based on some formal rule system. As one moves toward less adjudicative proceedings such as arbitration and mediation, the power of a third party to decide the case on the basis of some generalized (legal) rules diminishes. Successful outcome is more dependent upon conciliation and the mutual agreement of the parties. In an inquisitorial system the third party controls the process of investigation and fact finding, a pattern typical of several European legal systems. In adversarial systems the disputing parties control and are responsible for the production of evidence. Compared to the United States, the Japanese legal system appears to be more inquisitorial and much less adjudicative.[7]

Such differences as exist are no accident of history. As Haley (1982a) notes, during the interwar years in Japan the government acted to limit the growth of adjudicative alternatives to conciliation as the preferred method of dispute resolution. The Japanese deliberately turned their back on the liberal tradition of the West in favor of what Haley calls the neo-Confucian tradition, placing cohesion over conflict. Thus the development of Japanese law in the direction of conciliation was consciously planned by governmental actors.

More recently, Rosch (1987) reported on the evolution of the Japanese Civil Liberties Bureau (CLB). Founded to promote individual rights, it became an organization that mediates disputes between private parties. In this respect it is part of a large network of dispute settlement organizations and procedures designed to resolve disagreements through conciliation or mediation. These include the two formal alternatives to ordinary litigation: precommencement compromise (*wakai*) and civil conciliation (*minji chotei*). Together these two alternatives constitute a significant part of the caseload of the summary courts (Obuchi, 1987).

The summary courts and the district courts are the two major trial courts of ordinary jurisdiction in Japan. In 1983 the summary courts had jurisdiction of civil cases involving amounts less than 900,000 yen. Approximately 60 percent of cases in the civil docket were filed in summary courts (Hattori & Henderson, 1985, pp. 3–8). In 1983 there were 179,000 ordinary actions,

9,000 applications for compromise, and 130,000 applications for civil conciliation (Hattori & Henderson, 1985, sec. 9.02[3]). Outside the formal courts,
there are other public agencies like the CLB practicing mediation rather than
adjudication (Bryant, 1984; Gellhorn, 1966; Ishimura & Wada, 1984).

Informal, conciliatory proceedings are also encouraged in a wide range of
regulatory arenas. Upham (1987) reports on the efforts of the Ministry of
International Trade and Industry (MITI) to get a subcommittee of members of
the petrochemical industry to agree on the allocation of reductions in capacity in the early 1980s. As might be expected, firms found it difficult to agree to
an equitable system of contraction. "To break this impasse, MITI tried a
different approach: in early October it sent the subcommittee members to
Europe. The stated purpose was the study of structural reform in the European petrochemical industry, but the real purpose was to create personal
relationships among the company presidents conducive to the reorganiza-
tion of the industry. This approach seems to have worked. Participants
claimed that the experience of traveling together built mutual trust, and the
end of October marked a new flurry of activity" (Upham, 1987, p. 196).

This type of dispute resolution is to be found in non-industrial regulatory
settings as well. Young (1984) discusses the resolution of disputes that arose as
residents of large Japanese cities became concerned about the effect of high-
rises on ventilation and sunlight. After the national government failed to
respond to these concerns through appropriate changes in the Construction
Standards Law, several hundred local governments enacted what came to be
known as *outline guidance*. The outline guidance typically asked developers
"voluntarily" to reach an agreement with nearby residents concerning inter-
ference with light and air. The outline guidance was not legally binding, but
neither would it be fair to say compliance was fully "voluntary." For instance,
the outline guidance of the municipality of Musashino indicated that un-
cooperative developers would not receive water or sewage services and
would not be issued local construction permits required under the Construction Standards Law (Young, 1984, p. 932). The resolution of these disputes never involved direct governmental intervention, or even governmental regulation. There were no regulatory rules concerning the permissible
amount of intrusion on ventilation and sunlight of surrounding structures.
Instead, the outline guidance ordinances empowered local residents so that
the parties to the negotiation had to take each other seriously and reach a
mutually satisfactory solution appropriate to their particular circumstances.

These examples show that flexibility and use of input from the parties are
typical of administrative guidance by MITI and other governmental organizations. As Young (1984) notes, administrative groups "seek to enshrine bar-

gaining and negotiation between the parties as the principal device for allocating regulatory burdens" (p. 941). Informal "management" not only facilitates compromise, but also simultaneously impedes simple one-time contractual relationships. Recall the analysis of economic and social relationships in a Japanese fishing village presented above; each transaction was embedded in a series of similar transactions designed to foster long-term multiplex ties (Marshall, 1984). In this context even a utility-maximizing individual would not act to maximize immediate personal gain.

Juxtaposed to this elaborate network of informal remedies in the regulatory area is a relatively undeveloped and inaccessible set of formal adjudication mechanisms. Resort to the courts is made more difficult and more expensive by a set of barriers to litigation. Among the barriers are the following:

1. Administrative organizations are given wide discretion in the enabling legislation. For instance, the Foreign Exchange and Foreign Trade Control Law, a primary instrument of MITI, provides in part that MITI shall have the power to regulate imports. Article 52 reads, "For the purpose of sound development of foreign trade and the national economy, a person wishing to import goods may be required as stipulated by Cabinet Order to obtain approval therefor" (Upham, 1987, p. 170). By putting a good on the Cabinet Order proscribed list, MITI was able to gain control over any foreign transaction. The reasons for including a product on this list included "stability of the currency," "the most economic and beneficial use of foreign currency funds," "safeguarding the balance of international payments," and "rehabilitation and expansion of the national economy" (Upham, 1987, p. 170). Given such sweeping powers, plaintiffs find that many decisions cannot be challenged in court. They are beyond judicial review; in legal terms they are not justiciable.

2. Even when decisions are justiciable, there may be a problem of standing: Is this plaintiff the appropriate person to challenge some decision? Every legal system has standing requirements. For instance, in the United States an individual has no standing to challenge an appropriation of Congress as illegal or unconstitutional (see *Valley Forge College v. Americans United*, 1982). Japanese standing requirements, however, are a more frequent barrier to litigation. The Administrative Case Litigation Law limits standing to persons having a "legal interest" in an administrative decision. Upham (1987) notes that this implies that a mere "factual" interest will not create standing and that Japanese courts "have historically limited standing to individual interests that an administrative

agency has been specially charged by statute with protecting. Where an agency acts for the general public interest, therefore, personal interests injured by the government action are merely factual interests" (p. 172). A community facing a threat of economic disruption because of the placement of a factory would have only a "factual" interest in the decision, hence no standing. While there has been some loosening of Japanese standing requirements in the environmental law area, they remain a formidable barrier to litigation concerning industrial policy.

3. Even if a party has standing, a further limitation is created by the fact that the Japanese code of civil procedure does not permit mandatory class action: a procedure that can compel the joining of all interested plaintiffs in a single lawsuit. As a result, victims of some violations (e.g., antitrust or environmental harms), each of whom has suffered some real but minor harm, may be unable to raise the damage pool high enough to justify the cost of litigation.

4. There are barriers to proving one's case. The United States has elaborate rules allowing for discovery of documents and deposition of witnesses in advance of trial (see *Federal Rules of Civil Procedure*, 1987, Rules 26–37). These rules allow each side to know in advance what evidence and testimony the other side will present. Injured plaintiffs may be able to research defendant records and locate documents indicating defendant wrongdoing. Discovery proceedings are more limited in Japan, in turn limiting the ability of plaintiffs to build a case in complex regulatory areas (Ramseyer, 1985).

In regulatory cases as elsewhere, even when one does turn to court for a remedy, this frequently begins a process by which the dispute and the disputants are slowly brought into less adversarial relations. As Upham (1987) notes with respect to gender discrimination cases against employers in the 1980s: "There seems little doubt that the [Equal Employment Opportunity Act] is part of a government attempt to follow the time-honored Japanese pattern of dealing with social conflict by simultaneously ameliorating its causes and incorporating the antagonists into government-controlled mediation machinery" (p. 163).

Interestingly, in some circumstances even when adjudication does occur it is accompanied by an inquisitorial style of fact finding that facilitates settlements by minimizing the possible range of litigated outcomes. For instance, in the case of automobile accidents, the calculation of damages, including pain and suffering, is heavily influenced by the Guidance for Assessment of Damages setting forth nationwide standards for payments under compulsory insurance plans. The courts have adopted and encouraged the idea of standardized damage awards for various injuries and have further reduced the control of the litigants over the damage issue by acknowledging only damages proved by official or quasi-official documents (Tanase, 1990).

Japanese automobile accident law is superficially similar to U.S. law. It is a fault-based system accompanied by a compulsory insurance requirement. But the existence of high standards for driver behavior, as well as a provision that the victim's own fault will not be an offsetting factor unless he or she is more than 70 percent responsible for the accident, produce a system that approximates a no-fault insurance system (Tanase, 1990, p. 668). Injured victims receive compensation from the driver's insurance.

Consequently, factual issues concerning the causes of accidents are usually absent. Where they do occur, however, an inquisitorial style is reflected in the special weight given in court to the police report of the accident. Here the preferences for non-adjudicative and non-adversarial styles play on each other. The police report is not the simple citation we are accustomed to in the United States. In Japan, such a report is the work of officers who specialize in traffic accidents. Officers conduct a detailed investigation at the scene and record testimony of the parties (and often that of witnesses). Together, through a process that is a hybrid of inquisitorial and mediative styles, the parties and the police come to an agreement as to "what happened." The result for later adjudication is summarized by Tanase (1990): "Indeed, because the parties and the police, and often the witnesses as well, consult at the scene of the accident as soon as possible, and the police adjust differences in factual assertions of the parties and hammer out a consensual story as to what happened to which the parties agree and formally endorse by signing, it is very difficult for the parties later to refute the facts recorded in the police report" (pp. 673–674).

In sum, Japanese dispute processing structures tend to minimize adversarialness and adjudication while supporting inquisitorial and non-adjudicative mechanisms. They parallel Japanese social structure in the sense that they tend to treat people as connected rather than separated, and to encourage solutions that minimize conflict and reduce the probability that relationships between disputants will be permanently severed by the dispute. Some have argued that the relative inaccessibility of Japanese courts has impeded the development of a more individualistic consciousness of rights (Haley, 1982a; Henderson, 1965; Kidder & Hostetler, 1990; Ramseyer, 1985). According to this view, the Japanese are structurally incapacitated from suing, rather than personally or culturally disinclined to do so. This argument will be reconsidered in Part III.

Variations in Social and Legal Structure

Within each society there is variation in the relationship among individuals. All types of relationships—all combinations of hierarchy and solidarity—exist in every modern society. Specific relationships between people can be more or less equal and more or less interconnected. Likewise, there is variation in the way disputes are processed. Adjudications are not unknown in Japan, and Americans frequently employ mediation and other non-adjudicative mechanisms. If dispute settlement structures reflect the structure of social relationships, we should expect that dispute settlement structures within each society vary with social relationships. When parties find themselves in enduring, multiplex relationships they should be less likely to turn to law to settle disputes and should prefer dispute settlement structures that are less adversarial and adjudicative (Lempert & Sanders, 1986). Evidence from both the United States and Japan suggests that this is true.

Relationships and the Willingness to Litigate

There are places in the United States where relationships among individuals are remarkably similar to those found among the Japanese. Kai Erikson (1976), for example, describes the nature of community along Buffalo Creek, a narrow mountain hollow in West Virginia that was ravaged by a flood caused by a bursting dam in the winter of 1972: "People are identified by the place they occupy in the larger linkages of family and community rather than by the work they do or the way they live. . . . Relationships between people are thus based on a high degree of mutuality, and they emerge from a quiet agreement to look out for one another and to submerge one's separate sense of self into the large tissues of communal life" (p. 129). The reports of two residents capture the element of mutual assistance and the subtle ways in which self is part of community:

> "You just have to experience it, I guess, to really know. It was wonderful. Like when my father died, my neighbors all came in and they cleaned my house, they washed my clothes, they cooked, I didn't do nothing. They knew what to do. . . . The morning my daddy died—he died in Logan— my aunt called me and told me on the phone at about ten o'clock in the morning, and I had just got time to get off the phone and go set on the bed and in come three of my neighbors. They knew it that quick. I don't know how. They just knew." (pp. 190–191)
>
> "I knew everybody in the camp and practically everybody on Buffalo, as far as that is concerned. But down here, there ain't but a few people I know, and you don't feel secure around people you don't know." (p. 191)

Nor are the people of Buffalo Creek unique. The Baptists of Hopewell mentioned earlier are also closely bound by ties of religion, family, and friendship. So, too, are the Amish (Kidder & Hostetler, 1990). Their statements reflect a similar commitment to community and the concept of harmony, and more specifically a rejection of conflict as a rejection of God. For the Baptists, "an ability to get along, to preserve harmony, to *create* harmony, is . . . a sure and ready test of an individual's spiritual maturity" (Greenhouse, 1986, p. 105).

Variations exist in Japan as well. The village R. J. Smith studied for twenty-five years has suffered a greater loss of a sense of community than other nearby villages, he reports, in part because of a bitter controversy over the location of a factory to kill and dress chickens (1978, p. 233). Fukutake (1982) argues that there has been a decline in solidarity in new urban neighborhoods of Japan.

Differences in types of relationships in a society create a structural reality that is reflected in the way disputes are processed within and outside of the legal system. Miyazawa (1987) reports that a 1977 survey by the Kyoto University Faculty of Law asking people about their willingness to turn to law for a remedy found that "when a problem involves a continuing social relationship, the trouble is most likely to be ignored and a court is least likely to be used" (p. 227). Yet when there are no role relationships to maintain, disputants are more willing to use formal, adjudicative legal processes to resolve conflict. Recent work on Japanese legal disputes that involve groups, collectivities, and organizations involved in civil litigation finds relatively frequent use of the courts to settle disputes (Haley, 1982b; Krauss, Rohlen, & Steinhoff, 1984; Ramseyer, 1985; Upham, 1987). For example, Upham's (1987) discussion of the pollution cases in the 1970s and early 1980s indicates that courts may be used to exercise a Western concept of "rights," especially in disputes between strangers. Four famous pollution cases filed between June 1967 and June 1969, which came to be called the Big Four, are sometimes thought of as a watershed event in postwar Japan. They opened up a substantial volume of other pollution litigation, and together legitimized formal litigation procedures for many pollution victims (Upham, 1987, p. 37).

Kidder (1983) draws a relevant distinction between two of the Big Four cases. Both involved mercury poisoning of people who lived downstream from factories discharging the pollutant. Individuals were poisoned from eating contaminated fish. The illness was first discovered in the early 1950s in Minamata, a small city on Kyushu, Japan's southernmost main island. For years the source of the problem remained uncertain, due in part to the ability of the polluter, the Chisso Corporation, to buy time by making minimal payment to victims (who in return forfeited rights to future claims) and in part to the unwillingness of the government to determine officially the cause and the source of the victims' illnesses (Upham, 1987, p. 34). The government, abetted by the firm, engaged in a decades-long suppression and cover-up. Even in the face of this behavior, the victims did not turn to litigation until June 1969, and then only one faction of the Minamata disease victims did so.

The Minamata lawsuit followed by nearly a year the first of the Big Four suits, filed by residents in Niigata Prefecture on the island of Honshu against the Showa Denko Corporation. Problems in Niigata did not emerge until 1964. For three years they, like the residents of Minamata, "encountered corporate denials, collusive obfuscation by government and industry, and the intervention of 'objective' scientists who invariably supported the company's claims" (Upham, 1987, p. 35). In April 1967 a report from a team of researchers from Niigata University Medical School was made public over governmental objections. It linked the Niigata problems, and the Minamata problems as well, to mercury poisoning from the two factories. By June 1967, the Niigata victims had filed suit.

Kidder questioned why the Niigata victims were so much more willing to turn to law. At least part of the answer is that in Minamata, many of the victims and their families were directly or indirectly dependent upon the defendant. Many of the town's social services were provided by the company. Town-company relations, and to some extent injurer-victim relations, were multiplex and hierarchical. In Niigata, on the other hand, the victims lived a full forty miles downstream from the factory. There were no substantial ties between the community and the injurer. They were more nearly strangers (Kidder, 1983, p. 77).

Alternative Procedures

Procedures, like the willingness to litigate, vary as the relationship of the parties varies. In more mundane cases Japan, like the United States, has truncated proceedings to deal with routinized interactions. *Tokusoku tetsuzuki* is a special proceeding for summary debt collection. If a debtor fails to object within two weeks of a filing of a claim, the court, without a hearing, enters an order for the face amount of the debt plus expenses (Hattori & Henderson, 1985, sec. 9.02[4]). Whatever else may be said about this procedure, it is not conciliatory in nature. In 1983 there were 558,000 applications for summary debt collection (Hattori & Henderson, 1985, sec. 9.02[3]).

On the other hand, in the United States as in Japan, the use of adjudicative solutions diminishes as relationships become more solidary. The disputing parties are more likely to search for compromise and to consider a wide range of issues relevant to the relationship beyond their immediate dispute (Black, 1976; Ekland-Olson, 1984; Lempert & Sanders, 1986). Greater effort is likely to be directed to restoring or repairing the network itself—to effecting compromise or conciliation. This tendency causes the parties to seek alternatives to legal adjudication.

In the United States there is a long (albeit limited) history of special courts for special relationships. Perhaps the best known example is the juvenile court, which can usefully be thought of as an experiment to treat childhood criminals *as children*—part of a hierarchical, closely interconnected set of relationships—rather than as individual criminals who are connected to and dependent on no one (Lempert & Sanders, 1986). Such alternatives are increasingly gaining legitimacy in areas where the preservation of closely tied relationships is considered to be important. Communitarian and feminist legal scholars have argued for legal rules that more clearly recognize the special circumstances of highly solidary relationships in non-family settings (Macneil, 1980, 1985; Sherry, 1986; Yeazell, 1977). Danzig (1973), for example, argued that for those in highly solidary relationships the traditional judicial process "fails to be more than a 'Bleak House,' profoundly alienating, rather than integrating" (p. 44). At least part of the justification for these institutions is that they would be better able to strengthen communities as well as to settle disputes involving persons in ongoing relationships (Wahrhaftig, 1982).

The alternative dispute resolution (ADR) movement has been gathering increasingly powerful forces, including large segments of the American bar, toward the establishment of alternatives to formal adjudication. Alternative dispute resolution is a routine part of the law school curriculum with its own set of teaching materials (Goldberg, Green, & Sander, 1985). The American Bar Foundation and the U.S. Department of Justice have supported the growth of informal dispute resolution forums including neighborhood justice centers (Silbey & Sarat, 1989). Of course, this very process in which the ADR movement gains friends in high places dismays some supporters who fear that the infusion of lawyers will inevitably subvert ADR procedures.

Alternatives are not limited to the court context. People find private solutions outside of specific legal structures. For example, the seminal work of Macaulay (1963) on contractual relations in business indicated that American business people rarely turned to law to remedy disputes with those with whom they had an ongoing business relationship. The dangers to be avoided are the dangers of a general and relatively inflexible rule. As one businessman said: "You can settle any dispute if you keep the lawyers and accountants out of it. They just do not understand the give-and-take needed in business" (p. 61). The basis of this attitude is that some sales people and purchasing agents have dealt with each other for several years and hope to do so far into the future. The costs of litigation, monetary and otherwise, are too high a price to pay to settle a specific dispute. As Macaulay notes, "A breach of contract law suit may settle a particular dispute, but such an action often results in a 'divorce' ending the 'marriage' between two businesses" (p. 65). When future dealings are unlikely or when there are many alternatives in the marketplace, the parties appear more willing to hold each other to the contract (see Palay, 1984).

The Baptists of Hopewell also seek alternative ways to resolve their quarrels. They recognize that there may be conflict among themselves, but this does not lead to an adversarial or even a confrontational dispute resolution process. Narratives, joking, gossip, and prayer are used to resolve or defuse quarrels (Greenhouse, 1986, p. 110). Narratives are a way of communicating troubles and searching for solution without confrontation. They are first- or third-person, "I know someone who" or "Something once happened to me" statements that only obliquely call the listener's attention to his or her own situation: "Both teller and listener can achieve the results of a more direct confrontation without the costs: an ordinary conversation among equals potentially adjusts their relationship (by adjusting the offender's performance of his or her role) without any obvious application of authority or direct references to norms" (Greenhouse, 1986, p. 112).

Even when in conflict with outsiders in the community, as in the occasion of an automobile accident, people in Hopewell are unlikely to use law. Turning from law is part of what it is to live "in the world but not of it." As Greenhouse (1986) puts it: "The crucial element is adversarial conflict. The temptation to pursue one's own ends is continual—indeed, a premise—in modern society. If Baptists preclude disputes, it is not because they cannot conceive of self-interested remedial action but because they *can,* all too well. The effort of refraining from adversarial conflict forms the reservoir that feeds the transformation of meaning so crucial to their social relationships. In other terms, their refusal to dispute makes Christianity both important and possible for believers" (p. 116).

The Amish exhibit a similar attitude toward conflict with outsiders: "Amish are committed to a vow of 'nonresistance,' which means seeking always to be at peace with each other and with all others as well. . . . This doctrine means that they must not employ lawyers, or attempt to rely on litigation or legal threats, to defend their legal rights against challenges, because such actions would be resistance" (Kidder & Hostetler, 1990, p. 904).

Ultimately, the most extreme alternative in informal dispute resolution is simply to "lump it": to suppress or ignore a transgression for the sake of harmony or at least a tense peace (Felstiner, 1974).[8] In Japan, a survey of over 900 residents at the Tokyo area by Wada (1983–1984; cited in Miyazawa, 1987) indicates that concern for maintaining relationships prevented neighborhood and family disputes from escalating even to the level of actual negotiation, much less mediation or adjudication. In the United States, Baumgartner (1988) reports avoidance strategies both within families and between neighbors in the middle-class suburb she studied. Within families the extent of avoidance varied dramatically. At one extreme, avoidance was not particularly distinguishable from "cooling out," as in not speaking for a day or so. At the other extreme, Baumgartner reports long, hard silences. In one case a husband and wife intermittently quarreled about the husband's drinking, which the wife considered excessive:

> After verbal altercations—or sometimes with just a new annoyance and no discussion—Mrs. Moran inaugurates a state of avoidance. On one occasion, the couple persisted in this state for about six months. Mr. Moran went to work daily, while Mrs. Moran continued to care for the house. Mr. Moran deposited his checks in the couple's joint checking account, and his wife drew on them for household expenses as usual. She continued to prepare and serve meals which the couple ate together, silently. During their time together in the house, the pair exchanged no words and usually withdrew into separate rooms (each had a private bedroom). (p. 25)

Similar processes are at work between neighbors. Single incidents are simply allowed to pass. Persistent disruptions lead to more noticeable avoidance. For example, the Callaghans had a habit of sitting on their front porch and engaging in hours-long drinking sessions during which their conversations would become louder and more profane: "In response to the Callaghans' conduct, their near neighbors began, one by one, to avoid them. They rarely chatted with the Callaghans, never invited them over, and generally ignored them" (Baumgartner, 1988, p. 76). Nor is avoidance the solution chosen solely by the citizens. Baumgartner reports that "in the few cases in which individuals appeared in the municipal criminal courts to press grievances against neighbors or other acquaintances, the judge usually recommended avoidance as the optimal way to manage the conflict" (p. 76).

At the extreme, representatives of the legal system may choose to refuse to become involved. Not surprisingly, the area of life in the United States where the "rule of law" has been most successfully resisted is in the family, especially parental decisions with respect to their unemancipated children. As Coons (1987) notes in discussing the virtues of a lack of formal consistency in a legal system: "The legal hegemony of parents is a rule . . . so pervasive we tend to overlook its juridical status. 'Parents decide' is a rule of law (in many respects, of constitutional law) that shelters a potential infinity of inconsistent treatments. The classic citation is *Pierce v. Society of Sisters*, 268 U.S. 510 (1925)" (p. 94, n. 102).

This body of research suggests that in order to understand specific differences in legal systems and in culture, such as differences in how responsibility and punishment are determined, it is necessary to focus on differences *within* society as well as differences between societies. That is, we must explore how people and the law respond to disputes within different role relationships.

The Interplay of Social Structure and Individual Relationships

We have now examined Japanese and American dispute processing structures from macrolevel and microlevel perspectives. It would be an error to look only at differences between societies without examining the within-society impact of relationships among individual disputants, but it would equally be an error to believe that all between-society differences are solely the result of microlevel differences in disputant role relationships. In this section we discuss the interplay of micro and macro structures on disputing. In statistical terms, this amounts to looking for context effects in the operation of legal systems: that is, for evidence that the larger cultural context affects the meaning or impact of microlevel differences in social relationships.

The citizens of American communities such as Hopewell or Buffalo Creek find themselves in highly solidary networks at least as multiplex as most Japanese communities and therefore are likely to perceive adjudicative methods of dispute settlement as destructive. Many Hopewell Baptists are as committed to a non-adjudicative, mediative method of dispute processing as are many Japanese. Within similar circumstances, however, the overall legal structure of the United States makes it much easier for aggrieved citizens to turn to law. The accessibility of courts facilitates and *legitimizes* the resort to the legal system to resolve conflict. A comparison of Buffalo Creek and Minamata indicates the nature of the difference.

Both communities were in part "company towns." Buffalo Creek's relationship to the Pittston Coal Company, the owner of the burst dam, is not dissimilar to the relationship of the citizens of Minamata to the Chisso Corporation. Many of the victims were company employees. Pittston "was part of the life of the creek. It employed hundreds of people and was represented locally by officials who lived in the area, were known by first names, and were merged into the community as individual persons" (Erikson, 1976, p. 180). Yet within two weeks of the disaster, some of the citizens of the community were already organizing for litigation (Stern, 1976, p. 6).

How might we explain this rapid turn to adjudication? At least part of the answer may be found in the community's relationship to Pittston. Pittston had obligations that, in the mind of some citizens of Buffalo Creek, it failed to meet. Said one old man who lost everything in the flood: "I've often thought some of this stuff could have been avoided if somebody would have come around and said, 'Here's a blanket and here's a dress for your wife' or 'Here's a sandwich. Could I give you a cup of coffee?' but they never showed up. Nobody showed up to give us a place to stay. . . . The Pittston Company never offered me a pair of pants to put on, no shirt. . . . That's what gets you kind of riled up" (Erikson, 1976, p. 181). Chapter 1 noted that the supervisory role entails additional, often diffuse, responsibilities; here we can see that organizations as well as individual authorities can be seen to have supervisory responsibilities. When the dam broke on Buffalo Creek, Pittston was perceived to have violated its obligations, "first by building an unworthy dam and second by reacting to the disaster in the manner of a remote bureaucracy rather than in the manner of a concerned patron with constituents to care for" (Erikson, 1976, p. 180).

This alone, however, seems an inadequate explanation. In Japan, the disregard of the community by Chisso and its unwillingness to admit wrongdoing constituted at least as great a betrayal of trust as that of Pittston. Nevertheless, large numbers of victims refused to join the litigation against Chisso even in 1969, and some bitterly said that those who litigated were being selfish by pursuing their own ends rather than the concerns of the community generally (Upham, 1987, p. 38). Litigation was not viewed as a legitimate alternative. Those who turned to it were acting as individuals.

Differences between the Buffalo Creek and Minamata examples do not end with the reluctance to sue. The dissatisfaction of the Japanese plaintiffs with the litigation alternative continued. They objected especially to its formalism and impersonality: "As concerns the way the hearings went, we were made extremely anxious by the formalism. To take a living phenomenon like pollution, turn it into a series of documents, then discuss those while people are actually suffering and dying seems somehow arrogant or disrespectful" (Upham, 1987, p. 41, quoting a plaintiff). What many of the

Japanese litigants seemed to want even more than monetary compensation was an apology. In the end they got their wish, and this also says something about differences between the legal systems of the two societies. At the end of the Minamata trial Chisso agreed to a settlement that provided for a damage award larger than that granted by the court. In addition the agreement included a full apology by Chisso. After reciting a litany of Chisso's wrongdoing, it said in part:

> Chisso continued to maintain a regrettable attitude toward [a] solution. Chisso will reflect upon these actions with heartfelt sincerity. . . .
>
> Chisso deeply apologizes to those patients and their families . . . who suffered as a result of Chisso's attitudes. . . .
>
> Furthermore, Chisso deeply apologizes to all of society . . . for its regrettable attitude of evading its responsibility and for delaying a solution, as this caused much inconvenience to society. (Upham, 1987, pp. 48–49)

Nor did the apology occur only at a formal and impersonal level. Chisso's president, Shimada Kenichi, personally knelt before the pollution victims and apologized to them.

A Bridge to Culture: Apology

With apology we move to the edge of social structure. Apology, and the role it plays in dispute resolution, is better understood as a part of a society's culture. Culture involves ideas about the nature of persons and their proper place in the social order. The full importance of apology cannot be appreciated unless one understands the role of apology in the two cultures. The apology is itself tied up with a general Japanese cultural assumption that there are bonds to be restored between offender and victim and that individuals exist in a network of interlocked others. Apology for wrongdoing reinforces social harmony and order in groups. Wagatsuma and Rosett (1986) further contrast the role and meaning of apology in the two societies. They note, for example, that the sincerity of an apology is likely to have different connotations in the two countries that are related to different connotations of sincerity (p. 473). To be sincere in Japan is less a matter of acting from one's innermost feelings and more a matter of performing according to one's role. When speaking of the sincerity of an apology, Americans are more likely to stress its wholeheartedness (its revelation of individual regret), whereas Japanese emphasize the offender's submission to the normative order (its restoration of the relationship between offender and victim).

Apology, even on American terms, is sometimes thwarted by formal legal considerations. In American disputes apologies run the risk of being interpreted as admissions of responsibility, and clients who ask their lawyers whether they should apologize to someone they have injured are likely to be told that the wiser course is to say nothing and to have no contact with the victim or plaintiff. Indeed, one of the present authors has actually given such advice to an individual who wanted to know if it was wise and proper to show concern and sympathy to a youngster he had struck with his automobile. Even the potential for formal adjudication removed an alternative way of resolving the dispute. It pressured the actors to treat others involved in the dispute as strangers.

This incident stands as an example of a general point: Legal culture, just as much as legal structure, reflects general social patterns. For example, the influence of underlying culture on legal culture is reflected in Rosch's (1987) story of the Japanese Civil Liberties Bureau that was slowly transformed into a less adjudicative, more mediative forum. The U.S. legal system is less capable than the Japanese of creating community-based mediation services completely separated from the formal, individual rights-based legal system (Silbey & Sarat, 1989; Wahrhaftig, 1982).

American legal culture generates and supports substantive rules that tend to conceptualize disputants as equal, unconnected claims-making individuals. Individuals become identified by their rights. Joel Feinberg (1980) provides the extreme version of this legal culture: "Respect for persons . . . may simply be respect for their rights, so there cannot be the one without the other; and what is called 'human dignity' may simply be the recognizable capacity to assert claims. To respect a person, then, or think of him as possessed of human dignity, simply *is* to think of him as a potential maker of claims" (p. 151).

3

Culture and the Socialization Process

What makes a person responsible for harm done, for wrong committed? To answer this question we must consider how a culture envisions its actors, including its bad actors. The preceding chapter focused on social structural and legal roots of the image of the responsible actor. This chapter explores cultural roots of variation. We first examine the notion of the individual social actor and its alternative, what we term a contextual actor, as a framework for understanding differences in American and Japanese conceptions of responsibility and of the responsible actor.

Culture and the Social Actor

The general perspective on the social actor adopted here is the interactionist view outlined long ago by William James (1890/1981) and George Herbert Mead (1934). For James the self was both multiple and interactive. Selves are not *in* persons; rather, persons are selves as they act in social settings. An interactionist approach emerges even more strongly in Mead: "The self is something which has a development; it is not initially there, at birth, but arises in the process of social experience and activity, that is, develops in the given individual as a result of his relations to that process as a whole and to other individuals within that process. . . . The individual experiences himself as such, not directly, but only indirectly, from the particular standpoints of other individual members of the same social group, or from the generalized standpoint of the social group as a whole to which he belongs" (Strauss, ed., 1956, pp. 212, 215). Thus the human actor in any society is nurtured by and becomes a self within the confines of the surrounding social structure and the prescribed social roles. The question becomes one of how much, if at all, this actor differs from one society to the next. In order to draw as widely as possible on the pertinent literature, the following discussion avoids firm distinctions among such terms as "actor," "individual," "self," and "person," although for other purposes there may be important information carried by the choice of terms (Mauss, 1938/1985).

Any investigation into Japanese versus American conceptions of social actors must begin with the widely shared view about the general direction of difference: In the United States, the person tends to be perceived by self and others as an individual whose identity and sense of self stand apart from the group or the community; in Japan, the person tends to be perceived by self and others as a social participant whose identity is in large part defined by social relationships. The shorthand we use to describe the distinction is the contrast between *individual* actors in the United States and *contextual* actors in Japan.[1] In the sociological literature on self and self-concept, this distinction is probably closest to Rosenberg's (1979) contrast between selves that are grounded primarily in a psychological interior or a social exterior, or to Turner's (1976) concept of a "real self" that is realized in impulse as opposed to institutions. Here, the distinction is meant to capture the reactions of *other people* to a social actor as well as to describe that actor's self-concept. Note, however, that differences in conceptions of social actors in the United States and Japan are differences in degree, not in kind. Further, conceptions of the responsible actor vary *within* societies as well as between them. Certain kinds of relationships facilitate a focus on the actors as isolated individuals, whereas other kinds of relationships lead observers to focus on the interrelatedness of the participants.

Individualism

At root, *individuum* means "indivisible" rather than separate, distinct, or particular (Regamy, 1968). Therefore the individual is the smallest unit into which one can divide a social group. But to say that someone is an "individual" has considerable meaning, as signified by the existence of an associated "-ism" (Waterman, 1984). Individualism includes several distinct philosophical elements: "(1) accepting the intrinsic *moral worth* of individual human beings, (2) advocating the *autonomy* of individual thought and action, (3) acknowledging the existence and importance of individual *privacy,* and (4) espousing *self-development* or self-realization as a desirable goal" (Lukes, 1973). Across all of these elements, the fundamental unit of social life—of economics, ethics, and politics alike—is the individuum: the social atom.

The history of the word *individualism* parallels the economic and social transformations that underlie its coinage. The suffix "-ism" was first attached to the individual in reaction to the French Revolution, thereby transforming the social unit into an ideology about social units (Lukes, 1973). *Individualisme* was apparently coined in 1820 by a radical rightist, Joseph de Maistre, as a pejorative term, and it retained pejorative connotations in French usage into the modern era. To German romantics, in contrast, *Individualismus* and especially *Individualität* (individuality) had a positive ring. To English liberals, much the same was true, more for utilitarian than for romantic reasons. An American affinity for individualism was noted by Alexis de Tocqueville (1835/1981, p. 395).

The modern individual is in part the creature of the market economy, with its assumptions that land, labor, and property are all potentially alienable and that value should be a product of supply and demand. With the advent of industrialism in the nineteenth century, Western society has developed into a full-blown market economy (Polanyi, 1944; see also Heilbroner, 1970; Wolf, 1966, 1969). Market economies destroy differences as individuals become more economically interchangeable, as they become what economists term human capital; "labor" once referred to particular people tied to particular jobs, but the term is now an abstraction. Yet the new social relationship of contract between employer and employee creates the potential for formal legal equality and greater financial and geographic mobility (Maine, 1906/1963); a person's identity is less firmly tied to specific relationships. The philosophy and politics of individualism celebrate this "great transformation" (Polanyi, 1944).

Using Lukes' (1973) categories, individualism as autonomy and individualism as self-development most nearly seem to grow out of this economic transformation. The person is more autonomous in the sense of being freed from specific relationships, and one's position in the world is partly a function of self-development. The role of self-development or self-realization is in part contingent on the degree to which a society is a meritocracy that allows for social mobility based on personal skills. The ideology of self-realization, however, may exist as a cultural ideal in societies with varying degrees of meritocracy.

The development of human capital is a market idea. But the development of the idea of the individual did not occur during a single century, nor can it be explained entirely in economic terms. Research on the individuation of children and other household members indicates that a longer process incorporating more than economic change was involved in the growth of Western cultural notions of the individual, especially as these notions relate to the ideas of individual moral worth and individual privacy. When the "great transformation" occurred, many streams of Western culture channeled society toward an individualistic conception of the social actor.

In the classic *Centuries of Childhood*, for example, Philippe Aries (1962) argued that individuated actors, young or old, are relatively new. He traced the difference in conceptions of childhood in premodern and modern times in large part to the mortality that characterized society before the transition to the smaller families of the industrial era; this transition is itself related to economic changes outlined above. "Nobody thought, as we ordinarily think today, that every child already contained a man's personality. Too many of them died" (p. 39). Thus portraits of dead children tend not to be kept or remarked on until sixteenth-century European life, and portraits of children do not reach full flower until the seventeenth century. Even the names of these children were not "preserved." Whereas a modern family would be unlikely to give the same first name to a second child after the first had died, this was not unusual in the past (deMause, 1974); there might be several Marys or Johns before one survived. There appears to have been no sense that some unique personality or individuality was symbolized by a name.

Architectural evidence presented by Tuan (1982) suggests that adults as well as children have undergone individuation in recent centuries. For example, with regard to eating habits, Tuan concludes that for Europeans the passing centuries brought increasing "differentiation, order, understated elegance, and an extraordinarily inflated sense of human dignity, which implies not only the necessity to distance oneself from nature but from other human beings as well" (p. 50). The architecture of the house and the use to which rooms were put also shifted as Europe moved toward modernity. The household structures of Rome, Greece, and ancient China show that wealthy and poor alike led a relatively *public* life. Rooms were not differentiated by function, were typically interconnected, and were rarely if ever allocated for private or personal use. Rich or poor, people shared space during sleep: servants or same-sex relatives with one another, masters with servants (and parents with infants—see deMause, 1974). Even individuated furniture within rooms came late to Europe: "Upholstered chairs made an appearance in the middle of the sixteenth century" (Tuan, 1982, p. 78). As its members attained rooms and chairs, the biological family—as opposed to the household that included servants or workers—emerged in sharper relief.

Contextualism

Shweder and Bourne (1982, p. 126) have argued that one underlying factor producing a contextual conception of actors is *holism* as a "mediating world premise." In an organic or holistic view of society, the whole is greater than the sum of its parts (Phillips, 1976). Because society as a whole is primary and its individual parts are secondary, members value conformity of the parts to the whole (Dumont, 1970). A holistic view fosters a tendency to perceive things in terms of their concrete and immediate contextual features rather than in the abstract (e.g., Miller, 1984; Shweder & Miller, 1985). In the arena of person perception, this means "a tendency not to separate out, or distinguish, the individual from the social context" and especially from social roles held in that context (Shweder & Bourne, 1982, p. 104). A holistic view tends to be more sociocentric and less egocentric (Cousins, 1989). One difference between individualists and holists lies in the causal attributions that they make. Societies vary in the extent to which they attribute behavior to a person's traits instead of seeing events as environmentally caused or as an interplay of person and environment; the individualist is likely to focus on traits carried by the person, while the holist is likely to focus on the ways in which the person may be embedded in the context, the whole. Research in the United States and India by Shweder and Bourne (1982) indicates that American attributions emphasize context-free traits: causes that people carry inside themselves. Among the Oriya in India, emphasis is instead placed on specific actions in the context. Shweder and Bourne distinguish two aspects of this contextualism: references to "cases" (specific behavioral references) and to "contexts" (concrete reference to spatial, temporal, or social context), as opposed to traits. An American might say of another, "She is friendly." An Oriya Indian might say, "She brings cakes to my family on festival days." Contextual attribution here includes making more reference to actors' role relationships as well as emphasizing aspects of the physical or temporal surroundings.

Miller's (1984) related work comparing Chicago residents with Hindu residents of the city of Mysore indicates that the difference in worldview develops gradually. Adult attributions differ more sharply than do those of children. Miller argues that these findings show the impact of culture and is able to reject a number of potential alternative explanations for the results. Deficits in cognitive skills, intellectual motivation, pertinent information, or linguistic tools fail to account for a greater contextualism of Indian accounts of the person. The end result of development in the American case is an adult who can attribute to the context but in whom the predominant attributions are to stable traits or dispositions; the end result in the Indian case is an adult who can make trait attributions but who predominantly focuses on context. The American tends to see others as individual foci of experience and causation; the Indian tends to see others as existing in and shaped by a social web.

The citizen of India is far from alone. Most societies in history and most of today's living cultures appear to be more holistic or contextual than the United States. The anthropologist Clifford Geertz (1973, 1975) puts it this way: "The Western conception of the person as a bounded, unique, more or less integrated motivational and cognitive universe, a dynamic center of awareness, emotion, judgment, and action organized into a distinctive whole and set contrastively both against other such wholes and against a social and natural background is, however incorrigible it may seem to us, a rather peculiar idea within the context of the world's cultures" (1975, p. 48). Other writers provide support for Geertz's point with widespread evidence of holism across the globe. Shweder and Bourne (1982), for example, draw on evidence of contextualism in Tahiti (Levy, 1973), Bali (Geertz, 1975), the Gahuku-Gama of New Guinea (Read, 1955), and the Zapotec of Oaxaca, Mexico (Selby, 1974). From the perspective of these and other scholars (Gergen, 1984; Sampson, 1985), what begins to seem odd is the American insistence that some stable central core of self or personality underlies the ebb and flow of action across situations and circumstances.

Varieties of Contextualism

Contextualism often appears to be a matter of people who "are" their roles rather than acting them. Thus the Baining of Papua New Guinea describe self and others in terms of their roles or their social interaction. They avoid an "interiorized" description or explanation that focuses on subjective states, personal will, or experience (Fajans, 1985; cf. Rosenberg, 1979). Ochs (1982), for example, studied the verbal interactions of children and their caregivers in Samoa and the United States. Samoa, like other Pacific cultures, appears to be relatively contextual; for instance, the vocabulary does not include terms for "individual," "personality," or "self."

A second contextual theme consists of failing to recognize differences between self and other. For example, residents of Ifaluk atoll in Micronesia appear to perform a merger of self and other through the use of "we." An ethnographer reports making an error by asking "Do you want to come with me to get water?" when "We'll go get water now, OK?" was appropriate (Lutz, 1985, p. 44). For mental events and such emotions as love, "we" statements are more common in Ifaluk language than "I" statements. Internal as well as external experiences are presumptively shared beyond the boundaries of skin.

The nature of contextualism in modern market societies like Japan is not the same as in these traditional societies. Japanese culture is in fact deeply concerned with certain aspects of the individual, such as personal development. The Japanese social actor appears to be an actor embedded in roles; yet the individual is not lost in these roles.

Japanese Conceptions of Social Actors

Japan, a modern capitalist society, is generally perceived as standing on the contextual, holistic side of a great cultural divide. The United States seems to stand on the other side of that divide. But the development of capitalist economies promotes some aspects of individualism (e.g., M. Friedman, 1982; Hofstede, 1980). In what ways, then, are Japanese conceptions of the social actor individualistic?

To address this question it is useful to recall Lukes' dimensions of the individual: moral worth, self-development, privacy, and autonomy. Evidence suggests that in terms of moral worth and especially in terms of self-development, Japanese conceptions are decidedly individualistic. Concurrently with the United States, Japan experienced a boom in meritocratic beliefs about success in the later nineteenth and early twentieth centuries. Whether one argues that striving for success was a matter of self-interest in both countries (Yamamura, 1974) or that the Japanese achiever had to strive for family rather than self (Kinmonth, 1981), accounts of what people valued and of how they used education to attain their goals are remarkably similar.

One cultural hero in Japan is an American little remembered in his own land: "The greatest tourist attraction in the city of Sapporo . . . is the campus of Hokkaido University with its statue of Dr. William Smith Clark. The famous words he addressed to his students—'Boys, be ambitious'—are inscribed on many souvenir items. Indeed, the name of Dr. Clark has become so famous that more than 80 percent of Japanese high school and university students today can identify who he was and what he did in Hokkaido. It is doubtful if 10 percent of American intellectuals, or the students of Amherst College, where Clark was president in the 1870s, know his name" (H. Kato, 1979, p. 173). The founder of Hokkaido University, Clark remains a symbol of striving toward individual achievement. He was not the only popular foreigner urging Japanese toward individual success. British writer Samuel Smiles' *Self-Help*, a best-seller in the Japan of the 1870s and later, was a moralistic exhortation to virtue and achievement (and achievement through virtue). Magazines urging educational and economic attainment, such as the aptly titled *Seiko* (Success), reinforced this message within a modernizing Japan.

Individualistic tendencies in Japan should not be attributed solely to economic changes or to Western contacts. It has been argued, for example, that Confucian ethics and the samurai code of honor provided a "functional equivalent" to Protestant religious beliefs in spurring the development of Japanese capitalism (Bellah, 1957/1985; cf. Tawney, 1962; Weber, 1958). Whatever its social structural and cultural sources, Japanese attention to self-development and belief in meritocracy predates the Meiji Restoration (Dore, 1967; T. C. Smith, 1967). Well before Japan opened to the West, there was some opportunity for meritocratic advancement in the Japanese bureaucracy on the basis of education, and economic advancement was becoming possible through nascent market forces. Even in the first half of the nineteenth century, an egalitarian emphasis on merit served as an alternative, if not dominant, Japanese value, as the writings of Ogyu Sorai exemplify: "All human ability rises from the difficulties of life. . . . When Heaven would entrust men with great responsibilities, it first sends them troubles. Talent therefore develops below. . . . The wise and talented men of history rose from low rank" (quoted in T. C. Smith, 1967, p. 82). In the early 1800s such arguments were used to justify advancement by the lower ranks of the samurai. By the latter days of the nineteenth century, thanks to Japanese reformers and to visitors such as Clark, such relatively individualistic and meritocratic themes of "human ability" were widespread.

Thus American and Japanese culture seem to differ little in terms of the self-development or self-realization component of individualism. Indeed, Japanese respondents to a poll concerning their "favorite word" chose "effort," closely followed by "perseverance" (Shapiro & Hiatt, 1989). Or, as the American adage puts it, "If at first you don't succeed, try, try again."

Self-development need not, however, imply personal autonomy. This apparent paradox led Ruth Benedict (1946) to argue that Japan exemplified a shame culture, wherein the individual refrains from wrongdoing in response to the anticipated reactions of others, in contrast to a guilt culture such as that of the United States, wherein the individual avoids misdeeds because of their internalized psychological costs (the experience of guilt). Among the many criticisms of this shame-guilt dichotomy, George De Vos (1973) noted that in the arena of achievement, Japanese do appear to exhibit strong feelings of guilt over failure. What generates the guilt, however, is failure to meet the expectations of family members. In other words, the Japanese self develops with a more explicit interconnection to others and awareness of obligations to those others.

When asked in a social psychology experiment to describe their causal actions, Japanese research subjects essentially responded as interconnected individualists. Cousins (1989) summarized their responses: "Japanese subjects make use of an array of attributive terms suggestive of individuality, but this is an individuality expressed within, rather than beyond, the provinces of social context. . . . Japanese are less concerned with asserting themselves, through abstract summaries of behavior, as autonomous agents whose actions and feelings exist apart from everyday social setting and engagements with others" (p. 130). Japanese talk—and apparently think—about themselves as individuals-in-context. Thus it is hardly surprising that the philosopher Hajime Nakamura (1968) boldly concludes that "Japanese in general did not develop a clear-cut concept of the human individual *qua* individual as an objective unit like an inanimate thing, but the individual is always found existing in a network of human relationships" (p. 144).

Self-development coupled with lack of individual autonomy; guilt based on failing to meet obligations to others: Such are the apparently paradoxical conceptions of the individual that greet the observer of modern Japanese culture. Some light can be shed on this paradox by exploring the ways in which the Japanese language allows a speaker to talk about the social actor; the language both exemplifies and enforces a relational conception of the individual as residing in a social context.

Japanese Word Usage

Japanese word meaning and word usage reflect basic ways in which Japanese are nested within a network of social relationships.[2] "For the Japanese, selfness is not a constant like the ego but denotes a fluid concept . . . for Euro-Americans, 'the self,' even though it develops from relations from others, is, in the final analysis, one's uniqueness or one's substance. By contrast, *jibun*, the word for self in Japanese, originally meant 'one's share' of *something* beyond oneself. It is neither a substance nor an attribute having a constant oneness" (Kimura, *Hito to hito no aida,* quoted in Hamaguchi, 1985, p. 302).

The word for "self" is not the only example that reflects an understanding of social actors as contextual rather than individual beings. For example, to be *sincere* in English is to be oneself—to give one's views in the face of pressures to do otherwise, to play some part, or to curry favor. To be *seijitsu* (sincere) in Japanese often involves carrying out one's role obligations— doing or saying what one should in the face of pressures that could include one's own desires. Each word evokes or preserves the integrity of a culturally defined core. But the American core is closer to an individual attribute, whereas the Japanese core is closer to a social relation between individuals.

Several writers have focused on personal pronouns as a key difference between the Japanese and English languages.[3] Japanese and European languages share a basic set of dimensions to describe a person in different relationships (Brown, 1965); the dimensions of hierarchy and solidarity as depicted in figure 1.1 produce four logical combinations of relationships. These four types of ties in turn yield six basic ways of talking. A highly solidary relationship can involve equals, or a superior talking to an inferior, or the reverse; a relationship of low solidarity can also involve speech by an equal, a superior, or an inferior. Indo-European languages, like Japanese, have historically made some provision for hierarchy as well as solidarity through different "you" words (e.g., the French *tu* vs. *vous*, the German *du* vs. *Sie*). In these languages the pronoun historically used to address a superior is the one used for a stranger, and the term historically used to address an inferior is used for a friend; the direction of change has been toward varying one's pronouns solely on the basis of solidarity (Brown, 1965). But today, in English as well as other European languages, terms of address and titles serve many of the hierarchical functions once served by the use of different pronouns. In the West it is still one's superior who is Mr. or Ms.

Beyond this dimensional similarity are important differences that reflect the contextual nature of Japanese conceptions of the social actor. The Japanese language has a wider variety of words for "I," "you," and the like. A Japanese refers to self in a number of ways depending on horizontal and vertical dimensions of the connection between self and other (i.e., the relative familiarity of the other person and the relative roles or statuses of self and other). Various honorific or humble prefixes, words, and verb forms cause a person's conversation to vary dramatically as a function of the social status, age, and sex of the two parties involved, even though the formal content may remain constant. Technically speaking, in Japanese it is difficult to greet someone adequately, including bowing to the appropriate depth, without fairly substantial knowledge about the person being greeted.

As many as fourteen words for "I" may ensue; the contrast with English is profound. As one English phrase, made popular by Popeye, goes, "I yam what I yam and that's all what I yam." Passin (1980) notes, "While this is probably translatable into Japanese, I am not sure that the proposition would be true. In English, and in the European languages, in general, whatever it is that I am, I am always the same 'I.' In Japanese, this is not the case. What I am—and therefore what first-person singular pronoun to use—depends upon the structure of interpersonal relations in the situation in which the identification is required" (p. 1).

Suzuki (1978) has even suggested that it is wrong to categorize Japanese "I" words and "you" words as pronouns, and that to do so is a misplaced generalization from European languages: "First- and second-person pronouns in the Indo-European languages have nothing to do with the concrete properties (position, age, sex, etc.) that the speaker or the addressee possess" (p. 131). Suzuki adds, "In Japanese all terms for self-reference and for address are connected with the confirmation of concrete roles based on a superior-inferior dichotomy in human relationships" (p. 135). Words of self- and other-reference in Japanese serve "to specify and confirm the concrete roles of the speaker and the addressee" (p. 129). Moreover, there is even some quality of taboo about I-you words in Japan. Their use tends to be avoided whenever possible, and repeated use over time appears to degrade their meaning to lower politeness levels (Suzuki, 1978).

In word usage as in other ways, Japan remains a contextual culture despite its market economy and its tradition of individual achievement. It is, however, a contextual culture in which the rich texture of differences between the parties, instead of their autonomy *or* their oneness, is the social focus.

Relationships and Social Actors

Within as well as across cultures, the dimensions of social relationships outlined above—hierarchy and solidarity—appear to underlie conceptions of the actor just as they underlie the use of "I" or "you." Figure 3.1 summarizes the conceptions of social actors that are likely to emerge or to be perceived in different types of relationships.[4] At the microlevel, relationships within cultures are likely to differ in predictable ways. At the macrolevel, cultures themselves may be characterized as emphasizing one or more types of relationship. This argument allows for something like a "modal (typical) personality" (or, in this case, a modal attribution about someone else's personality) across a large-scale unit such as a nation, but does so as a function of the nature and distribution of underlying social relationships.

Two key distinctions among social actors can be built from the dimensions of solidarity and hierarchy: the distinction between separate and connected actors (based on their solidarity) and that between equal and unequal actors (based on their hierarchy). In figure 3.1, solidarity and hierarchy are reflected by the horizontal and vertical dimensions, respectively. The critical dimension for distinguishing individual from contextual cultures is solidarity. Logically, individuation is consistent with low solidarity because a separate entity can be more sharply defined or more distinct when ties are of low solidarity. It is difficult to conceptualize and apparently impossible to find a contextual culture where low-solidarity ties predominate. Contextualism also has an empirical connection to high solidarity because conditions of high interconnectedness are likely to foster sensitivity to the connection (the relationship itself). Hence individuated (low-solidarity) actors are placed on the left of the figure, and contextual (high-solidarity) actors are on the right.

The second distinction is that between equal and unequal. There is, however, an asymmetry between relationships of low and high solidarity in terms of their likelihood of also involving equality or inequality. In societies where relationships are characteristically low in solidarity—as is often true in the United States—the actor is typically thought of as an equal individual,

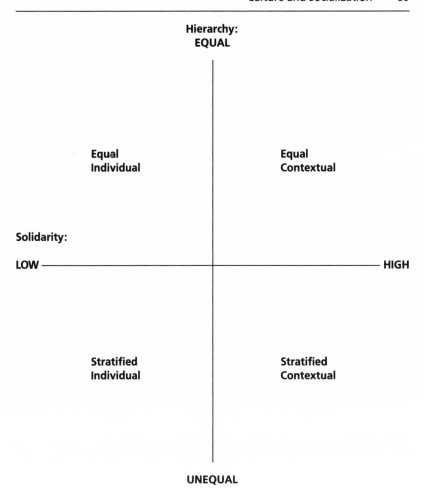

Figure 3.1   Dimensions in the Conception of Self

at least as reflected in formal legal structures and political identities. (Of course, within these societies many role relationships are between unequals, and some institutions such as the military might be thought of as promoting stratified individuals.) Thus we believe that one quadrant of the figure, the lower left quadrant representing the stratified individual, is of minimal interest and may be essentially a null category (at least with reference to legal rights and activities).

High solidarity is different. Relatedness may be expressed by *not* distinguishing between "I" and "you," as in the Ifaluk "we"; in such societies contextuality can mean some degree of fusing of identity, a failure to see differences, a "we-ness." On the other hand, relatedness may be expressed by *carefully* distinguishing among participants to reflect their connection. This is the contextualism that characterizes Japan: a fine-tuned sensitivity and adjustment to the nuances of similarity and difference between parties. The Japanese actor in a social network is literally subject to revision. Because Japanese identity is always framed in a specific self/other context, it is automatically redefined when in a new frame with a new other.[5] In this respect the fourteen "I"s of the Japanese and the "we" of the Ifaluk differ from each other nearly as much as each differs from Popeye's "I yams."

It is this distinction that is represented in the contrast between the upper right quadrant of figure 3.1—equal contextualism, or lack of differentiation of the parties—and the lower right—stratified contextualism, or fine-tuned differentiation among the parties. Equal contextualism is associated with communal, equal social relationships, while stratified contextualism is associated with social differentiation and inequality. The Japanese form of stratified contextualism suppresses ideas of individual autonomy separate from social relationships but encourages self-development and mobility within the bonds of hierarchical relationships.

Such cultural conceptions must originate somewhere; we have argued that their roots lie in characteristic social relationships. But they must also go somewhere; that is, they must be transmitted to new generations in order to constitute a stable culture. Socialization is the way structural and cultural relationships are maintained and reproduced in each new generation.

Socialization into Structure and Culture

Socialization is the concrete manifestation and transmission of social order. Socialization and educational practices typically reflect and reproduce the social structure of the larger society, and Japan is no exception.[6] Japanese socialization practices serve to introduce an individual into a world where the self is typically thought of as a stratified contextual because the "normal" relationship between people is one of high solidarity nested within hierarchies. Resulting relationships often permit little autonomy and require high levels of conformity.

The following anecdote indicates the level of nonconformity that may result in a sanction by the time a Japanese child reaches high school level:

> Naoko Kakesu's offense was to bring a portable hair dryer to high school. For this minor violation of school rules, she was smacked on the head with a magazine, berated by some teachers for her delinquent ways and then slapped five times across the face.

The only unusual thing about this incident was its ending: Kakesu quit the school instead of accepting her treatment as an all-too-normal fact of life in Japanese schools. . . .

Japanese schooling has a dark and authoritarian side. . . . There are rules governing the color of underwear, rules banning dates or visits to coffee shops, rules mandating shaved heads for boys and forcing girls to choose short bobs or modest braids with only black, brown or navy blue rubber bands. Harsh enforcement, often relying on corporal punishment or public humiliation, discourages any attempt to deviate from school-mandated norms. (Shapiro, 1989a, p. A1)

Recently, a more tragic incident made the news. A fifteen-year-old schoolgirl, late to school for the first time, was crushed to death by the five-hundred-pound iron gate of the school, which a teacher swung shut just as the 8:30 bell indicating late arrival was tolling. Some parents and the liberal *Asahi* newspaper immediately complained. The principal stated that in the future the gate would not be closed until 9:00. But at an assembly held to express his regret, the principal also remonstrated: "If more of you would come 10 minutes earlier, teachers wouldn't have to shout, 'Don't be late!' I have no intention of denying my responsibility, but I would like all of you to think again about your basic lifestyle" (Hiatt, 1990).

In its "basic lifestyle," Japanese society enforces a level of conformity and compliance that Americans would find highly uncomfortable. Furthermore, the coercive formal apparatus enforcing school discipline has an underlying base of ideological support. As one Japanese teacher put it, "Parents want the rules to be more and more strict. . . . One statistic said that 70 percent of [teachers] agree with corporal punishment. . . . Mothers seem to like to see school rules applied very severely" (Shapiro, 1989a, p. A27). Thus the coercive rules applied to Japanese high school students represent a restrictive social structure, but they flow from the culture with the approval of its day-to-day forces of authority: parent and teacher.

Conformity means behaving as one's peers do; compliance means doing what authority says to do. This discussion treats the issues under the rubric of conformity because for the most part what the school authority demands *is* conformity. But what does it mean in its Japanese context, and how is it generated?

American social scientific models of human motivation, mirroring the culture's understanding of the individual and of conformity and obedience, tend to depict human motivation as an either-or choice. Either we do as we wish, or we do as we are told or led to do by others; control of self is either internal or it is external.[7] However, the dynamics of conformity and obedience to authority do not necessarily correspond to this model, even in the American context—and certainly not among the Japanese.

Although Americans who see behavior in terms of a dichotomy between internal and external control might assume that the conformity of Japanese teens and their elders is externally driven, coerced, or "for show," this would be a mistake. A conforming behavior does not necessarily imply anything about the thoughts, feelings, or motives of the actor. To understand motivations, one must reexamine the assumption that individual desires necessarily stand in opposition to conformity or compliance. The type of commitment fostered in Japanese schools and workplaces is captured in the concept of *sunao*. To be *sunao* is a goal of Japanese socialization, with complex connotations that rest on Japanese socialization strategies. Often translated as "obedient" when used to describe a child, *sunao* actually implies a more active engagement, an unfolding of self in the approved direction (White, 1987). The *sunao* adult is obedient, prone to accept others, dependent, not self-centered, honest, and free from antagonisms (Murase, 1982). This combination does not evoke a cultural goal in the United States. Our attempts to think of comparable images included "Boy Scout" (which has a pejorative connotation when used to refer to an adult) and "wimp" (whose connotation is unambiguously negative at any age). But in Japanese culture the connotation is both complex and positive.[8]

In sum, obedience and independence need not have the same implications or even the same meanings from one culture to the next. In Japan, obedience and self-actualization do not stand in necessary opposition to one another; more often, self is to be actualized through obedience. Understanding this, however, still does not tell us how it comes to pass. One might surmise that the harsh sanctions meted out to high school students are the culmination of a long childhood of strict discipline and demands for obedience and conformity. In fact, a very different path is followed. Parents (and later on, teachers) slowly, incrementally tighten a web of expectations that are finely calibrated to what the child is developmentally capable of and personally inclined to do.

Mother-Child Relations

Japanese who play a role in childrearing appear more likely than their U.S. counterparts to "let nature take its course." Befu (1971) and Lebra (1976) have argued that the result is a child who is quiet, dependent, and conforming. This is especially true in the all-important first social context: the relationship of mother to child.

Japanese and American mothers talk and act differently toward their babies even at very early stages when the child can contribute relatively little to the interaction. Caudill and Weinstein (1969), who observed sixty infants with their caretakers during typical daily activities in middle-class homes, found differences in patterns of mother-child interaction for infants as young as four months. (Caretakers were mothers more than 90 percent of the time in both cultures.) The authors found American babies to be more active, exploratory, and happily vocal. American mothers, correspondingly, were more lively and verbal in approaching the baby. The American mother talked to elicit happy chats from baby; the Japanese mother talked to soothe complaints.[9] The Japanese mother was "there" more: physically present, lulling, soothing.

The American mother might be said to practice kinship with her child. The Japanese mother regularly practices what Japanese refer to as "skinship": the closeness one experiences when touching (White, 1987, p. 36). Mother and child are in regular contact. Mother takes baby along rather than relying on baby-sitters—even relatives—and baby rides on mother's back rather than in a stroller.

At night, mother sleeps on the floor beside baby on the traditional Japanese bedding, *futon*. Thus the Japanese family extends the closeness of child to adult throughout the day. In a landmark study of sleeping patterns in urban Japanese families, Caudill and Plath (1974) reported that family members voluntarily "co-sleep" to a dramatically greater degree than Americans. Perhaps their most startling datum is that not only do infants sleep in the same room right beside parents, but when a second child comes it is not uncommon for the parents to separate, mother sleeping with infant and father with older child. They summarize the life cycle of sleep and its implications for Japanese personality thus: "An individual in urban Japan can expect to co-sleep in a two-generation group, first as a child and then as a parent, over approximately half of his life. This starts at birth and continues until puberty; it resumes after the birth of the first child and continues until about the time of menopause for the mother; and it reoccurs for a few years in old age. In the interim years the individual can expect to co-sleep in a one-generation group with a sibling after puberty, with a spouse for a few years after marriage, and again with a spouse in late middle age" (p. 301).

Of course, these widely cited data are now more than two decades old. As the "nuclearization" of the family has continued in Japan, opportunities to co-sleep have probably declined. However, one recent study indicates a strong tendency to retain co-sleeping arrangements. Hendry (1986) remarks about a group of high-income kindergarten children: "Out of a total of 176 children, 37 slept regularly in the same bedding as their mothers, 118 slept in the same room, and only 20 in separate rooms. One child slept with a grandmother" (p. 44).

In sum, the Japanese sleep interdependently and across status hierarchies rather than individually; their sleeping hours mirror their waking selves.

Sanctions

This early maternal indulgence and familial closeness may make the Japanese child more susceptible to external social sanctions that involve a threat to closeness (De Vos, 1973). The most severe forms of punishment for a Japanese child involve isolation or threat of abandonment. Where Americans might shut or lock a child in, Japanese shut or lock a child out (Befu, 1971; Lebra, 1976; Vogel & Vogel, 1961). Aside from the severe sanction of some form of isolation or abandonment, the Japanese mother tries to socialize by means of rewards; when faced with misbehavior she may tease, ridicule, wheedle, bribe, or appeal for the child's empathy.

When a child has misbehaved, the Japanese mother's response is typically solicitous: "The Japanese mother typically approaches a demanding or disobedient child with solicitude rather than with authority, with as much reasoning and explaining as the child is capable of understanding. . . . A Japanese mother might even plead and beg the child to do as told, rather than resort to physical punishment or other authoritarian methods. . . . In extreme cases, if the mother fails at all other methods, she is prone to give sweets to the child as a method of appeasing him—even minutes before mealtime" (Befu, 1971, pp. 156–157). The child, in turn, becomes highly sensitive to maternal desires and maternal assessments that behavior is or is not acceptable to others.

Love

The Japanese language has words for love that English lacks. These words capture the mutual interdependency of parent, especially mother, and child. The psychiatrist Takeo Doi (1973) argued that the concept of *amae* is a core element of Japanese culture. According to Doi, *amaeru* (the verb form of *amae*) means "to depend and presume on another's love," "to seek and bask in another's indulgence." It might be called an "active passivity" that is initially characteristic of the infant vis-à-vis its mother. It is reciprocated by the mother's *amayakasu*, or indulgent treatment of one who shows amae. There is no English equivalent to these terms. These concepts evoke a Japanese sense of identity as contingent on being embedded in a group that affords an opportunity to depend on other group members (Hamaguchi, 1985). Despite the poverty of Western languages in trying to describe it, *amae* appears to be a universal sentiment. "Why, even a puppy does it," is how his colleague reacted to Doi (1973, p. 15). For the Japanese this emotion has a cultural centrality that it lacks in the West.

To those who would argue that obedient adults are best created by imposing obedience on the young, the Japanese mother offering sweets provides a powerful counterexample. Socialization to "oneness" with mother is also socialization into dependency upon and solidarity with a fundamentally benign authority. Hierarchical and solidary ties are one and the same where a child's dependency on a mother is concerned. Thus, instead of forcing the young to toe the line, the indulgent Japanese mother who sketches a hazy boundary between self and child fosters an adult offspring who is enmeshed in a web of vertical and horizontal social interdependencies.

Children at School

During the years between early childhood socialization and the exacting discipline of the Japanese high school,[10] the motivational foundations for modern Japanese citizenship and scholarship are laid (Hamilton, Blumenfeld, Akoh, & Miura, 1989a, 1989b). In early elementary school, overt coercion plays little part in the process. The Japanese teacher builds upon what the parents—primarily the mothers—have already done. This building is done carefully, step-by-step, starting from a presumption that the Japanese child sees authority as essentially benevolent. This presumption rests upon the indulgence of mothers and upon the respect accorded to teachers as authority figures throughout Japanese society. Authority that already has respect and goodwill does not need to instill fear.

When children enter first grade, teachers spend considerable time— weeks—teaching them simple procedural tasks such as how to stand, bow, and line up. The basic expectation is simple: Everyone is presumed to be capable. The teaching strategy is equally simple: Learning to perfection requires practice. As White (1987) notes, the teacher's philosophy is part of a broad cultural heritage. It echoes traditional Zen archery training. If one practices long enough at drawing the bow, the arrow will eventually fly true. Actual performance is seen as deriving from perfect procedure. By the early school years, Japanese students become adept at handling themselves in the classroom.

From the beginning, Japanese education draws on the strengths of the group to assist the individual member. One key goal of education is social: to teach the child to cooperate with others. Much of the routine of daily classroom life and the maintenance of order is handled by job assignments and children's self-policing. Work groups (*han*) are responsible for the product of their individual members. Children are grouped together in the *han* heterogeneously, so that the more facile students will assist the slower ones. The teacher's goal is to shape a group of cooperative children who have high average achievement with little variation in performance among them. The goal is regularly met.

All this does not mean that the Japanese elementary classroom is an orderly place. Western observers are often dismayed by the levels of noise and apparent confusion. Perhaps the most succinct way to describe the contrast with American elementary classrooms is to say that Japanese teachers are not afraid of losing control. Instead, they see the children as naturally amenable to control. A classroom incident witnessed by one of the present authors illustrates this point:

It was a hot July day. Our group of researchers was videotaping a lesson. The teacher, whom we will call Mr. Tanaka, was in shirt-sleeves. He occasionally wiped sweat from his face as he lectured. The subject was reading comprehension, and Tanaka was asking students to describe in their own words the flow of the argument in what they had read. He urged them to express themselves simply, so that "even a third-grader could understand." Most of the forty or so pupils in this fifth-grade classroom participated actively in this exercise.

As the lesson was drawing to a close, some of the students became restless, giggling and looking out a window that overlooked an internal school corridor. They were watching another class that was streaming down the corridor toward recess. Faced with this budding disruption, Tanaka made an instant decision. He quickly suggested to the children that they yell their explanations of the reading passage to the students who were passing by. He had noticed that these passers-by were third-graders. His students gleefully began to wave and yell, and the bedlam continued for the one to two minutes that Tanaka knew it must. He stood laughing, hands on hips, until the children began to subside. Then he gradually brought them around to the lesson.

Within one or two minutes after the last third-grader had rounded the corner, the children in Tanaka's class were quite orderly, quietly receiving an assignment and preparing for their own recess. At the end of the lesson, instead of pupils bowing to teacher and vice versa, as is usually done, both pupils and teacher turned to bow to the observers. Then recess began and bedlam broke loose once more.

Tanaka's handling of a small disruption consisted of *creating* a major disruption, preempting any involuntary loss of control and having fun in the process.

This incident illustrates an important lesson from the indulgence of Japanese authority toward the child. Authority cannot be defied (or even really tested) if the authority is aware enough and skillful enough at channeling the natural urges and interests of the child. The child's elementary school experience is consistent with and builds upon the naturally hierarchical and intimately contextual authority of Japanese mothers. In the context of this benevolent authority, the child is further socialized into a society where normal relationships are solidary hierarchies and where the self-other boundary between child and authority may not be as rigid as it is in the United States.

Recent quantitative research also serves to illustrate the inadequacy of sharp distinctions between internally and externally controlled behavior. Hamilton et al. (1989b) asked Japanese and American fifth-grade children to provide reasons for academic achievement and good behavior. The answers of the Japanese fifth-graders indicated that they were more internally motivated than their American counterparts. For example, they were less likely to refer to fear of punishment and were more likely to refer to the value of learning for its own sake. However, the emotional wellspring of this motivation—what would make the Japanese child feel bad in response to failure and good in response to achievement—centers on pleasing parent and teacher. These results are consistent with De Vos' (1973) argument that Japanese achievement motivation is a "family affair." In contrast, American children rarely said that they would obey *or* achieve to please a parent or teacher. It appears that among American children this middle ground between internal values and external sanctions—the middle ground of pleasing mother and imitating father and occasionally hero-worshipping teacher—is suppressed if not lost. This middle ground is at the core of Japanese socialization. Benign authorities—parents and teachers—are its catalysts.

Adult Socialization

The socialization process does not end with childhood.[11] As might be expected, the "firm as family" does more than offer a one-day orientation and a sharpened pencil to its new employees, especially where white-collar workers are concerned. Businesses have three goals in their orientation periods: to provide new workers with necessary technical information; to introduce them to their community of fellow workers; and to build motivation or spirit in a process known as *seishin kyooiku,* or spiritual education. Spiritual education, not technical detail, is seen as the key to membership in the corporate community. (Younger workers may tend to find spiritual education old-fashioned; nevertheless they undergo versions of it and they work for people who believe in it.)

Anthropologist Thomas Rohlen's *For Harmony and Strength* (1974) is a compelling account of corporate orientation practices. Rohlen participated in orientation activities while studying the organization of the bank whose motto forms the book's title. Training was carried out in groups. Trainees stayed in a special dormitory for a period that usually lasted from two days to a week. Rohlen reports:

> Each morning the trainees are awakened at 6:30, and, dressed in athletic outfits, they soon assemble in front of the institute where the bank and Japanese flags are raised, the bank pledges are recited, and exercises are conducted. . . .
>
> Rakes are occasionally taken along for the purpose of cleaning up a section of the park. The president and other top executives will sometimes show up before seven to join in the effort. . . . At sunset, a flag-lowering ceremony is accompanied by exercises and announcements similar to the morning ceremony. . . .
>
> During introductory training considerable time is devoted to teaching everyone a number of songs, and as a result training groups are able to sing together when traveling on a bus, during an evening's recreation, or around a campfire. . . .
>
> Strict attention to detail and propriety is constantly encouraged. People who dress in a sloppy manner or fail to comb their hair can expect to be sent back to their rooms. (pp. 196–198)

To American readers, this account is likely to conjure up an image not of a business, but of a religious summer camp.

During this indoctrination period, trainees also participate in special exercises intended to inculcate company values. Rohlen (1974) participated in two such exercises. The first exercise took place while the training group was staying at a government youth center near a town: "Early one morning the trainees were instructed to go down into the town and find work from the residents. Instructions were to go singly from house to house offering to work without pay. They were to do whatever their host asked of them. It was strongly emphasized that this was not to be a group operation. Each was to go alone and work alone for the entire day" (p. 203). This task was psychologically difficult for at least two reasons. It was to be carried out alone, rather than in the company of one's now-close fellow group members. It was also to involve approaching strangers with an odd request even though Japanese generally attempt to ignore strangers. When the trainees returned from this difficult day, the discussion theme was: "What is the meaning of work?" The message the company executives wanted to convey was that no form of work is intrinsically good or bad, but pleasure in work depends on the worker's attitude.

The second exercise, an endurance walk, was also a test for the individual rather than the group. Within the bank, it is a legendary part of this bank's training regimen, at least in part because of its twenty-five-mile length: "The trainees were to walk the first nine miles together in a single body. The second nine miles were to be covered with each squad walking as a unit. The last seven miles were to be walked alone and in silence. . . . It was forbidden to take any refreshment. . . . A dozen or so young men from the bank were stationed along the route to offer the trainees cold drinks which, of course, they had to refuse. . . . The walk began around seven-thirty in the morning and finished around three in the afternoon" (Rohlen, 1974, pp. 205–206). The point of this exercise was the central importance of spiritual resources; related to this is the notion that one's most important competition is with oneself, not others. The themes were hammered in during the last seven miles:

Each individual, alone in a quiet world, was confronted by the sweep of his own thoughts as he pushed forward.

My own experience was to become acutely aware of every sort of pain. Great blisters had obviously formed on the soles of my feet; my legs, back, and neck ached; and at times I had a sense of delirium. . . . Other moments brought feverish dreams of somehow sneaking away. . . . I kept going, I suppose, because I feared discovery.

I could see that I was easily tempted and inclined to quit. Under such stress some of my thoughts were obviously not serving my interest in completing the course. Whatever will power I had arose from pride and from an emerging, almost involuntary belief in the spiritual approach. If I was to finish I needed spiritual strength. It angered and amused me to realize how cleverly this exercise had been conceived. (Rohlen, 1974, p. 207)

Orientation without follow-up is unlikely to lead to long-term commitment. As noted earlier, permanent employment and organizational emphasis on seniority help to cement the individual into a highly solidary hierarchy. Workers progress through the ranks both by seniority and by sensitive use of the mentoring that is provided in the *oyabun-kobun* relationships that commonly form. Authorities' decision making is also considerably more consensual in Japanese firms than in their American counterparts. Quality control circles and other techniques such as the *ringi-seido* procedure for decision making are part of a process of consensus building through the use of informal networks. In the *ringi* system decisions are made through a process that can be initiated by low- or middle-level managers, who may draft a petition and see that it works its way up through the firm's hierarchy. By this process the top management bears formal responsibility for all decisions while the firm formally delegates authority to lower management (Allston, 1986; Lincoln & McBride, 1987). One result of such programs is to build commitment to the organization and to place responsibility for decisions with hierarchical groups rather than individuals (Lincoln & Kalleberg, 1985, 1990; Sasaki, 1981; Vogel, 1975).

Resocialization

Social scientists speak of *re*socialization when people are identified as not having adequately "learned their lesson" and when society is called upon to do something about it. Unlike the sometimes haphazard or unorganized primary socialization that occurs in homes and schools, resocialization is organized and often occurs in formal institutional settings. Every society has its failures, its deviants, its outcasts; Japan is no exception.[12] What is exceptional about Japan is the small number of such failures and the way in which Japanese attempt to deal with various forms of deviance.

For deviants of various kinds, one important goal of Japanese resocialization efforts is restoration of *sunao*. One resocialization technique that seems to epitomize the Japanese orientation to deviance is Naikan therapy, which is widely used for such problems as delinquency and addiction. Naikan therapy explicitly trades on the person's guilt at failure to fulfill obligations—in particular, obligations to parents and other authorities (Lebra, 1976; Murase, 1974). To many of its successful patients, the main goal is "becoming *sunao*" (Murase, 1982).

In Naikan the person undergoes seven days of meditation in long daily shifts from dawn to near bedtime. The person sits in a quiet place, cut off from distractions by a screen, interrupted only by short visits from the therapist to guide meditation. The subject to be addressed is the benefits received from others and the obligations owed to them. This subject is attacked along two dimensions: persons to whom obligation is owed and the life cycle during which the obligations have accrued. The meditation typically begins with and centers on mother as the person to whom obligation is owed and the time period of childhood as the period in which obligations are incurred. The procedures and even the goals of Naikan could not be mistaken for those of a Western therapeutic procedure. Identity is smoothed out—made *sunao*—through thankfulness for others' indulgences. With this therapeutic approach to resocialization, we symbolically come full circle to a sleepy Japanese child carried on its mother's back.

Conclusions

In microcosm—a Japanese mother lulling her baby, a Japanese teacher-managing rowdy behavior in a classroom—such structural concepts as solidarity and hierarchy and such cultural concepts as "stratified contextual" come to life and take on meaning. To be less-than-separate from mother is a first version of a culture's contextualism and may be its cornerstone. To be guided by a confident teacher who channels rather than suppresses the inevitable flow of childish energy is to experience formal authority, authority other-than-parents, as fundamentally benevolent and reasonable. The American experience with parental and educational authorities is often different from this. It would be surprising if these different experiences were not reflected in views of the person. Our concern is how these different experiences, and the different cultural conceptions that shape them, are reflected in judgments of the responsibilities of persons who do wrong and cause harm.

PART TWO

Responsibility and Sanction

4

Responsibility:
A Research Agenda

In this chapter we lay out the variables in our empirical studies of responsibility. Our predictions about these variables take into account the microlevel of differences between roles within a society as well as the macrolevel of differences between American and Japanese societies. The challenge is to build and test a coherent theory about what makes people responsible when things go wrong and what should then be done about it: a theory of responsibility and sanction.

Having said that responsibility is a matter of action and obligation, roles and deeds, there remains a broad range of issues one might examine empirically. As Lloyd-Bostock (1983) notes, "an almost unlimited programme of experiments could be devised simply by browsing through [legal] material" (p. 264). The research described below required selection of a small, manageable number of dimensions or aspects of roles and deeds. The discussion that follows focuses on those variables that we chose to examine, and should not be construed as an inventory of all factors that might affect responsibility judgments.

Deeds

"If we conceive of a person as an embodied mind and will, we may draw a distinction between two questions concerning the conditions of liability and punishment. The first question is what general types of outer conduct (*actus reus*) or what sorts of harm are required for liability? The second question is how closely connected with such conduct or such harm must the embodied mind or will of an individual person be to render him liable to punishment?" (Hart, 1968, p. 221).

The law commonly distinguishes between a person's overt act and its consequences on the one hand, and the state of mind in which the person performed the act on the other; the mental elements in action are central to the process of determining liability for sanctions. Psychological research on judgment of wrongdoing has similarly emphasized the contrast between *consequences* of action and the actor's *intent*. The seminal research of Piaget (1932/1965) stressed developmental progression from judgment focused on the objective consequences of action to judgment focused on the actor's subjective intent. Piaget's attempt to outline a broad two-stage or two-level moral development process—of which the shift from consequences to intent is an important component—was later expanded into a six-stage, purportedly universal model by Kohlberg (1969, 1981, 1984).

Piaget's influence was felt in social psychology through the work of Heider (1958). Heider proposed five levels in the attribution of responsibility (see table 4.1). The first level, Association, describes a type of vicarious liability. As indicated above, this sort of liability is involved when the law uses role relationships between an actor and some other to determine the other's responsibility for the actor's conduct. The second, third, and fourth levels—Causality, Foreseeability, and Intentionality—concern the mental state that must accompany an act for the actor to be responsible. In legal terms, Causality is strict liability, Foreseeability is negligence liability, and Intentionality is essential for criminal liability. Heider's fifth level, Justification, concerns some of the excuses and justifications an actor may advance to defeat attributions of responsibility.

For the most part, psychological research on responsibility judgments has made use of Heider's levels by presenting subjects with stories that represent varying levels of an actor's mental state and seeing how much difference this makes in the responsibility allocated. The results are consistent with Piaget's (1932/1965) suggestion of developmental trends in how responsibility is judged, with adults more sophisticated at taking the actor's mental state into account.[1] In addition, situations themselves differ in the level of responsibility they imply. For example, adults are capable of using rules that exemplify each of Heider's levels, however developmentally "primitive," depending on the case. Thus even vicarious responsibility, Heider's Association level, is readily attributed by adults to certain people under certain circumstances. Because our research concentrates on actors who are in some way causally connected to outcomes, this level assumes less importance here. Heider's three middle categories define the central component of an actor's deed: mental state. These form the core of our research into the impact of mental state.

In theory, another key aspect of deeds is the nature and severity of an act's *consequences*. Piaget's (1932/1965) early work indicated that young children, using what lawyers would call a strict liability rule, tend to say that a child who accidentally broke fifteen plates was "naughtier" than a child who neg-

Table 4.1 Heider's Stages of Responsibility Attribution

Level*	Definition	Approximate legal equivalent
I. Association	A person is "held responsible for each effect that is in any way connected with him or that seems in any way to belong to him" (Heider, 1958, p. 113).	Vicarious responsibility
II. Causality	Anything "caused by [a person] p is ascribed to him. Causation is understood in the sense that p was a necessary condition for the happening, even though he could not have foreseen the outcome however cautiously he proceeded . . . The person is judged not according to his intention but according to the actual results of what he does" (p. 113).	Strict liability
III. Foreseeability	Here "p is considered responsible, directly or indirectly, for any aftereffect he may have foreseen even though it was not a part of his own goal and therefore still not a part of the framework of personal causality" (p. 113).	Negligence
IV. Intention	At this stage "only what p intended is perceived as having its source in him" (p. 113).	Criminal responsibility
V. Justification	In this final stage "even p's own motives are not entirely ascribed to him but are seen as having their source in the environment. The responsibility for the act is at least shared by the environment" (p. 114).	Legal justifications, excuses, mitigations of III or IV (e.g., duress)

Source: Reprinted from Hamilton, 1978b, by permission of the publisher
*Labels originally applied by Shaw and Sulzer (1964) and Sulzer (1971)

ligently broke one. Social psychologists' interest in consequences grew when a finding by Walster (1966) suggested that the degree of responsibility attributed to an actor who is involved in an accident is a function of the severity of the consequences of the accident: the more serious the consequences, the greater the responsibility attributed. But Walster's consequence effect has been difficult to reproduce. Burger (1981) found that only six of twenty-one studies he surveyed had found this effect. A number of writers have expressed reservations about this line of research (e.g., Fincham & Jaspars, 1980; Vidmar & Crinklaw, 1974). Nevertheless, this hypothesis continues to have some supporters (see Burger, 1981; Semin & Manstead, 1983).[2]

The severity of consequences was included as a "deed" factor in this study of responsibility largely because of the controversial role that consequences have played in psychological research on adult judgments of wrongdoing. In addition, the small amount of cross-cultural evidence on the relative importance of mental state versus consequences made the question of consequences an interesting one.

Predictions

With respect to mental state, we expected that an actor would be held more responsible for acts described as negligent than for accidental outcomes, and in turn more responsible for intentional acts than for negligent acts. This prediction represents a linear progression: At the level of accidents (Causality), there is no control and no intent; at the level of negligence (Foreseeability), there is negligence over what was presumed controllable, but with no intent; and at the level of intent (Intentionality) there is both controllability and intent.[3] We did not necessarily expect any impact of consequence severity on responsibility; if an effect appeared, we expected that actors would be held more responsible for actions that had more serious consequences.

Context

Some factors in responsibility judgments are best identified as aspects of the *context* within which an act occurs rather than aspects of deeds or roles. The context of an act offers the observer potential clues as to the purposes and meaning of behavior. This research focused on two such aspects.

One aspect of context is brought to the situation by the actor: the person's *past pattern* of similar wrongful behavior. In Kelley's (1967, 1971, 1973) terms, a past pattern of similar acts provides consistency information: It demonstrates that the actor behaves in the same way in response to a given stimulus across time and situational contexts. Information about past pattern facilitates attribution to the actor's internal disposition or trait (e.g., Ajzen & Fishbein, 1973; Monson, 1983; Nisbett & Ross, 1980; Ross, 1977). Where there is no past similar behavior, this contextual information invites the observer to find something distinctive in the situation that explains the behavior. Information about past pattern is context information about the individual actor and the meaning of the actor's deed; it is information about what kind of person this is.

A second important contextual factor is the *influence of another person* on the actor. Extreme versions of influence take the form of coercion and duress:

"He made me do it, officer." Such an excuse essentially amounts to the removal of agency from the actor (Hart & Honoré, 1959). Coercion and duress are less interesting to us than are more subtle and situationally legitimized influences from others—situations in which another involved person attempts to make the actor behave in a certain way. When such influences are hierarchical, they are often called orders. When they occur among equals, they may be interpreted as social pressure. In both cases, the person exerting the influence has some "standing" in the situation, hence the action can be called influence rather than coercion.

Influence from another, in all its forms, enables a judge to conclude that an act was less than fully "owned by" the person who performed it; the actor can then be deemed less responsible than would otherwise be the case. The relative impact of the influence of another person is contingent upon the relationship of actor and other. For example, influence from equals or inferiors provides individuals with less of an excuse than influence from superiors. In contrast to variations in the actor's past pattern, other's influence is a contextual factor that is linked to the role relationships of actor, victim, and other.

Predictions

In this research, one contextual factor—past pattern of behavior—primarily concerns the actor and the type of person he or she is. An actor with a past pattern of wrongdoing can be expected to be held more responsible for a new misdeed. The second contextual factor—influence from another person—primarily concerns the nature of the actor's role relationships. A *lack* of influence from another person is expected to produce higher levels of responsibility.

Role Relationships

Imagine you are walking down a neighborhood sidewalk on a spring morning. Coming toward you is a small boy, perhaps five or six years old, skipping down the sidewalk and bouncing a ball. About thirty feet behind the boy a woman is walking. Suddenly the boy darts out into the street after his ball; he is hit by a car rounding a curve in the road. How responsible is the woman for what happened?

One of the present authors has tried this thought experiment regularly in classes and has just as regularly obtained the expected result: It is necessary to know *who* the woman is before we can determine her responsibility. If she was the boy's mother, we are likely to hold her more responsible if only because we expected more of her in the way of attention and foresight. What she did—or, in this case, failed to do—cannot be fully evaluated except in the context of who she was.

As this example suggests, social roles can have two kinds of impact on judgments of wrongdoing. First, roles may have a direct impact on a judgment of responsibility or a decision about sanction. As Hart's (1968) story of the captain in chapter 1 teaches us, a person in one role, or one type of role, may be held more responsible than a person in a different role vis-à-vis some victim of an action. A mother may be held more responsible simply because the harm involved her child. Second, the actions of people in different role relationships may be weighed differently. For example, the actor's mental state may be more or less important to our judgment of responsibility depending on that actor's role. A mother's inattentiveness to her child may be seen as more serious than that of a stranger. In the real world, it is not always easy to tell when a role per se is making a difference in a person's responsibility and when that role is causing others to weigh information about deeds differently. Our study assesses each of these effects of roles. Roles can be described and analyzed into a bewildering variety of categories (Biddle, 1979; Biddle & Thomas, 1966; Heiss, 1981; Sarbin & Allen, 1968). We used the dimensions of hierarchy and solidarity as the framework for our analysis.

Hierarchy

In typical hierarchical relationships one party is seen as having the right or power to direct the actions of the other party, and generally as being responsible for actions that may be performed under that person's orders or instructions. Within the context of ongoing relationships, authority is not simply a matter of greater power to coerce or reward. It is authority's legitimacy, not its power, that places duties on subordinates and obligations on superiors (Blau, 1955; French & Raven, 1959; Kelman & Hamilton, 1989). When two people stand as equals in a relationship, in contrast, there is no special, asymmetrical web of obligations and responsibilities between them.[4]

Predictions about Hierarchy

Hierarchy is not simply a question of power. Within the context of ongoing interactions, legitimate hierarchical relationships create a set of expectations about likely behavior derived from an actor's social characteristics. These expectations influence our judgments of the actor's behavior (Jones & McGillis, 1976). In hierarchies, superiors are held responsible for actions at lower levels of intentionality. Vicarious liability and strict liability rules are typically reserved for corporations, employers, generals, and parents.

These legal tendencies have parallels in everyday judgments. Superiors tend to be subject to diffuse standards for their actions; they are supposed to oversee the actions of others and to exercise such qualities as good judgment, caution, and control. Most important, they are expected to foresee problems and respond to them. Failure to meet these diffuse expectations is less readily excused by a reference to the actor's mental state. "I didn't mean to do it" and "I couldn't help it" excuses are less acceptable. Because superiors are held to stricter standards of accountability than subordinates, it can be expected that ordinary citizens will judge superiors to be more responsible than equals who are involved in wrongdoing, holding constant the actors' mental states. That is, for a deed of a given level of intentionality, a superior who wrongs a subordinate should be held more responsible than an equal who wrongs an equal.[5]

Solidarity

Equal and authoritative relations occur throughout social life, but the ways in which they manifest themselves are governed by the types of ties between individuals. In general, Japanese relationships seem to exhibit higher solidarity than similar American relationships. Within each society, however, some relationships are typically of higher solidarity than others. All modern societies reflect the entire continuum of relationship solidarity. Here our concern is with these microlevel effects of solidarity.

Predictions about Solidarity

In Japan and the United States, as in other advanced industrial societies, relationships between people range from interactions between strangers to closely knit, long-term, complex relationships. The impact of varying solidarity on responsibility judgments is less straightforward than the impact of hierarchy because of the role of the victim in acts of wrongdoing in high-solidarity relationships. The actor is likely to have two believable defenses in such cases: "he/she deserved it" on the one hand, and "I didn't mean to" on the other.

The argument that the other party deserved it need not be explicitly made for it to play a part in the judgment of closely tied parties. In Collingwood's (1940) terms, one causes a person to act by providing him or her with a motive for the action. In close relationships it is often as accurate to describe a behavior as a *reaction* as it is to call it an action: "If I provide you with the motive to commit a crime, then I have caused you to engage in the offense. Even though you freely and deliberately committed the crime, I should share the responsibility" (Shaver, 1985, p. 26). In highly solidary relationships, it is often the case that the victim is involved in the wrongdoing in the sense of providing the actor a motive. For example, some women who commit murder engage in what is called "victim-precipitated homicide": They kill a male who has been threatening or attacking them, usually their spouse or lover. In general, the presumption of involvement of the victim in an act of wrongdoing can follow simply from the extended interaction and generalized exchanges that characterize highly solidary relationships. Actions become reactions in such long-term exchanges. Our research focused on typical instances of wrongdoing in the relevant settings. Hence it could be expected that victims might be seen as sharing responsibility to a greater extent in incidents that represented highly solidary ties.

Moreover, the excuse "I didn't mean to" need not be explicit. An actor may not need to deny intent when a closely tied person has been harmed because outside observers may be ready to believe that an injury or harm had to be accidental, or at most careless, rather than malicious. Recent legal and social arguments about the problem of child abuse reflect the state's difficulties in invading the realm of family life, part of which involves the usual presumption that parental intent is benign.

Overall, we expected that less responsibility would be attributed to the actor in highly solidary relationships, either because the actor's intentionality would be assumed to be low or because the victim's participation would reduce the actor's responsibility, or both. Had the incidents represented clearly unprovoked wrongdoing, in contrast, we would have expected responsibility to be judged more severely where relationships were highly solidary.

Combining the two role relationship dimensions, hierarchy and solidarity, yields the four types of relationships outlined in chapter 1 (figure 1.1). Figure 4.1 summarizes the combinations of relationships investigated in our research, including the aspects of deeds and contexts studied. On the right side of the figure are examples of highly solidary social ties. Bonds between siblings, for example, are equal relations of high solidarity; a parent is an authority in a high-solidarity relationship with children. Intermediate in the figure are relationships in which solidarity is low but some sort of relationship or at least exchange can be said to exist. Representing equal relations, buyers and sellers are in the quintessential equal, low-solidarity relationship; representing hierarchical relations, bosses and workers are in a low-solidarity, authority relationship.

The left side of figure 4.1 presents the limiting case: situations where there is no relationship between the parties, in which solidarity could be said to be nonexistent and hierarchy to be indeterminate. Crimes and auto acci-

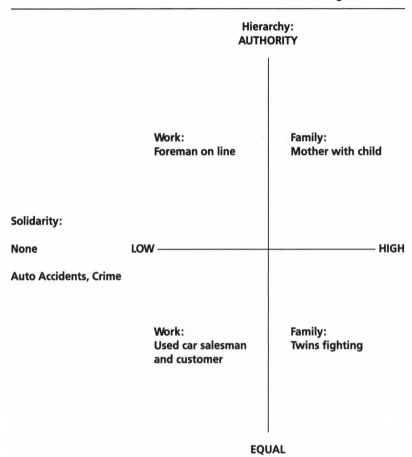

Hierarchy:
AUTHORITY

Work:
Foreman on line

Family:
Mother with child

Solidarity:

None   LOW ———————————————————— HIGH

Auto Accidents, Crime

Work:
Used car salesman
and customer

Family:
Twins fighting

EQUAL

Note: In the four everyday life incidents where there was some sort of role relationship, stories were varied on four dimensions: actor's mental state, act's consequences, actor's past pattern of behavior, and the presence or absence of another person influencing the actor. Three of these factors were also varied in the "no solidarity" stories: mental state, consequences, and past pattern. (In one auto accident, past pattern was replaced by actor's status (clerk/professor).)

Figure 4.1   Diagram of Story Types and Variations within Stories

dents "bring together" such people. In two of the surveys in our research, each respondent also judged one incident involving an automobile accident and one street crime. As is discussed below, such limiting cases are useful in testing our macrolevel arguments about whether cultural differences between Japan and the United States really reflect differences in characteristic social ties.

The Interplay of Roles and Deeds

Attributions of responsibility are a result of deed information, role information, and their interrelation. If we are correct about the importance of social ties in attributing responsibility, the relative impact of potential excusing conditions should vary across relationships. This has already been suggested with respect to influence from another person. The impact of another's influence can be expected to depend on whether that other is our boss, our spouse, our friend, or some random acquaintance. We are expected to listen to some people's opinions and suggestions but not to those of others. Our responsibility for having listened therefore varies.

This interdependence of roles with deeds and contexts is true of most excusing conditions. Roles are guides as to what people ought to do, and different obligations and different standards of accountability may attach to different roles (Hamilton, 1978a, 1978b; Jones & McGillis, 1976). The research was designed to test for differences in the impact of deed and context for actors in different role relationships. In particular, we expected that dimensions of social roles would affect use of information about the actor's mental state. In addition, as already noted, influence from another person has an impact on responsibility that varies depending on that person's role.

Hierarchy and Mental State

The interrelationship between hierarchy and mental state has a twofold nature. Both the meaning of information about the actor's state of mind and the effect of this information on responsibility attributions are likely to differ for authorities. First, because of the special obligations of authorities, information about mental state bears on a superior's unfulfilled role obligations as well as on subjective involvement in wrongdoing per se. A careless boss whose worker thereby is harmed can be characterized in three ways: careless (mental state), a boss (hierarchy), and a "careless boss" (because mental state information also reveals unfulfilled obligations to exercise foresight).

Information about an authority's state of mind therefore has a meaning over and above what it literally implies for such questions as whether the person "meant to do it." For authorities, mental state information can alter responsibility in two ways: by affecting the actor's perceived mental involvement, or by evoking unmet obligations. For equals, the only anticipated impact of mental state information is through perceived mental involvement.

In addition to the different paths that information about mental state may take in influencing the responsibility of an authority versus an equal, the responsibilities of authority and equal may diverge more under certain mental state conditions than under others. Because of their diffuse role obligations, we may attribute responsibility to superiors for accidental or negligent behavior, but we would not do so if the participants were equals. This suggests that differences in responsibility between authorities and equals should be greatest at low levels of mental state involvement: when nobody "meant to do it." In Heider's (1958) terms, the responsibilities of authorities and equals are most different where mere association with an act or accident is involved (vicarious or strict liability), are more similar where questions of negligence arise, and converge toward full responsibility for both authorities and equal actors when actions are intentional. The pattern of responsibilities should form a sort of fan, with responsibilities of authorities and equals most divergent where the actor is least intentionally involved.

Solidarity and Mental State

Although the actor's mental state is an important element in all adult responsibility judgments, it plays a different role in highly solidary relationships than in relationships of low solidarity. The more diffuse and longstanding obligations characteristic of highly solidary ties may, as in the case of authority relationships, create an "obligation of foresight." If so, this implies that the same pattern presented above for hierarchical versus equal relationships would hold for highly solidary versus less solidary relationships. When solidarity is high, mental state information is evaluated against a backdrop of the actor's obligations; when solidarity is low, information about an actor's state of mind should simply indicate whether the actor could or could not have avoided the outcome and to what degree, if at all, the action was intentional.

Relationships that differ in solidarity also differ in a second respect. In highly solidary relationships the persons have greater knowledge of each other's past and greater concern with the relationship's future. This leads participants in such situations to take a more subjective orientation to each other's deeds, using information about the actor's state of mind to a greater extent (Jones & Nisbett, 1971). If this argument is correct, then the effect of variations in the actor's mental state will be greater in highly solidary relationships than in less solidary relationships.

Hierarchy and Other's Influence

The expected pattern here is straightforward. Direction from a superior reduces an actor's responsibility more than direction from an equal.[6]

The Macrolevel: Cultural Differences

This study was guided by a central belief that judgments of responsibility involve a consideration of both deeds and roles; this does not mean, however, that deeds and roles play an equal part in the attribution processes of all individuals. We wished to study the issue in both the United States and Japan because of an expectation that citizens of the two countries would differ systematically in how they judged responsibility and how they assigned sanctions. According to the theoretical model, people in both countries judge people in high-solidarity (or hierarchical) relationships differently from people in low-solidarity (or equal) relationships. Roles matter; but the two countries differ in the extent to which and the ways in which roles matter, reflecting broad differences in the distributions of social ties and social experiences.

Roles

To the extent that a society's legal culture treats each actor as a formally equal individual, role differences—both solidarity and hierarchy—are relatively less important factors in the judgment of wrongdoing. The United States is an example of such a society. Japanese formal law often treats actors as separate individuals, but we have seen that both the legal structure and the legal culture still embed actors in a highly solidary and hierarchical network that discourages litigiousness. In our terminology, the type of culture that is expected to yield the greatest sensitivity to variations in role obligation is a stratified contextual culture. Stratified contextualism is highest where relationships are highly solidary and where sensitivity to inequalities in status between parties is maximized. Japanese society is an example of this configuration. Thus Japanese judging wrongdoing can be expected to make greater use of information about the roles of actor and victim than do Americans.

One competing argument can be made about the impact of roles in the two countries. Even if a Japanese perceiver is more likely to be sensitive to differences in role obligation than an American counterpart, it can still be asserted that the ways in which roles differ among themselves are not necessarily the same in the United States and Japan. Relationships in Japan may be relatively higher in solidarity overall. If firm is like family and family is like firm in Japan, then judgments of wrongdoing may be more convergent along this dimension than they are in the United States. That is, a smaller between-role difference within Japan would tend to diminish the relative importance of role information in Japanese as compared to American legal culture. Therefore one might expect to find a *smaller* difference between high- and low-solidarity ties in the judgments of Japanese.

This argument is reasonable, but we are not in a position to test it directly. The research design enables us to test whether Japanese and Americans differ in their allocations of responsibility in low- versus high-solidarity relationships and, if so, in what direction. But it does not allow us to test "how low is low" or "how different is high" with regard to the perceived solidarity of the relationships being scrutinized by the respondents.

Our prediction of greater sensitivity to variations in roles among Japanese assumes that the solidarity of ties may be greater in the typical Japanese relationship, but that Japanese are more sensitive to differences in role obligations, however slight. Nor apparently is their sensitivity entirely misplaced. For example, Argyle, Shimoda, and Little (1978) found that compared to England, in Japan the situation accounts for more variance in social behavior than does the person. In sum, we expected that the Japanese sensitivity to role relations would create a larger impact of differences in role relationships, even if the difference between low and high solidarity is smaller in absolute terms in Japanese culture.

Deeds

In a society where actors are viewed as isolated individuals, information about individual attributes and deeds, especially about the actor's mental state, should be relatively more important in assessing responsibility than in societies where actors are viewed as contextuals—especially stratified contextuals. Therefore it can be expected that Americans are more likely to be sensitive than Japanese to differences in deeds, especially when the actor's mental state is taken into account.

Contexts

With respect to the two aspects of context with which we are concerned—the presence of another person influencing the actor and the actor's past pattern of behavior—cultural differences can also be expected. Because other's influence is perceived as both more real and more legitimate in a contextual culture, Japanese should be more sensitive than Americans to the impact of influence from others on responsibility. The probable effect of an actor's past pattern is more difficult to determine than the effect of other's influence because past behavior is both an actor-held characteristic and part of the act's context. We expected that the linkage of past pattern to the actor would be the more salient feature of this information, meaning that Americans would be expected to emphasize an actor's past pattern of action more than Japanese in evaluating responsibility.

Interrelationships

Finally, the ways in which roles serve to change the impact or meaning of deeds and contexts may also vary across cultures. Because Japanese are expected to be more sensitive to both role relationship information and other's influence, the joint effect of hierarchy and other's influence is likely to be stronger among Japanese than among Americans. However, it was less clear what to anticipate about the interrelationship of mental state with hierarchy or solidarity. We expected Americans to be more sensitive to mental state information and Japanese to be more sensitive to role information. It was not clear that there would be any cultural differences in their combination.

Implications

Before turning to a description of the methodology of our study, certain implications of the theory and the research should be put into perspective. This research deals primarily with ordinary citizens' judgments of responsibility for everyday-life incidents. That is, the central focus was informal rather than legal adjudication. Because the judgments to be discussed exist outside of formal legal procedures and forms, they should more nearly capture differences in culture and legal culture between the two societies. Our social structural approach to understanding cultural differences, however, does not imply that we see culture as playing no independent role of its own. Let us consider briefly the implications of the potential disconfirmation or confirmation of our macrolevel hypotheses.

If the predictions prove to be incorrect, this might suggest that cultural differences between Japan and the United States are not that great. It might also provide support to those who argue that the observed differences between the two legal systems are primarily the product of differences in legal structures per se and reflect the impact of the costs and benefits of the various legal and extralegal alternatives (e.g., Haley, 1978, 1982a). If, on the other hand, the predictions are confirmed, this lends support to those who argue for the existence of genuine *cultural* differences, insofar as our predictions imply differences in individual respondents' conceptions of the responsible actor. Our model asserts that this cultural difference has a structural underpinning: differences in the distribution of social ties. Close, hierarchical ties lead to close attention to the social bonds of others, whereas looser, egalitarian ties lead to a slippage in this attention. Further, once it is in existence, a legal culture can play an active role in maintaining, justifying, and directing legal structure.

5

Methods:
Experiments in
Surveys

The preceding chapters suggest *why* we chose to carry out research in the United States and Japan on issues of responsibility and punishment. This chapter addresses *how* we did so: the methodology of the research project. We have attempted to make the discussion accessible to readers who lack statistical backgrounds. Discussions of the findings about responsibility and punishment in chapters 6 and 7 require some familiarity with the survey sites and the content of each survey; these are reviewed below. Readers who wish to move on to the findings can return here for information about particular survey questions or statistical issues.

Experiments in Surveys

To learn how people judged incidents of wrongdoing, we told them hypothetical stories and asked them to assess responsibility and assign punishment. Since Piaget (1932/1965), psychologists have used such strategies to explore the cognitive structure of moral judgments. When hypothetical stories are told, they can be varied experimentally—that is, each story represents an experiment in meaning. One group of people hears one variation, and another group hears another; the researcher then determines statistically whether the variation in the story led people to react to it differently. This strategy has also been used by sociologists in survey research. The resulting interview has come to be called a *factorial survey,* referring to the presence of experimental variations or factors (Rossi & Anderson, 1982). The stories are usually called vignettes or scenarios. Our study follows this tradition; it nests a set of experiments within a survey format.

The vignette method addresses a fundamental problem of survey research. Unlike laboratory experiments, surveys must frequently contend with factors that are inextricably and intimately interrelated, such that their separate impacts are difficult or even impossible to determine. In statistical terms, they exhibit multicollinearity. For example, in studying crimes, key factors such as the perpetrator's intent and the act's consequences are often so closely related that it is difficult to separate the influence of each on the judgments that third parties make.

In hypothetical stories, experimental design can make these factors orthogonal: each independent of the other. By manipulating several dimensions that describe a situation, we can assess how each dimension is used to construct judgments. Because the vignettes are presented in surveys, inferences can be made about a far wider population than is usually possible in psychological research. Therefore vignettes in surveys combine the experiment's advantage of clear causal inference with the survey's advantage of wide generalizability. (For examples, see Alves & Rossi, 1978; Jasso & Rossi, 1977; Rossi & Nock, 1982.)

Vignettes: A Technical Exposition

Following Rossi and Anderson (1982), an *object* may be defined as a unit being judged that consists of a single level for every manipulated dimension. The factorial object universe is the set of all unique objects formed by all possible combinations of one level from each dimension. Each respondent judged six vignettes. The stories involving everyday-life incidents each contained four dichotomous experimental manipulations (variations). The stories involving strangers, to be reviewed in chapter 8, contained three experimental manipulations each.

Each everyday-life vignette comprised 16 objects in a $2 \times 2 \times 2 \times 2$ matrix; mental state, consequence, past pattern, and other's influence were each varied dichotomously. Because each respondent heard six stories, however, the number of total potential combinations of objects across all stories in all possible orders (the object universe) was very large, making a fully counterbalanced design impossible. Instead, we employed an algorithm to generate for each respondent a random variation among the possible variations in each story. Together these individual subsets constitute a sample of the universe of unique objects. This process generates dimensions that are approximately orthogonal, each level in a dimension appearing equally frequently with each level in every other dimension (Rossi & Anderson, 1982). The order of presentation of stories was then varied according to a Latin square design to control for possible order effects. Preliminary analyses uncovered no significant effects based on story order.

Data Analysis

The discussion of responsibility judgments in chapter 6 is based on analysis of variance (ANOVA) and regression. These statistical techniques were advantageous because we judged responsibility on a continuous 0-to-10 scale. The design of the ANOVA, which is used to test the basic experimental predictions, is described below. (Details of the ANOVAs are available from the authors.) In contrast to responsibility, punishment decisions are either/or choices, and punishments themselves fall into qualitative types. Therefore the discussion of punishment judgments in chapter 7 makes use of statistical techniques based on cross-tabulation of categorical variables. Although presentation of results is generally restricted to basic and descriptive statistics, such as the chi-square test of association, overall logit analyses using maximum likelihood estimation were always carried out. (Details of these statistical procedures and results are also available.)

The basic experimental design for the core everyday-life stories consists of five between-subjects factors (city, mental state, consequence, past pattern, and other's influence) and two within-subjects factors (hierarchy and solidarity of the role relationship). A between-subjects factor is one for which each person can have only one datum: A person must live in either Detroit, Yokohama, or Kanazawa. A within-subjects factor is one for which each person may have many values; for example, as was done here, several stories can be judged by each individual. All factors are varied dichotomously except for city, which has three levels. Note that the auto accident and crime stories are not included in this analysis but are treated separately in chapter 8.

Each respondent in a particular city heard four sixty-fourths (or one-sixteenth) of a fully repeated design. Because versions were randomly assigned and hence were not typically the same across stories for a given respondent, observed differences across stories can be due either to differences between the stories themselves or to differences in versions of the story heard. Because a particular respondent heard only one of sixteen possible combinations of the between-subjects variations in each story, the effect of the combinations and the effect of the story cannot be completely disentangled. In statistical terms, this design's highest-order interaction terms would be confounded. A conventional mixed-model ANOVA (in which city, mental state, consequences, past pattern, and other's influence are between-subjects factors and role dimensions are within-subjects factors) is inappropriate in this case.

Our main approach to the analysis of these data was to treat the problem as a 2^7 design in which the units are not persons but person-stories. Each respondent is therefore represented four times in this design, once for each of the core stories. The highest-order interactions in such a design are, of course, still confounded. However, because we had no predictions regarding interactions above three-way, all four-way, five-way, six-way, and seven-way interactions were combined with the error term instead of being tested in the model. This approach to high-order interactions is consistent with common practice in survey experiments (see Alves & Rossi, 1978; Nock & Rossi, 1978; Rossi & Anderson, 1982) and with recommended practice in the adaptation of experiments to regression analysis (Cohen & Cohen, 1983).[1] Because the research was conducted in the field and respondents were given simple random assignments to versions of stories, cell sizes were slightly unequal. The computer program for the ANOVA, BMDP2v, uses dummy variable regression to accommodate unequal cell sizes.

The Surveys

The Cities

Detroit and Yokohama were the original choices for comparison, not because each was strictly representative of its country but because each presented comparable similarities and dissimilarities to its nation.

DETROIT. Detroit is America's sixth largest city. Like other older industrial cities of the Northeast and Midwest, Detroit has in recent decades suffered from population losses, "white flight" to the suburbs, and industrial decline. The incursion of foreign automakers—notably, Japanese companies—has had a special impact on the city that stands at the hub of American automaking. Detroit is, after all, Motown. The world headquarters of General Motors is so prominent on one approach to the city that a dissident executive entitled a book *On a Clear Day You Can See General Motors* (DeLorean & Wright, 1979). The Ford Motor Company world headquarters building that dominates the Detroit suburb of Dearborn is known simply as the Glass House. From two freeways billboards continually proclaim the number of cars produced in the United States during the current year; the figure is updated every few seconds. The economic fate, physical layout, and political rhythms of Detroit rest on industry—primarily on one old, powerful, and recently faltering industry.

Like other older cities of the Northeast, Detroit is a polyglot mix of ethnic groups and minorities. Although its largest group of foreign nationals is Canadian, it has one of the largest concentrations of Poles outside of Warsaw and includes a major Middle Eastern community. The Metropolitan Statistical Area (MSA), used by survey researchers, includes the city and some of its suburbs. As is true of many older American cities, Detroit's core and suburbs differ enough that one demographic discussion was called "Chocolate City, Vanilla Suburbs" (Farley, Schuman, Bianchi, Colasanto, & Hatchett, 1978).

Detroit is heavily black; the Detroit MSA is not. The sample in our research, for example, was 19 percent black; thus its concentration of minorities is not much different from any major urban area, nor from the profile of the nation as a whole.

On balance, Detroit resembles other older American cities in its appearance, its industrial character, and its populace. It stands out mainly in its dependence on the auto industry.

YOKOHAMA. Yokohama differs from Detroit partly on the basis of location. (For general reference, see *City of Yokohama, 1985.*) Although it had a mid-1980s population of approximately 3 million, Yokohama is part of the urban sprawl around Tokyo Bay—part of a blend of industry and port activity that stretches from Yokohama on the west, through Tokyo, and around to the newer industries and facilities of Chiba port and its environs. Thus Yokohama is less a stand-alone city than a part of a megalopolis dominated by Tokyo. But Yokohama has always had purposes and a personality that set it apart from Tokyo.

When Admiral Perry's steamships opened Japan to the West in 1853, Yokohama was eventually designated as the place where foreigners would meet, greet, and trade with Japanese. In an earlier era of the shogunate, Nagasaki to the west had been a point of contact, mainly with the Dutch and Portuguese. Now Yokohama on the eastern rim of Honshu island became the port of foreign trade and an enclave for Europeans (especially British) and Americans. Today the special cosmopolitanism that emerges from such contacts can be sensed in such areas as restaurants and night life. But physical evidence of this history is relatively scanty from the point of view of Westerners used to visiting European ruins. Such Westerners fail to take into account the impact of fire bombing on a city of wooden buildings. Much of Yokohama, like much of Tokyo, burned in the latter days of World War II. The traveler who searches a standard source such as *Fodor's Guide* for things to see in Yokohama will find the sobering summary: "Yokohama is not exactly a prime sightseeing destination for foreign tourists" (Narain, 1985, p. 237).

Thus one characteristic that Yokohama shares with Detroit is a certain lack of glamour. Like Detroit, it is a port—a considerably more important one for Japan than Detroit is for America. Like Detroit, it is industrial. Although the auto industry is less all-encompassing in Yokohama, the city is a major site of Japanese car production. The reputation of the Yokohama area as a center of older industry and older port facilities, in comparison with newer industry in the Chiba area on the eastern rim of the bay, closely parallels Detroit's industrial reputation and reality.

To study work and mobility in Japan versus the United States, Robert Cole (1979) conducted the Detroit Area Study, a survey that compared Detroit and Yokohama.[2] Our choice of a Detroit-Yokohama comparison was in one sense directly influenced by his choice, as we also were to carry out a Detroit Area Study survey. Thus the advantages of replication for social science were a methodological reason for the comparison. In addition, Cole's discussion of the cities and his findings about their industrial and other work life convinced us of the substantive appropriateness of the comparison. It would be difficult to find a better match for Detroit than Yokohama, and vice versa.

KANAZAWA. Kanazawa was selected by our Japanese colleagues as a site for a further survey in order to find a more traditional Japan. It was felt that residents of Yokohama might prove to be only trivially different from Detroiters, whereas it seemed likely that traditional Japanese moral sensibilities about responsibility and sanction would survive in Kanazawa.

Kanazawa is a small city on the Sea of Japan, westward and across the Japan Alps from the bustle of Tokyo Bay. (For general reference see *Introducing Kanazawa Japan*, 1983). It gained major historical importance as a feudal provincial capital, especially in the seventeenth century during the heyday of Japanese feudalism (McClain, 1982). Kanazawa was a major castle town, the headquarters of the powerful Maeda clan. At the end of the feudal period, Kanazawa was Japan's fourth largest city.

Kanazawa's mid-1980s population was about 500,000. Although its economic and political role is smaller than it was during the feudal period, Kanazawa remains an administrative, manufacturing, and educational center for its area. The tourist guidebooks have more to say about the modern-day attractions of Kanazawa than those of Yokohama. Partly because it was the second largest city (after Kyoto) *not* to be firebombed during World War II, more antiquities survive: more physical evidences of its earlier role. At the city's center, on the grounds of Kanazawa University, stands a remnant of the Maeda castle (ruined long before World War II). Nearby is Kenrokuen Park, one of the three most famous gardens in a country notable for its landscapes. In the vicinity of the city center, narrow streets and canals that speak of long-past efforts at defense, of moats and ramparts, wind around the castle ruins; traditional pottery is produced; and examples of samurai houses are preserved. Although modern commerce is never far, it is possible in Kanazawa to lose oneself in a bygone Japan. Perhaps for these reasons Kanazawa enjoys a reputation of relative traditionalism, rather like Kyoto does in comparison to Tokyo or Osaka.

For these reasons, our Japanese colleagues felt that Kanazawa might represent a starker contrast to Detroit than Yokohama represented. Residents of what is still thought of as a castle town might judge wrongdoing in ways more characteristically or traditionally "Japanese" than residents of Japan's Motown.

Samples and Survey Instruments

DETROIT. The initial survey was a 1977 probability sample of the Detroit Metropolitan Statistical Area ($N = 678$). Approximately half of the interviews were conducted face-to-face and half were carried out over the phone.[3] Respondents heard six vignettes that had been developed in consultation with Japanese researchers in order to make their elements appropriate to both societies.

Four "core" stories concerned wrongdoing in everyday life. Two of these stories represented high-solidarity ties and two represented low-solidarity ties. (Although the vignettes selected represent *relatively* high rather than low solidarity, it should be remembered that Japanese social ties are likely to be more solidary than those of Americans in absolute terms.) At both levels of solidarity we varied a second dimension: hierarchy. Either the actor and victim were equals, or the actor had authority over the victim. The vignettes themselves are described in more detail below. The Detroit survey also featured two "no-solidarity" vignettes (stories involving strangers), described below. Detroit respondents were also asked to complete a mailback questionnaire that included additional vignettes as well as attitudes about such issues as reasons for imprisonment. (See chapter 7 for results involving imprisonment.) The questionnaire was completed and returned by 50 percent of the overall sample ($N = 339$). The Detroit respondents who returned questionnaires were significantly more educated and were more likely to live in the suburbs than in the city. There were also trends involving gender and age—females and older people were more likely to return the questionnaire—but these differences were not significant (Adams, 1977).

YOKOHAMA. The first Japanese survey was a 1978 probability sample of Yokohama ($N = 600$). Sampling procedures in the Japanese cities differed from those in Detroit; for example, Japanese survey researchers were able to sample respondents from government lists of residents instead of compiling their own listings of residents by block. These differences could be expected to have an inconsequential impact on the inferences to be drawn. (See Cole, 1979, for a discussion of differences in survey procedures in an earlier Detroit-Yokohama comparison.)

The Japanese researchers carried out their own translation of the relevant Detroit materials, consulting with Americans in the Tokyo area and with teachers of Japanese who had advised the American researchers. The Yokohama survey replicated the four core vignettes involving everyday-life wrongdoing as well as the additional vignettes about offenses between strangers. In Yokohama, unlike Detroit, it was possible to include items about rationales for imprisonment in the main survey.

KANAZAWA. The Japanese researchers also conducted a further probability sample survey in Kanazawa in 1979 ($N = 640$). This survey included the four everyday-life vignettes from the previous two studies. Items about rationales for imprisonment and the vignettes about strangers were omitted from this survey.

Although each sample represented its city, the cities themselves differed demographically. The key demographic variables that can be readily compared across the cultures are gender, age, and education level (see table 5.1). Race and religion are obviously noncomparable, and equivalences are difficult to determine for such variables as income and occupation (see Cole, 1979; Lincoln & Kalleberg, 1990). The Detroit sample was relatively female, young, and well-educated; Kanazawa, in keeping with its image as a traditional rather than a growing industrial city, had respondents who were both older and less educated than those in either Detroit or Yokohama. These differences among the cities would threaten the validity of our conclusions about responsibility and punishment judgments only if these demographics themselves somehow affected people's judgments. Our previous research indicates minimal impact of demographics and essentially no interaction of demographics (including income and occupation) with city in determining responsibility and punishment (Sanders & Hamilton, 1987). Therefore, although the samples and the cities from which they were drawn differ in predictable ways, these differences in demographic composition do not threaten our inferences.

To summarize, all three surveys included four key vignettes depicting variations in wrongdoing within everyday social life. In addition, the Detroit and Yokohama surveys each contained the automobile accident and crime vignettes about incidents involving strangers as well as items about rationales for imprisonment. It is important to emphasize that statistically the results cannot be generalized to the United States and Japan as a whole. However, these surveys are representative of the cities in question (within sampling limits) and are likely to be representative of large urban areas in either country (cf. Cole, 1979).

Table 5.1   Demographic Characteristics of the Samples

Demographics	Detroit (%)	Yokohama (%)	Kanazawa (%)
Gender: male	44.2	54.8	48.4
female	55.8	45.2	51.6
Age: < 33	41.0	36.8	30.0
33–49	29.3	40.8	37.8
50+	29.6	22.3	32.2
Education: < 12 years	25.3	27.2	31.6
12	36.1	48.2	50.5
> 12	38.6	24.7	17.8

Note: In each case, the overall difference among the cities was statistically significant by chi-square test. For gender, *N*s included the full sample (Detroit = 678, Yokohama = 600, and Kanazawa = 640). For age, Detroit's *N* was 675, whereas there were no missing data in the Japanese cities; for education, *N* = 676 for Detroit, 600 for Yokohama, and 639 for Kanazawa.

The Vignettes: Everyday Incidents

The four core stories in each survey involved questions of everyday wrongdoing. Each of the stories was intended to represent an ideal-typical combination of the two dimensions of roles: hierarchy and solidarity. As discussed above, hierarchy and solidarity are conceived of as *dimensions*, not dichotomies. However, in order to test the usefulness of these dimensions in research on responsibility, we chose relatively clear-cut examples of the combinations of these dimensions: exemplars of each general combination of high versus low on each dimension. In sociological terms this represents use of the method of *ideal types* (Weber, 1949). From the standpoint of psychology, it represents use of *prototypes* to illustrate the concepts in question.

Although clear-cut examples were selected, the vignettes do not represent logical extremes of the role dimensions. For example, hierarchy between master and slave is an extreme that we did not choose to represent. What we sought instead were realistic, commonly observed examples of each combination of hierarchy and solidarity. To avoid cumbersome labels, the two high-solidarity stories will be referred to as *family* stories (rather than high solidarity–equal and high solidarity–authority) and the two low-solidarity stories will be referred to as *work* stories. These labels reflect the stories' settings.

Within each story the four aspects of deed and context discussed in chapter 4 were manipulated: the actor's mental state, seriousness of consequence, past pattern, and other's influence. Logically, the other person influencing the actor could have been in any sort of relationship with the actor. To simplify the design, the other party consistently stood in the same type of relation to the actor that the actor stood in relative to the victim. The texts of all versions of the stories are reproduced in appendix A.

In the *family/equal* story, twin brothers are playing baseball with a friend. Either Billy, the protagonist, or the friend (when other's influence is present) decides that it is Billy's turn to bat. Billy grabs the bat and the brothers begin fighting. The brother is then hit with the bat; the hit is described as accidental (low mental state) or done out of anger (high mental state). Billy has either often or rarely gotten into fights before (past pattern manipulation). The consequence is a head injury or a large bump on the head.

In the *family/authority* story, a four-year-old child is crying and will not sleep. The child's mother either goes to quiet him or is told to do so by the father (when other's influence is present).[4] The child either struggles in her arms and slips, hitting a chair (low mental state), or is shoved into the chair (high mental state). The injury is a sprained ankle (low consequence) or a head injury (high consequence). The mother is described as either frequently or rarely getting angry at her child (past pattern manipulation).

In the *work/equal* story a salesman, Dave, sells a customer a used car that he either thinks has not been inspected (low mental state) or knows to have a hidden defect (high mental state). It turns out that the car needs fifty or five hundred dollars' worth of repairs (consequence manipulation). Dave is described as honest or sometimes dishonest with his customers in the past (past pattern manipulation). He either sells the car on his own initiative or at the urging of another salesman (when other's influence is present).

In the *work/authority* story, Joe is a foreman on an assembly line. The company is trying to fill a large order, and Joe either does not want to stop the line or is told by his supervisor not to let the line stop (when other's influence is present). Joe is described as always being careful about safety procedures in the past or sometimes being careless (past pattern manipulation). Either he becomes busy and does not notice that a safety guard is improperly attached (low mental state) or he notices the safety guard problem but decides to do nothing until the end of the day (high mental state). A worker then suffers a bruised hand or loses two fingers (consequence manipulation).

Incidents Involving Strangers

The two automobile accident stories were part of the Detroit and Yokohama surveys. Because respondents were told one story or the other, N was only half as large as for other stories. For this reason, and because influence from another party is less interesting theoretically in this context, three rather than four dichotomous manipulations were introduced in each vignette.

In the Child vignette, a man is driving down a one-way street when he strikes an eight-year-old child who has stepped from between parked cars. The man is either driving above (high mental state) or below (low mental state) the speed limit. This has been his first or fourth accident in twelve years of driving (past pattern manipulation). The child is only bruised or suffers several broken bones (consequence manipulation). In the Adult vignette, a housewife is walking across the street at a stop sign when she is hit by a car; she either receives a broken leg or is killed (consequence manipulation). The driver strikes her either because his brakes fail and he cannot stop in time (low mental state) or because he fails to see the stop sign (high mental state). In this vignette the third manipulation was a new one: the status of the actor. The driver is either a clerk at the university (low status) or a professor (high status). This manipulation was analogous to the everyday-life stories' variation in hierarchy, except that the incident took place outside the actual context in which the actor would have authority (or lack it). We were curious as to whether the professor would be judged more responsible than the clerk.

Finally, in the crime story (Robbery), the protagonist Thomas Wilson is robbing a store. Either he shoots the store owner upon leaving (high mental state) or the store owner tries to overpower Thomas and take the gun, and during the struggle the owner is shot (low mental state). The owner is killed (high consequence) or wounded (low consequence). Thomas has no prior record or had been imprisoned for assault with a deadly weapon (past pattern manipulation).

Manipulation Checks

After hearing a version of a story, each respondent was asked a series of questions. Several of these questions were designed to serve as what experimental psychologists call *manipulation checks* of the within-story variations. These are simply checks on whether the manipulation—the variation in the story—worked. For a manipulation to work means only that the versions were different and noticed as such by the respondent; it need not mean that these differences had their predicted effect on, for example, responsibility judgments.

For two of the variables a single question was asked as a manipulation check. The consequence manipulation was checked with an eleven-point item asking about the *seriousness* of the consequences, ranging from 0 (not at all serious) to 10 (extremely serious). In this case an effective manipulation would be one in which the "high" condition of consequences was judged to be significantly more serious on this question than the "low" condition. The past pattern manipulation was checked with a dichotomous item asking whether the actor's deed was or was not *predictable* based on the information given. An effective manipulation would be one in which the presence of a bad past pattern led significantly more often to respondents' saying that the deed was predictable, in comparison to respondents who heard the alternative. For a third experimental variation, presence of influence from another, there was no readily appropriate manipulation check, as this other person was missing in half of the versions of each story and present in the other half.

The crucial manipulation of the actor's state of mind, in contrast, required *two* manipulation checks. Because the difference between accidental and negligent acts is not the same as that between negligent and intentional acts, two items were included to assess these distinctions. To measure negligence, a dichotomous item asked whether the actor "could have avoided" the act. To measure purposiveness, an eleven-point item (0 to 10) asked the extent to which the actor "didn't mean to" or did "on purpose" the act in question. Responses to these two questions about mental state can be combined so as to characterize a response in one of three ways: as a judgment that the wrongdoing was accidental, a result of negligence, or intentional. An accidental act is neither avoidable nor purposive; a negligent act is avoidable but is not purposive; and an intentional act is both avoidable and purposive. The results of the manipulation checks are discussed below.

The Problem of the Actor's State of Mind

Together the four core stories describe the hierarchy and solidarity dimensions discussed in chapter 4. One of our central hypotheses was that superiors in hierarchies are subject to more diffuse standards for their actions and are expected to foresee and respond to problems. They are held to stricter standards of accountability and should therefore be expected to be held more responsible than equals for an action of any given degree of purposiveness (Hamilton, 1978b; Kelman & Hamilton, 1989). This fact produces a methodological difficulty: The same variation in state of mind theoretically should not produce the same outcome in authoritative and equal relationships. How one manipulates mental state thus becomes an issue in comparing authorities and equals. The original objective in the four core stories was to manipulate mental state between negligence and intentionality. Pretests in Detroit, however, indicated no appreciable variance in responsibility judgments in authority stories unless mental state was varied around lower levels: essentially, accident versus negligence. This result supports the original hypothesis—that is, actors in superior positions were invariably being assigned the highest levels of responsibility for intentional acts, while equal actors were not.

We eventually settled on variations between what we thought of as negligence (carelessness) and intentionality in the equal stories, while the authority stories varied between accident and negligence or recklessness (but with no direct intent to harm the victim). For example, in the low mental state versions of the work/equal story, Dave the used-car salesman thinks the car has not been inspected, but does not check (negligence). In the high mental state condition Dave knows the car has a hidden defect but sells the car anyway (intentional harm to victim). In contrast, in the low mental state condition of the factory foreman story (work/authority), Joe the foreman becomes busy and does not notice the safety guard (accident with some hint of negligence). In the high mental state condition, Joe notices the safety guard but does not stop the line (recklessness, but no intention to harm). As illustrated below, the manipulation checks can be used to assess the accuracy of these assumptions about variation in mental state.

This presumed difference between equal and authority stories means that statistical techniques must be used to control for differences in the actor's mental state, as *perceived* by the respondent, when testing differences in responsibility between equals and authorities. The statistical procedure is described in chapter 6.

Dependent Variables
The central dependent variables measured respondents' attribution of responsiblity and assessment of punishments. In all vignettes the respondent was asked to judge the responsibility of the actor for what happened on an eleven-point scale (0 = not at all responsible, 5 = somewhat responsible, 10 = fully responsible). Punishment judgments are discussed in chapter 7.

Issues of Translation
The translation of survey instruments across cultures is a delicate task. Literal comparability invites the danger that the same words connote different things in different societies. (To take a trivial example, names had to be changed from English to comparable Japanese terms. Instead of hearing about a child called Billy in the family/equal story, Japanese respondents heard about "Yasuhiko.") Attempts to achieve substantive comparability, on the other hand, entail the risk that it will prove impossible to apportion the differences that are discovered between substantive differences in the society and language differences across instruments.

Translation issues may arise at several levels: pure errors in translation, differences in the meaning of words or phrases, and differences in the connotations of various scenarios. Our project incurred two translation problems that deserve mention concerning the stories in Detroit versus those in Yokohama.[5] In the family/equal story there was a pure error in translation. The Yokohama translation added a phrase to the Detroit vignette indicating that Billy's (Yasuhiko's) brother held onto the bat when Billy grabbed it—an addition that potentially reduces Billy's responsibility for the outcome. This vignette was changed in the Kanazawa instrument to be consistent with the original Detroit wording.

A second translation issue occurred at the level of word meaning. In the work/equal story, the term the Yokohama survey used to describe the used car retranslates into English more accurately as "broken down" than "defective"; the obviousness of a "broken-down" car might be seen as reducing the salesman's liability. The Kanazawa survey also corrected this wording. Therefore, the Kanazawa results provide a check that results in Yokohama-Detroit comparisons are not a function of translation.

A third, more global, issue of the genuineness of equivalents can be seen at the vignette level. For example, the work/equal story involved the sale of a used car. A used-car salesman stands in a special position in American culture that may not have an equivalent in Japanese society. In the United States the unsavory reputation of used-car salesmen puts all buyers on some notice and thus may make buyers who are cheated seem to be in part responsible for their loss. This may be less true in Japan, where perhaps a salesman of some other type of product would be the substantive equivalent of a used-car salesman in the United States. In that case a better measure of cultural differences would be to use a used-car salesman vignette in the United States and a salesman of another product in Japan. At this level, however, it seemed to us that literal comparability was preferable to substantive comparability; in any case, our Japanese collaborators thought the used-car sales parallel to be appropriate.

Finally, it is important to remember that when two languages are as different as English and Japanese, concepts sometimes do not translate precisely. One minor example emerged in the attempt to translate one of the manipulation checks for the actor's state of mind, the question whether the actor could have *avoided* what happened. It turned out that a literal translation using the word *avoid* was a rather uncharacteristic sentence in Japanese but that a natural-sounding alternative could be produced if the Japanese survey asked whether the actor could or could not have *helped* it that the result occurred. Later discussions will use the English wording (avoid) for simplicity, but it should be remembered that the Japanese wording was—of necessity—subtly different. The summary of effects of the manipulation checks, presented below, suggests that the item tapped the same construct in the two languages.

A more intriguing example of linguistic nonequivalence occurred in the case of the second manipulation check for mental state, which concerned the actor's intent. The Detroit survey used the contrast between "didn't mean to" and "on purpose" to capture the concept of degree of intentionality. We avoided the word *intentional* because standard practice in the Detroit Area Study is to prepare survey items at a level comprehensible to an American seventh-grader. This created a problem in Japan, where the antonym for "on purpose" (*waza to*) is not "didn't mean to" but "nature did it." However, because literacy levels in Japan are high, the Japanese researchers reassured us (correctly) that their respondents would understand what *intentional* meant. Therefore, the final questionnaires in both Japanese cities used the "intentional/unintentional" dichotomy to capture a contrast that Detroiters heard as "on purpose/didn't mean to." The data reviewed below indicate that this question also seems to tap the same basic concept in the two countries.

Checking Whether the Experiments Worked

The items labeled as manipulation checks serve at least three functions in the analysis of these surveys. Their first function, the one that gives them their name, is to test whether the experimental variations in the stories meant the same thing to the survey's respondents as we anticipated—that "low" and "high" had the intended meanings. The results of the relevant tests are summarized below for the four manipulation checks: seriousness, the manipulation check for consequences; predictability, for past pattern; and avoidability and purposiveness, for mental state.

The additional functions of these items also involve meaning. Their second function is to diagnose differences among stories. For example, as noted, we found it necessary to vary the actor's mental state around different levels in the stories that involved authorities and the stories that involved equals. The manipulation checks for mental state can be used to assess whether the respondents perceived variations among stories as they were expected to do. A final use of the manipulation checks is in the analysis itself. They can be used to take account of and adjust for respondents' perceptions of the vignettes. By moving beyond straight ANOVA methodology, the traditional statistics for experiments, models can be built that include both the "objective" reality of the manipulation and the person's own subjective interpretation of that reality, each serving as predictors of such judgments as responsibility. This third use of the manipulation checks will be discussed in chapter 6.

Results of the Manipulations

A successful manipulation involves a significant difference between the experimental conditions. The condition that was "low" should be significantly different from the condition that was supposed to be "high" on the relevant dimension. In this case, where there are multiple manipulations and multiple questions about them, a second criterion should also be applied. A manipulation check should be significantly related to its manipulation *and* be more powerfully related to that manipulation than to any other. For example, even if seriousness of consequences was significantly lower in the "low" conditions than in the "high," we would have some difficulty in believing that the manipulation had been effective if seriousness was even more strikingly affected by another manipulation, such as the actor's past pattern of behavior.

By these criteria, the manipulations in the Detroit, Yokohama, and Kanazawa surveys were almost always successful, and almost equally so in all three cities. In all cases the manipulation of consequences significantly affected seriousness judgments; in all cases the manipulation of mental state affected purposiveness judgments, avoidability judgments, or both; and in almost all cases the manipulation of past pattern affected predictability judgments. The effects of the "appropriate" manipulation on its manipulation check were always more significant than those of other manipulations, and the effects were generally much stronger. Some cross-relationships of manipulations to other manipulation checks were of substantive interest. For example, the actor's manipulated mental state had regular effects on whether the action was judged as predictable, with intentional action seen as more predictable. Conversely, an actor with a bad past pattern was sometimes judged to be more purposive.

The weakest manipulation check was the predictability question, which was supposed to reflect the variations in an actor's past pattern of behavior. In three stories in Yokohama—the family/authority story (mother harming child), one of the auto accident stories (Adult), and the crime story—the past pattern manipulation did not relate significantly to the predictability item, although it approached significance in the case of the accident ($p = .06$). Two considerations lead us to believe that this represented a failure of the manipulation *check* rather than the manipulation. First, the Japanese researchers felt that asking about the predictability of behavior was an odd construction in Japanese. Indeed, they eliminated the item in the Kanazawa survey, so that this later survey lacks a manipulation check for that issue. Second, as reviewed in more detail below, the past pattern variable *was* significantly related to responsibility in all three instances. That is, a manipulation that apparently did not "work" (insofar as its manipulation check was not affected as it was supposed to be) nevertheless had the predicted impact where it mattered: on responsibility judgments. The imperfect relationship of past pattern to predictability appeared, overall, to be a problem with the question rather than the stories themselves. It is reasonable to conclude that the predictability manipulation check represents another instance of the impossibility of exact translation between the two languages. Unfortunately, in this case the insight came after the fact.

Manipulation Checks and Story Differences

If our impressions about experimental variations in the authority stories versus stories that involved equals were accurate, confirmation should be found in the pattern of responses about whether the actions were done "on purpose." Although in both types of stories the "low" and "high" mental state versions differ from one another, the absolute amount of purposiveness attributed to actors in the equal stories should be greater. In contrast, there was no reason to expect that survey respondents would see these two types of story as appreciably different with respect to other issues, such as the seriousness of the consequences depicted.

Figures 5.1 and 5.2 show, for all three surveys, the extent to which respondents saw the action as purposive and, on the same 0-to-10 scale, the extent to which they thought the consequences were serious. Stories involving authorities and stories involving equals are summarized in figures 5.1 and 5.2, respectively. The seriousness data on the right side of each figure indicate that in all cities, for both equal and authority stories, "low" and "high" seriousness conditions indeed differed. More important for the present purposes, the general level of seriousness was quite similar in stories involving equals and stories involving authorities.

The left sides of the two figures, in contrast, do not look the same. It is true in all cities that conditions that were supposed to be low on our mental state variable were judged as less purposive than stories that were supposed to represent high mental state. But in all three cities the absolute amount of purposiveness is noticeably (and statistically significantly) less in the stories about wrongdoing by authorities. Thus our initial estimates of the variations that had been created prove to be accurate. In considering the impact of role dimensions or of mental state on responsibility in chapter 6, these results also show that it will be necessary to take into account the respondent's own perceptions of the actor's state of mind.

Although detailed results from the Detroit and Yokohama surveys' stories

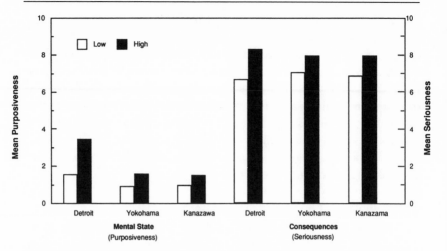

Figure 5.1 Manipulation Checks for Purposiveness and Seriousness in Stories Involving Authority

about auto accidents and crime are presented in chapter 8, this is a convenient point at which to demonstrate the ways in which these stories about strangers differed from the stories about everyday-life role relationships as well as from one another. Figure 5.3 presents data on the low versus high versions of mental state and consequence severity for the auto accident

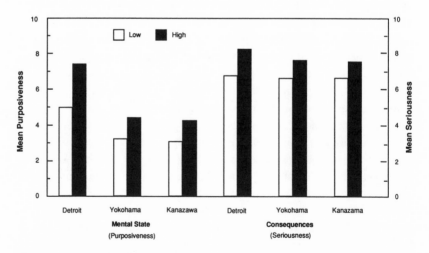

Figure 5.2 Manipulation Checks for Purposiveness and Seriousness in Stories Involving Equals

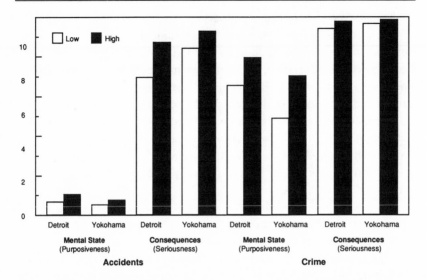

Figure 5.3   Manipulation Checks for Purposiveness and Seriousness in Stories Involving Strangers

stories on the left and the crime story on the right. Purposiveness and seriousness data are presented for each type of incident. (The two alternative auto accidents are averaged together to simplify the presentation.) The patterns of results for each variable are of interest, as are the differences between the two.

The seriousness levels are noteworthy; they are extremely high for the crime, as anticipated, and are also quite high for the auto accidents. These stories, as a group, are clearly the most serious in their consequences of any heard by the Detroit and Yokohama residents. In contrast, the accidents and the crime diverge almost perfectly in their purposiveness. As we had planned, the accidents were considered accidents; negligible levels of purposiveness were attributed in either city. Indeed, in Yokohama the low and high mental state conditions did not differ significantly with regard to the purposiveness assigned. Respondents instead differentiated between the versions on the basis of the avoidability manipulation check, which had been constructed with the issue of accident versus negligence in mind. The crime was, in contrast, judged to be the most purposive act in either survey.

Taken together, then, the accident vignettes and the crime vignette serve to frame the everyday-life vignettes with regard to the question of mental state and its effects on responsibility. Auto accidents stand at one end of a continuum of purposiveness, the crime stands at the other end, and the everyday-life role relationship vignettes stand in the middle.

Mental State: Accident, Negligence, and Intent

We have repeatedly referred to differences among categories of the actor's potential state of mind—fundamentally, accident (strict liability) versus negligence versus intentionality. Taking the two manipulation checks together is one way to operationalize these concepts. An accident can be defined as an event in which the actor could not avoid the occurrence and in which there is no purposiveness; negligence can be defined as an instance in which the outcome is avoidable but not purposive; and intent can be defined as an instance that is both avoidable and purposive. To simplify the argument, purposiveness is considered to be absent only when a respondent rated it as zero.[6]

Table 5.2 summarizes the percentages of respondents who made each type of judgment about mental state, by city and by story.[7] This table serves to flesh out what the figures showed about mental state, both by drawing on the two manipulation checks together and by presenting all stories separately. Certain patterns already shown in the figures also emerge in this table. The actors in the two stories involving equals, taken together, are judged as more intentional than in the two stories involving authorities. The auto accidents are the least intentional vignettes; the work/equal vignette, involving a used-car salesman selling a defective product, and the crime, a shooting during a robbery, are the most intentional.

In addition to the difference already discussed between the authority and equal stories, there is a subtle difference in intentionality between the low- and high-solidarity stories. We expected that incidents involving persons closely tied to one another often evoke less blaming of a wrongdoer, for any of a variety of reasons. For example, people appear less willing to believe that harm to an intimate was intended. In these surveys, consistent with this expectation, respondents in all three cities judged the actions of persons in low-solidarity ties as more intentional than actions of persons in highly solidary relationships (see table 5.2).

Two other issues are raised here. First, the Japanese respondents were generally less likely to judge acts as intentional than their counterparts in Detroit. This difference is particularly striking in the case of the family/equal story, in which a child harmed his brother. It is evident that Detroiters are willing to find intent in a ten-year-old whereas residents of both Japanese cities are not. Chapter 6 will return to the question whether there is something special about this story, perhaps because of the choice of a child as a protagonist. This result again serves as a caution that comparing responsibility judgments across stories will require consideration of what the respondent thought of the actor's state of mind. Both the manipulation checks and the manipulations will be needed to analyze responsibility adequately.

that authoritative actors were allocated *less* responsibility, contrary to our expectation. The average responsibility score of equals was 7.09, but the score for authorities was only 6.91. However, as chapter 5 discussed, "all things were not equal" in the case of authority stories versus stories involving equals. This was true in two senses. First, the actor's mental state had to be manipulated around lower levels in the authority stories: Authorities were depicted as at worst negligent, at the same time that equals were depicted as at worst fully intentional in their harmdoing. Thus a true picture of the effect of hierarchy requires taking into account the perceived mental state of the actor. Second, influence from another party was consistent in type within stories rather than across stories. That is, authorities who were influenced by another were influenced by someone in authority over them, while equals were influenced by equals. This difference means that the purest test of the responsibilities of authority versus equal is to be found in the vignettes in which other's influence was *absent* from the story.

We adjusted for these differences in a follow-up analysis. Effects of hierarchy on responsibility were assessed controlling for the respondent's perceptions of two aspects of the actor's mental state: the actor's *purposiveness* and the act's *avoidability*. As noted above, these two measures served as the manipulation checks to assess whether the variations in mental state had their intended impact. These responses carry all available information about what the survey respondent thought was true of the actor's state of mind. Analyses were carried out separately for story versions in which other's influence was present and versions in which it was absent (see table 6.1).[2]

The fact that the effect of hierarchy is positive in this table means that authorities are seen as more responsible than equals. When other's influence is absent, the average difference exceeded 1 point on the 11-point responsibility scale. Thus, when the perceived mental state of the actors is taken into account, authorities are noticeably *more* responsible for wrong or harm done than are equals. A comparison of the left and right sides of the table shows that this difference is more profound when there is no other person present influencing the actor.

These results suggest that the hierarchy and solidarity of social ties have a direct impact on the responsibility of the actors involved. First, at least in these ideal-typical stories, family relationships meant lower responsibility for the actor involved in wrongdoing than did work relationships. Second, when we introduced the appropriate statistical controls to make the situations equivalent (by controlling the extent to which the deed was seen as purposive and by controlling for the presence of another party), authoritative actors were more responsible than equals.

Table 6.1   Effect of Hierarchy on Responsibility, Controlling for the Extent to Which Action Was Seen as "On Purpose" and Outcome Was Seen as "Avoidable" (Unstandardized Coefficients)

	Other's influence	
	Absent	Present
Hierarchy	1.02	.31
Mental state	.31	.50
"On purpose"	.25	.24
"Avoid"	2.14	1.60
Constant	4.23	4.49
R^2	.26	.20

Note: N for tables 6.1, 6.2, 6.3, and 6.5 is based on the person-vignette: persons × vignettes judged. Overall N = 6,972 (Detroit = 2,537; Yokohama = 2,191; Kanazawa = 2,244). Hierarchy, Mental state, and "Avoid" were coded as dummy variables (authority = 1, high mental state = 1, avoidable = 1); "On purpose" and the dependent variable, responsibility, ranged 0–10. All variables had highly significant effects on responsibility ($p < .01$), both when other's influence was absent and when it was present.

Role-Deed Interrelationships

We predicted that roles would affect the use of deed information in three ways. Both hierarchy and solidarity were expected to affect the use of information about an actor's mental state, and hierarchy was also expected to affect the impact of other's influence. We shall discuss the statistical tests for each issue in turn.

Hierarchy and Mental State

We thought that information about an actor's mental state might have both a different impact and a different meaning for authorities and equals. A first indication that this is so emerged in the basic ANOVA in the form of a statistical interaction between hierarchy and mental state. Varying the mental state of the actor had a much greater effect on responsibility when that actor was an authority.

These results pertain to the sheer *size* of the impact of mental state information for authorities versus equals. But further examination is warranted for two reasons. First, as noted in chapter 5, "low" and "high" did not have the same meaning for authorities' and equals' mental states. Therefore it might be argued that these results simply show that the difference between accident and negligence is greater than the difference between negligence and intent. In addition, our theoretical expectations referred not to the sheer

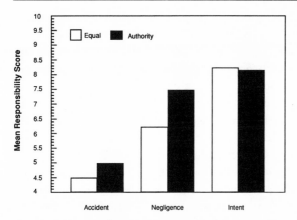

Figure 6.2   Responsibilities of Equals versus Authorities for
Accidental, Negligent, or Intentional Acts

size of the impact but to its *location*—that is, where on a spectrum from
accident to intentionality the difference between authorities and equals
would be at a maximum—and to its *meaning*—that is, how information
about the actor's state of mind is interpreted when that actor is an authority
as opposed to an equal.

Overall, authorities are more responsible than equals for acts that are
equivalent in terms of the actor's mental state, as indicated by the significant
hierarchy effect in table 6.1. Our model further predicted that the difference
in responsibility between authorities and equals should be greatest at lower
levels of mental state involvement, where harmdoing was accidental or
negligent, and that judgments of authorities and equals would tend to converge when actions were fully intentional. An appropriate test of this expectation requires taking into account how the survey respondent perceived the
actor's mental state.

Figure 6.2 presents the responsibilities of authorities versus equals when
the incident is perceived to be an accident, when the actor is seen as negligent,
and when at least some intentionality is perceived. These divisions into
mental state categories are made by combining respondents' answers about
purposiveness and avoidability. Accidental means neither avoidable nor purposive; negligent means avoidable, but not purposive; and intentional means
both purposive and avoidable. Here we combine conditions where other's
influence was absent versus present to simplify the presentation. The distinctions between equals and authorities that appear in this figure are sharper
when other's influence is absent.

The figure is broadly consistent with expectations. Authority-equal differences are larger (and statistically significant) for accidental or negligent acts; they converge for intentional acts. However, the shape of the trend is not the slowly closing fan that the theoretical discussion suggested. That is, we do not observe a gap that gradually closes as one moves from accidental to negligent to intentional deeds. Instead, authorities and equals diverge most when action is seen by the respondent as negligent rather than accidental. This result suggests that ordinary citizens may not apply a genuine strict or vicarious liability standard of accountability to authorities. Instead, the judgment of authorities is more stringent mainly in the case of actions deemed to be at least somewhat negligent (that is, where outcomes were avoidable).

Information about the mental state of authorities may also be construed differently from information about equals. In particular, it may have implications for whether they have met role obligations. These surveys provided at least some opportunity to test this notion. We examined whether there was any statistical effect of the mental state manipulation on responsibility, this time controlling for the manipulation checks that tapped perceived purposiveness and avoidability. If information about an actor's mental state has a different meaning when that actor is an authority, then there should be some impact of an authority's mental state on responsibility that is not captured by these manipulation checks. As noted earlier, a boss who has been careless is three things: careless, a boss, and a careless-boss (who should have known or done better by virtue of his or her role). The purposiveness and avoidability questions capture the carelessness; the effect of hierarchy captures the "bossness." Any impact of mental state that is not accounted for by perceived purposiveness or avoidability potentially captures the "careless-boss" aspect. In stories involving equals, in contrast, the effects of mental state should be fully accounted for by the way in which they alter the actor's judged purpose and the act's judged avoidability.

Table 6.2 shows the effect of mental state on responsibility for equals versus authorities. The left side of table 6.2 shows that for equals, the unstandardized regression coefficient for mental state is not significant when we take into account the respondent's perception of whether the act was committed on purpose and whether it was unavoidable. In other words, these two manipulation checks are what mental state means when an equal harms an equal. In contrast, the right side of the table indicates that variation in an authority's mental state has an important effect on responsibility even after taking into account how that mental state was perceived. We interpret this effect as reflecting the unmet obligations of this authority. It is as if the survey respondents were asking themselves an extra question about such

Table 6.2 Meaning of Mental State Information for the Responsibility of Authorities Versus Equals (Unstandardized Coefficients)

	Equal	Authority
Mental state	.06	.70
"On purpose"	.31	.16
"Avoid"	1.45	2.16
Constant	4.56	4.83
R^2	.29	.18

Note: See table 6.1 for coding and *N*. All effects on responsibility judgments were highly significant ($p < .0001$) except for the nonsignificant effect of mental state when actors were equals.

actors as Joe, the foreman whose worker gets hurt: not just "was he careless" or "did he mean it," but "was he a careless boss?" As table 6.2 shows, the statistical trace of this extra question appears in the form of an impact for mental state information that cannot be explained by direct questions about avoidability and purpose.

Solidarity and Mental State

The actor's mental state was expected to have a greater impact in stories involving family ties, where solidarity is high, than in work-related incidents where actor and victim are less closely tied. The results confirmed this expectation. Figure 6.3 presents the average allocation of responsibility for low versus high solidarity: work versus family roles. The placement of the two lines for low versus high solidarity reflects our finding that the actor's responsibility is lower when incidents involve highly solidary ties. The slopes of the lines from left to right of the figure show that the actor's mental state had a greater impact—a steeper slope—in the highly solidary bonds of families.[3] Thus when sibling hurts sibling or mother harms child, those who stand in judgment care more about whether the perpetrator meant to do it than in the more impersonal world of work.

Hierarchy and Other's Influence

Other's influence depends on the role of the other. Specifically, influence from another person who was an authority was expected to have a greater impact in reducing an actor's responsibility than influence from another who was an equal. The left side of figure 6.4 presents results confirming this expectation. The right side indicates that the impact of other's influence on responsibility also varied depending on the solidarity of the relationship.

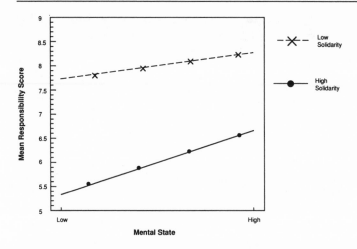

Figure 6.3 Effect of Mental State on Responsibility for Low versus High Solidarity

Influence from another had a more profound influence in work than in family incidents. This pattern may reflect the fact that people in family relationships are seen as having greater potential to exert countervailing influence. Thus they share in the responsibility for an action, even if it was influenced or ordered by another, to an extent that is not true at work, where solidarity is lower.[4]

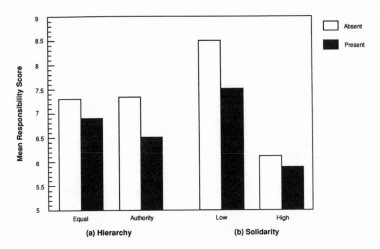

Figure 6.4 Impact of Other's Influence on Responsibility by (a) Hierarchy and (b) Solidarity

In sum, the data support each of our expectations about the texture of responsibility decisions when things go wrong in everyday life. Deeds affect responsibility; roles affect responsibility; and roles affect how information about deeds is interpreted and used.

Deeds, Contexts, and Roles: Macrolevel Differences

Thus far we have looked at patterns of judging wrongdoing as if no differences existed between Americans and Japanese. Statistically speaking, the discussion has considered the general results that obtain when we average *across* the cultural divide. Some things, however, are true in one country but not the other, or in one country more than the other. The impact of deeds, contexts, and roles might vary cross-culturally, in response to macrolevel differences in the overall distribution and meaning of social relationships. *Macro* here refers to data that characterize Japanese as a whole, in contrast to Americans as a whole; it refers to the effects of nation on responsibility judgments. We interpret these effects in terms of national differences in the structure and distribution of social relationships.

At the center of the theoretical model stands the actor who produces the harm. This responsible actor is likely to be viewed by Americans as more of an isolated, equal individual. Japanese, in contrast, are likely to view the responsible actor as what we have called a stratified contextual: a person embedded in a web of close and hierarchical ties with others, even victims. If these images capture important elements of how Americans and Japanese judge wrongdoers, they should be reflected in the use of information about deeds, contexts, and roles. Americans should be more sensitive to immediate aspects of what an actor did, especially the actor's subjective state of mind, than Japanese. This sensitivity may extend to aspects of the context of action that are "actor-carried," such as the past pattern of behavior. Japanese should be more sensitive to variation in the roles of the parties and to the influence of other parties in the social context. Each of these predictions is basically of the form "X matters to citizens in both countries, but X matters more in country Y than in country Z." The argument is that certain basic elements determine responsibility everywhere but that variations in social structure and in cultural experience may modify the weights that citizens place on these elements.

Overall Responsibility

American respondents assigned more responsibility overall than the Japanese. The averages fell in a stairstep pattern: Average responsibility scores assigned were 7.29 (out of a possible 10) in Detroit, 6.99 in Yokohama, and

6.70 in Kanazawa. Statistically, each of these averages differs significantly from the other two. It is tempting to interpret this result in terms of cultural differences. For example, it may be interpreted as evidence of a greater American focus on the responsibility of the individual who is called to account. In addition, since Yokohama's data are intermediate, this pattern is consistent with our Japanese colleagues' expectation that Yokohama might be more Westernized than Kanazawa. Cross-cultural researchers, however, warn that it is important not to read too much into variations in overall average scores or percentages from one culture to another. These may be due to different ways of using or conceptualizing the scales of measurement rather than to substantive differences. It is safer to look for cultural differences in *patterns* of response or patterns of relationships among more than one variable, such as our predictions about the effects of different factors on responsibility allocation (Przeworski & Teune, 1970).

Deeds and Contexts

Significant differences in the impacts of deeds and contexts are summarized in figures 6.5 and 6.6. Figure 6.5 shows that the actor's mental state was considerably more important to the American respondents than to residents of either Japanese city; the slope as one moves from low to high mental state is far steeper for Detroiters. Yokohama and Kanazawa did not differ in this regard. This confirms the expectation that Americans would pay more attention than Japanese to whether the actor "meant it" and whether the deed was an accident.

Figure 6.6 indicates an opposite pattern: Influence from another person was more important to Japanese than to Americans. The slope showing a drop in responsibility attribution from left (other absent) to right (other present) was steeper in both Japanese cities than in Detroit. Again this was consistent with expectations about a greater Japanese sensitivity to social context. Further, the cities fell into line in terms of their presumed Westernization. Although Yokohama residents were significantly more likely than Detroiters to consider the presence of another person who influenced the actor, Kanazawa residents were even more likely to take other's influence into account. The two remaining aspects of deed and context—the seriousness of consequences and the presence of a bad past pattern of behavior—are not presented because neither had an impact that varied significantly among the cities.

Overall, American and Japanese respondents differed most strikingly in their attention to the mental state of a person who commits a misdeed or causes harm. Especially because Western research has for decades empha-

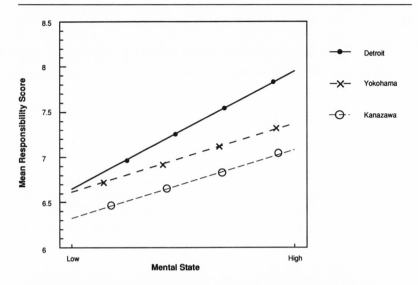

Figure 6.5   Impact of Mental State Information on Responsibility Judgments, by City

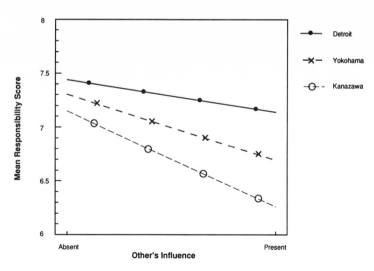

Figure 6.6   Impact of Other's Influence Information on Responsibility Judgments, by City

sized the importance of intent in mature moral judgments (Piaget, 1932/1965), it is worth reflecting on these results. The actor's state of mind when wrongdoing or harmdoing occurred was *approximately twice as important* a determinant of responsibility for Detroiters as it was for Japanese respondents. Chapter 5 also showed that Detroiters rated actions in these everyday-life incidents as much more purposive overall than did residents of either Japanese city. Taken together, these two findings mean that American respondents were both considerably more likely to see the same action as intentional and more sensitive to any variation in the intentionality of that action.

The picture of cultural differences in deeds and contexts that emerges from this analysis is quite consistent with our argument that Americans are likely to see the responsible actor as an isolated, purposive entity, whereas Japanese respondents tend to use information about influence from another to a greater extent and to make less use of mental state information, consistent with an image of the responsible actor as embedded in roles and contexts.

Roles

Significant cultural differences in the impacts of roles were found. Figure 6.7 shows that the overall effect of solidarity on responsibility—the harsher judgment of actors in less solidary, work relationships—is greater in the Japanese cities. Each Japanese city differed significantly from Detroit in this regard, but the larger gap between work and family—the steeper slope in the figure—appears in Yokohama rather than Kanazawa. Thus, as expected, Japanese respondents were more sensitive than their American counterparts to the nuances of relationship closeness in deciding about an actor's responsibility.

Table 6.3 reports the effects of hierarchy for each city. It parallels table 6.1 but splits the overall finding into three components: Detroit, Yokohama, and Kanazawa. In order to examine the differences between authorities and equals, we again present the data controlling for the perceived mental state of the actor. The left side of the table shows the pattern for situations in which other's influence was absent; the right side shows the results when this influence was present. The "pure" effects of hierarchy appeared most strongly where other's influence was absent.

In all three cities, authorities were more responsible for their misdeeds than were equals, but this pattern was significantly stronger in both Japanese cities than in Detroit. Like the effect of solidarity, the effect of hierarchy was most powerful in Yokohama. Thus the expectation that Japanese would be

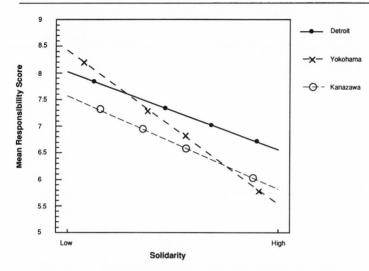

Figure 6.7   Impact of Solidarity on Responsibility, by City

more sensitive than Americans to nuances of relationships between people was confirmed for both the hierarchical linkages and the horizontal ties of everyday life.

These findings for hierarchy and solidarity did not suggest that Yokohama was more Westernized than Kanazawa. If anything, Yokohama residents appeared to be more sensitive than their counterparts in Kanazawa to the variations in role relationships. These results stand in contrast to the results

Table 6.3   Basic Effect of Hierarchy on Responsibility: Comparing American and Japanese Cities (Unstandardized Coefficients)

	Other's influence					
	Absent			Present		
	Detroit	Yokohama	Kanazawa	Detroit	Yokohama	Kanazawa
Hierarchy	.70	1.50	1.08	−.33ns	.70	.70
Mental state	.39	.27ns	.16ns	.71	.42	.28ns
"On purpose"	.25	.27	.25	.25	.23	.24
"Avoid"	2.32	2.06	2.44	2.30	1.54	1.46
Constant	3.79	4.24	4.23	3.91	4.64	4.46
R^2	.21	.29	.32	.27	.17	.16

Note: See table 6.1 for coding and *N*. *ns* = nonsignificant effects. All other coefficients were significant at $p < .05$.

for other's influence. On balance, Yokohama residents show no clear pattern of difference from Kanazawa residents in the "Japaneseness" of their responsibility judgments.

Macrolevel Differences in Role-Deed Interrelationships

In addition to expectations about deeds, contexts, and roles per se, we have discussed the interrelationships between mental state and solidarity, mental state and hierarchy, and other's influence and hierarchy. Results have already shown that each of these interrelationships is true in general. The next question is whether each is *equally* true among American and Japanese respondents. As noted above, we had no clear expectations that either of the interrelationships involving mental state would be more pronounced in one country than the other. For example, if Americans are more sensitive to mental state and Japanese are more sensitive to solidarity, what should be expected about the *joint* effect of solidarity and mental state? The joint effect of hierarchy and other's influence, on the other hand, was predictable, because each of its components were aspects to which Japanese were expected to be more sensitive. Therefore, Japanese were expected to show a more powerful interaction of other's influence and hierarchy than Americans; theoretically, the fact that a person influencing the actor was an authority rather than an equal should matter more to the Japanese.

Solidarity and Mental State

Differences between Japanese and American judgments of responsibility were found for all three of the role-deed interrelationships. Figure 6.8 shows the patterns of response to mental state information by city and by work versus family relationships. It indicates that in Japan, variation in the actor's state of mind was important only in the highly solidary relationships of family. In the United States, however, mental state was important in both work and family ties. This pattern is consistent with a picture of American responsibility decisions as dominated by perceptions about the actor's state of mind.

Hierarchy and Mental State

Cultural differences in the mental state–hierarchy interrelationship are more complex. The overall data analysis did not show a significant difference among the cities in average responsibility in terms of combinations of hierarchy and mental state (that is, statistically, there was no three-way interaction among hierarchy, mental state, and city). But the expectations about

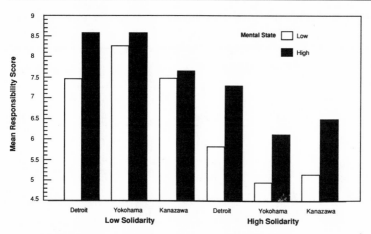

Figure 6.8 Effects of Mental State on Responsibility for Low versus High Solidarity, by City

mental state/hierarchy interrelations involved more subtle questions: the impact of hierarchy at different levels of mental state and the meaning of information about the mental states of authorities versus equals.

LEVELS. The first of these questions was again addressed by comparing actions that the respondent judged to be accidental, negligent, and intentional. Results for the two Japanese cities mirrored the overall pattern observed in figure 6.2. That is, authorities were more responsible than equals for accidental or negligent acts, but judgments of authorities and equals were indistinguishable when acts were seen as intentional. In Detroit, in contrast, the pattern for accidents was insignificant and for intentional acts the responsibility of equals was higher than that of authorities.

Further exploration indicated that this pattern among Detroiters actually reflected the inadequacy of the initial three-way categorization of acts as accidental, negligent, or intentional. Detroiters tended to perceive action as more intentional than the Japanese did (that is, they perceived relatively few "accidents"). Two changes in the coding were thus called for. First, because Detroiters saw most outcomes as avoidable, it was more appropriate to categorize perceptions of mental state by using only the "on purpose" question. In addition, because Detroiters saw so much action as purposive, the data were more evenly divided if the trichotomy stretched the "low" category to include scores of 0 to 2 on the 10-point purposiveness scale (rather than solely scores of 0).

Table 6.4 summarizes the results of the reanalysis of American responses

Table 6.4 Effects of Hierarchy and Mental State on Detroiters' Responsibility Judgments

A. Low purposiveness (0–2 on 0–10 scale)

| | | Other's influence | | | |
| | Absent | | Present | |
	Equal	Authority	Equal	Authority
Low	6.01	5.79	5.86	5.13
Mental state				
High	5.31	7.17	5.86	6.51
Total	5.83	6.36	5.86	5.67

B. Medium purposiveness (3–7 on 0–10 scale)

| | | Other's influence | | | |
| | Absent | | Present | |
	Equal	Authority	Equal	Authority
Low	7.09	7.60	7.55	5.93
Mental state				
High	7.09	8.27	8.12	7.78
Total	7.09	7.98	7.79	7.01

C. High purposiveness (8–10 on 0–10 scale)

| | | Other's influence | | | |
| | Absent | | Present | |
	Equal	Authority	Equal	Authority
Low	9.01	8.88	8.53	8.78
Mental state				
High	8.89	9.33	9.10	8.93
Total	8.93	9.21	8.91	8.90

Note: Overall, 1,113 of the Detroit responses (43%) involved ratings of low purposiveness, 685 (26%) medium purposiveness, and 811 (31%) high purposiveness. Entries refer to average responsibility (0–10 scale).

with this coding change made. The effects of hierarchy and of mental state variations on responsibility are summarized for actions seen by the respondent as low, medium, or high in purposiveness. On the left side of the table, where other's influence was absent, the relatively pure impact of these variables appears. On the right, where other's influence was present, a dampening of the effects is evident.

What are these effects? For acts they judged to be low in purposiveness, Detroiters rated authorities as more responsible than equals, and they were more sensitive to variations in authorities' state of mind. For acts they judged to be medium in purposiveness, Detroiters were sensitive mainly to mental state. They did not rate authorities and equals as different in overall responsibility, but they were again more sensitive to variations in authorities' mental states than variations in those of equals. Finally, for acts judged high in purposiveness, judgments of authorities and equals converged, and no significant differences were evident.

In sum, it appears that when the research question is tested appropriately, the results for Detroit are in many ways comparable to the Japanese results. American respondents judge authorities more harshly where acts are less purposive, and their judgments of authorities and equals converge for purposive acts (see table 6.4). The same fundamental tendencies in using information about the mental states of authorities and equals are at work in both cultures.

MEANING. The other question about cultural differences in the hierarchy-mental state relationship involved the meaning of the actor's state of mind for authorities versus equals (see table 6.2). For equals, information about the actor's state of mind could be reduced to information about purposiveness and avoidability: State of mind was a matter of what a person meant to do and what that person could have avoided doing. For authorities, "something more" was involved, an effect of mental state over and above what could be attributed to the act's purposiveness and the outcome's avoidability. We interpreted this effect as reflecting the fact that responsibility for authorities involves at least three elements: mental state, role, and their interrelationship. This interrelationship refers to the ways in which the role changes the meaning or impact of mental state information because of role-generated obligations, such as greater foresight.

Table 6.5 splits the pattern of table 6.2 into its three component cities. When the issue is judgment of actors who were their victims' equals, the three cities produce virtually indistinguishable patterns. In all cases there is no significant impact of the mental state variation once the respondent's perceptions of purpose and avoidability have been controlled. More detailed tests showed that the size of effects did not differ significantly among the cities.

Where authorities are involved, a somewhat more complex picture is revealed (table 6.5). One key similarity is present: In all three cities, when actors are authorities there is a "something more" that is communicated when information is provided about state of mind, beyond what such information evokes when equals are involved. In statistical terms, there is a significant effect of the actor's mental state on the responsibility of authorities, controlling for perceptions of purposiveness and avoidability. However, the right side of table 6.5 also shows substantial variation in the size of effects of mental state, purposiveness, and avoidability from city to city. A follow-up

Table 6.5 Cultural Differences in the Meaning of Mental State Information for the Responsibility of Authorities versus Equals (Unstandardized Coefficients)

	Equal			Authority		
	Detroit	Yokohama	Kanazawa	Detroit	Yokohama	Kanazawa
Mental state	.15ns	.22ns	−.17ns	.87	.48	.51
"On purpose"	.29	.30	.35	.21	.17	.13
"Avoid"	1.37	1.62	1.26	2.73	1.99	2.45
Constant	4.69	4.46	4.65	3.62	5.48	4.96
R^2	.20	.29	.31	.24	.16	.21

Note: See table 6.1 for coding and *N*. *ns* = nonsignificant effects. All other coefficients were significant at $p < .05$.

analysis (not shown) tested whether the cities differed significantly in the size of these effects involving authorities. All the effects—mental state, perceived purposiveness, and perceived avoidability—were significantly larger in Detroit than in either Japanese city. Thus Detroiters were significantly more sensitive than Japanese respondents to both the direct and indirect impacts of information about authorities' mental state.

Overall, a pattern of cultural differences has begun to emerge with regard to judging authorities, especially with regard to the processing of information about mental state. The differences basically revolve around sensitivity to states of mind: "Did he mean to?" "Did she know what she was doing?" To both Americans and Japanese, these questions were important but quite straightforward when judging equals who had harmed equals, and they became more complex when an authority caused harm to someone under their care or supervision. But Americans both saw more purposiveness in the deeds they judged and remained more sensitive to any differences in this purposiveness than did Japanese.

Certain of the features that make the responsibility of authorities distinctive were seen in both countries. The responsibility of authority and equal differed most where action was less intentional, and the meaning of mental state information for authorities differed from the meaning for equals. The cultural differences that were observed refer to the weight placed on the components in the interrelationship. They are matters of degree rather than of kind.

Hierarchy and Other's Influence

The possibility of cultural differences in the hierarchy-other's influence linkage was the most readily predictable of the linkages considered (fig. 6.9).[5]

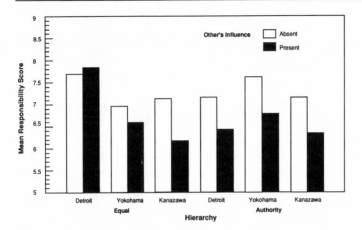

Figure 6.9 Effects of Other's Influence on Responsibility for Equals versus Authorities, by City

As anticipated, Japanese were sensitive to the presence of influence from another person both when actors were equals (who were influenced by equals) and when they were authorities (who were influenced by someone in authority over them). American respondents showed no effect of other's influence on an actor's responsibility unless the other person was an authority. Even then, the impact of other's influence on responsibility was slightly lower for American respondents than for the Japanese.

In sum, the nature of social ties affects the processing of information about deeds in three ways. Hierarchy affects use of information about the actor's mental state and about influence from others; solidarity affects use of mental state information. Americans and Japanese differ in the extent to which this processing is affected. For Americans, information about mental state is particularly salient, and it is relatively resistant to reinterpretation as a function of actors' social roles. For Japanese, information about roles and about others' influence is particularly salient. Insofar as all deeds are committed in roles and in contexts, Americans appear to focus on the deed and resist the reinterpretation that can occur because of role or context; Japanese focus on the context and shift their interpretation of the deed accordingly.

Evaluating the Findings

These results suggest that the basic model of how people judge responsibility is correct: Responsibility is a matter of people's roles as well as their deeds. In everyday incidents, this means that responsibilities are determined on the basis of people's obligations as well as their actions. The cross-cultural contrasts, which also fell closely into line with predictions, further suggest that Americans and Japanese perceive the responsible actor differently. The actor tends to be viewed by Americans as an isolated entity whose mental state matters greatly; the same actor is viewed by Japanese as a part of a context, and the influence of role and context matters greatly. We have argued that this difference flows from macrolevel (national) differences in social structure—in the distribution of types of social relationships and in the socializing experiences of the citizens.

How general are these conclusions? Like any social scientific research, this study has certain limitations. Some limitations and concerns involve the basic microlevel responsibility model; these include threats to the internal validity of the study. Other concerns involve the generalizability of the findings, primarily with respect to the macrolevel arguments about national differences.

Internal Validity

A major concern is the internal validity of the experiments: whether our purported causes really produced the purported effects (Cook & Campbell, 1979). Because the study was a survey and time and cost limitations dictated the use of a small number of stories, two internal validity issues arise:

1. Only one story was used to represent each type of role relationship. This is an issue because it is possible that any given story is idiosyncratic; if so, the results obtained are really due to something special about the story (e.g., the actor was a child, or the victim was a child) or the setting (e.g., the used-car lot or the factory production line) rather than the generic type of relationship.

2. Variations in role dimensions were made within-subject (i.e., with each person hearing all stories), so that responses to later stories could have been influenced by having judged earlier stories.

Both of these issues might be addressed by using multiple examples of each type of role. Variations in type of role would then be created by varying only one piece of information—the role—within an otherwise constant context. Ideally, each respondent would judge only one of these quite similar stories. To our knowledge no one has yet carried out such a study, but a promising beginning has been made by Jonathan Haidt (1988).

In Haidt's research, undergraduates and law students in the eastern United States responded to vignettes constructed in similar fashion to our own. That is, stories about wrongdoing were varied experimentally so that the different respondents did not necessarily receive the same version of the story. The research was a paper-and-pencil questionnaire rather than an interview, and the dependent variable was the actor's immorality rather than responsibility. Haidt varied hierarchy in a story concerning an injury at a construction site and solidarity in a story concerning the sale of a defective car. Hierarchy referred to whether the injured party was the boss, co-worker, or subordinate of the actor. Solidarity referred to whether the victim was a good friend of the actor, an acquaintance, or a stranger. Only one "deed" variable was represented, analogous to our mental state manipulation. But Haidt compared omission with commission, whereas we were concerned with accident versus negligence versus intent.

The most direct parallels between Haidt's work and our study concern the main effects of hierarchy and of omission versus commission, as well as the interaction of omission-commission with hierarchy. Haidt found that authorities were judged more immoral than subordinates for negligent action and that the question of whether the harm resulted from an omission or commission mattered less in the case of authority. These results correspond to our findings that authorities are more responsible than equals, holding mental state constant, and that authorities are held to more stringent standards than were equals, insofar as they are more responsible for negligent acts or accidents. Haidt also found that intentional harm by a person in a highly solidary relationship was judged more harshly than the same harm by a stranger, and that omission-commission differences were less important in judging a friend than a stranger. These results appear consistent with our finding that variation in mental state had a greater impact when solidarity was high (in families) than when it was relatively low (in work relationships).

Haidt's research has its own limitations. For example, some of its variations were within-respondent, so that the person judged two very similar stories in turn.[6] Under those circumstances the first response can influence or contaminate the second. However, the consistency between the study's findings and our own is noteworthy. Further, a number of characteristics of the Haidt study—including its limitations—complement our work:

Generalizability across samples. Haidt used a different pool of respondents (students rather than random samples of adults) from a different region of the United States.

Generalizability across methods. The research involved a different procedure, questionnaire rather than interview.

Internal validity. The experimental design differed; variations in roles were introduced by making only minimal changes in a single scenario. This provides greater experimental control—greater chance of being sure what causes one's effects—than did the broad differences in our vignettes. One can more confidently say that the difference between two stories that differ only by the change of a few words (e.g., friend vs. acquaintance) is due to that specific alteration. Overall, although any particular example of a role may not represent an ideal-typical example of that type of role, comparisons between roles are "clean."

Overall, the studies provide converging evidence, across varied experimental methods and varied samples, in support of the basic argument that roles matter, deeds matter, and roles and deeds interact in determining responsibility.

Generalizability and the Issue of Prosocial Norms

An additional concern is the generalizability of the results. This issue is particularly relevant to the macrolevel comparison made between the countries. At a concrete level, generalizability involves such issues as whether the cities studied here truly allow us to draw conclusions about the countries involved. Chapter 5 indicated ways in which the cities in question were and were not "typical." Yokohama and Kanazawa were chosen purposely for their contrasts, but in many ways the results from these cities are closely parallel, providing evidence that the overall conclusions about "Japanese" are likely to be a reasonably faithful image of the cultural realities. Because Detroit was the sole U.S. city, it was necessary to draw on data from other sources, some of which are discussed below. Overall, we believe that the allocation of responsibility and conceptions of the responsible actor in the United States and Japan as a whole are likely to follow the outlines that are suggested in these data.

The question of generalizability can also include potential comparisons between the United States and Eastern countries or between Japan and Western cultures. In one such study, Miller, Bersoff, and Harwood (1990) compared American adults and children with adults and children in India with respect to moral judgments involving norms of prosocial behavior: helping others. Miller (1984) had demonstrated that Indians, as would be anticipated of a contextual culture, made attributions about others that were more situational and behavioral, in comparison to Americans' tendencies to paint the sources of behavior as lying inside the individual. Miller et al. (1990) considered whether research subjects (college students, sixth graders, and second graders) would perceive helping others as a general norm, regardless of a person's role, or whether they would differentiate the obligation to help on the basis of a person's relationship to the person who needed that help. For example, when someone is in need, should it matter whether that someone is a friend or a stranger?

Miller et al. asked research subjects to judge hypothetical incidents where people refused to help others. They found that Americans were *more* likely than Indians to use information about roles: to perceive differences in people's obligations to give help based on their relationships. They interpreted these results in terms of a contrast between general moral norms and what they called personal-moral norms. Moral norms are obligatory and are seen as legitimate matters for social regulation; personal-moral norms are seen as personally obligatory, but not as matters for social regulation. In their interpretation, these results indicated that for Americans this prosocial behavior was a personal-moral norm, whereas for Indians prosocial behavior was a general moral norm.

Is this finding consistent with our evidence that Americans were *less* sensitive than Japanese to the impact of roles on responsibility for wrongdoing? We think so for two reasons. First, our data do not show Americans to be insensitive to role obligations; they merely show them to be less sensitive than Japanese where judging wrongdoing is concerned. In that sense, it could be said that the Miller et al. data constitute further evidence that Americans do make use of information about role obligations.

More substantively, if Americans have a role-differentiated version of the norm of helping others, it means that they have a limited responsibility to act. In this arena it is omission that is potentially blameworthy. Consider the implications of such positive responsibilities for the freedom of action of the individual. If there is some general American cultural tendency to view the social actor as an isolated individual, as we have argued, then a *role-differentiated* norm regarding prosocial action is likely to preserve that isolation better. The social actor has to take steps only in a delimited realm, rather than toward everyone. Conversely, the issue in our research has been a responsibility for misdeeds committed, and role obligations have served to excuse or exacerbate this responsibility. In the case of the commission of wrongdoing, it is an *undifferentiated* norm that preserves the individual actor's isolation.

The American respondents' use of role information to judge duty to act in the Miller et al. (1990) study is consistent with American tort law. As Keeton, Dobbs, Keeton, and Owen (1984) note, "for 'nonfeasance' it is necessary to find some definite relation between the parties" (p. 374). Moreover, the traditional legal justification for this rule is consistent with our interpretation of their results. Thus, according to Keeton et al., "the highly individualistic philosophy of the older common law . . . shrank from converting the courts into an agency for forcing men to help one another" (p. 373).[7] On balance, the findings of Miller et al. seem consistent with an image of Americans as relatively reluctant to acknowledge ties to others, whether they promote prosocial action or excuse antisocial action. But social scientists are only beginning to grapple with cross-cultural differences in prosocial action. Direct comparisons between Americans and Japanese on this issue would be a natural direction for future research.

Conclusions

Our survey results support the microsociological model of responsibility presented in chapter 4 and are consistent with our macrosociological arguments about the interplay of social structure and culture in Japan and the United States. Responsibility is a matter of what a person did and what that person was expected to do. However, cultures differ in how they reach conclusions about responsibility: Japanese tend to emphasize role-based expectations, whereas Americans tend to emphasize the actor's concrete deeds. Although differences are invariably a matter of degree rather than of kind, the pattern of findings is consistent with the idea that the responsible actor in Japan is more contextual and the responsible actor in the United States is a more isolated individual. This pattern, in turn, is consistent with the more tightly woven web of hierarchical and solidary relationships that characterizes Japanese social life.

Much remains to be discovered about how roles and deeds shape responsibility and other moral judgments, as well as how these judgments vary across cultures. The combination of Haidt's (1988) work and our own, and even the contrasting patterns found in Miller et al.'s (1990) work, leave us confident that our picture of responsibility decisions and of the responsible actor is correct in its broad outlines. But the picture is not yet complete. We next ask how these decisions about responsibility translate into choices about sanction.

7 Punishment

Offenses in a family are normal, expected oc-
currences. Punishment is not something a
child receives in isolation from the rest of his
relationship to the family; nor is it something which presupposes or carries with it a
change of status from "child" to "criminal
child." When a parent punishes his child,
both parent and child know that afterward
they will go on living together as before. The
child gets his punishment, as a matter of
course, within a continuum of love . . . and
he is punished in his own unchanged capacity as a child with failings (like other children) rather than as some kind of distinct
and dangerous outsider. (Griffiths, 1970,
p. 376)

In the last chapter we focused on the
attribution of responsibility. We turn now to the question of sanctions.[1]
Sanctions routinely presuppose responsibility (Hart & Honoré, 1959), and
many of the hypotheses we have raised with respect to responsibility also
apply to sanctioning. As the epigraph indicates, wrongdoing that may be the
occasion for punishment has community attributes as well as individual
attributes. For example, harm may be perpetrated against a stranger or an
acquaintance (a community attribute) as well as perpetrated unintentionally
or intentionally (an individual attribute). Correspondingly, sanctions for
wrongdoing have consequences for communities as well as for individuals.
Thus, like responsibility decisions, everyday sanctioning decisions may be
influenced by the actor's deed and the context within which the act occurred,
as well as by the relationship of the parties in dispute. The microsociology of
punishment, like the microsociology of responsibility, needs to take account
of people's roles and social ties as well as their deeds. Furthermore, at the
macrolevel, we have suggested that the legal culture and its conceptions
of the responsible actor may vary in different societies as a function of the

types of relationships and the nature of community typical of each society; this legal culture, too, may find reflection in the judgments of individual citizens.

A variety of evidence is available about the impacts of deeds and roles on sanctioning. With respect to deed information, there is evidence that information about the actor's mental state is relevant in assessing sanctions (e.g., Shaver, 1985; Shultz, Wright, & Schleifer, 1986). Likewise, there is evidence that the degree of punishment increases with the severity of harm, both for criminal acts (De Jong, Morris, & Hastorf, 1976) and for everyday misdeeds (Shaw & Reitan, 1969). The importance of consequence information may vary, however, depending on the objectives of the sanctioner. When the objective is retribution—"an eye for an eye"—this information may be more important than when the objective is rehabilitation, which focuses on the actor's subjective understanding of deeds. Vidmar (1977) found a stronger effect of the seriousness of consequences on punishment among individuals classified as high on retribution motivation (see also Shultz & Schleifer, 1983).

The nature of relationships also affects sanctioning decisions. People behave differently toward others' wrongdoing as a function of the high, low, or nonexistent solidarity of their ties. When ties are of higher solidarity, acts of wrongdoing threaten, in Ekland-Olson's (1984) terms, to create relatively greater *relational disturbance*. They more fundamentally disrupt the fabric of social life. Not only can the wrongdoing itself disrupt networks, but so can the response to wrongdoing. Within societies, where highly solidary ties exist between actor and victim and where the nature of wrongdoing has not irrevocably destroyed the relationship, a concern for the relationship should evoke sanctioning choices that are less destructive of the network. This concern is reflected in relative rates of use of law. Partly because formal legal proceedings are thought to strain or sever ties (Kawashima, 1963; Lloyd-Bostock, 1983; Macaulay, 1963), people are less likely to sue friends than strangers (Black, 1976; Ekland-Olson, 1982; Gottfredson & Hindelang, 1979; Nader, 1969).

Punishment practices are likely to be most sensitive to rebuilding relationships of actor and victim where relationships are initially highly solidary, as in family ties. Conversely, punishment practices are likely to be most isolative and indifferent to relationships where the parties are strangers. In Braithwaite's (1989) terms, people in highly solidary ties are more likely to make punishment an occasion for *reintegrative shaming*, whereby the offender is taught to "shape up," as in Griffiths' (1970) family model of justice; the alternative, *stigmatizing shaming*, with its potential for rejection of the offender, becomes more likely as social ties become weak or nonexistent.

The effect of roles—especially the contrast between relationships of high versus low solidarity—is thus not primarily to produce a difference in the *level* of sanctions. Rather, it is to produce a difference in the *kinds* of sanctions. The sanctions appropriate for a child are not appropriate for an employee; one neither fires a child nor spanks a worker. And neither of the repertoires of sanction used in home or workplace is appropriate for a criminal.

Finally, sanctioning decisions are influenced by the legal culture (e.g., the conceptions of the responsible actor that exist in different societies) as well as by deed and role information. Like role relationship differences, legal culture should affect not only the extent of punishment but the repertoire of punishments proposed. To the degree that American culture views the individual as an isolated entity, a consistent mode of punishment is to isolate rather than reintegrate the offender, and a consistent goal is to seek retribution or incapacitation for what has happened rather than rehabilitation or restitution and the restoration of ties. In contrast, to the extent that Japan can be characterized as a culture of differentiated contextual actors whose social ties are high in solidarity, sanction is likely to be used to reintegrate contextuals who stray from the prescribed pattern of behavior.

This account of how legal culture relates to punishment therefore rests on structural differences between the societies concerned, not simply on cultural proclivities such as a Japanese emphasis on restoring harmony. To the extent that our results show that punishment patterns within *and* between societies differ as a function of relationship types, the structural interpretation is strengthened and explanations that simply invoke "culture" or "custom" become implausible.

Two Models of Punishment

Japanese can be expected to recommend sanctions that restore the status quo to a greater extent than Americans across all types of relationships. Restoration as a goal of punishment can include a literal focus on restoring ties, as in the use of apology, as well as a more impersonal focus on restoring prior conditions through various forms of restitution. The former can be said to stress emotional restoration; the latter, financial restoration.[2] Substantial indirect support exists for our hypothesis that restoration is a more dominant aim of punishment among Japanese than among Americans. Chapter 2 showed that across a wide variety of situations, the Japanese legal system uses a set of procedures and sanctions that are less adjudicative and less adversarial, hence less destructive of networks. We have also noted that when wrongdoing occurs in Japan, apology has an important function in both criminal and everyday-life incidents; punishment is reduced or eliminated accordingly (see Haley, 1982b, 1986; Wagatsuma & Rosett, 1986). Japanese seem to assume that *there are bonds to be restored* between offender and victim, as if the individual exists in a network of interlocked others.

American and Japanese formal discussions or analyses of punishment also tend to support this hypothesis. In the United States such discussions typically occur in the context of the criminal sanction and usually focus on an individual in isolation. Exceptions, such as Brickman's (1977) suggestion that restitution may be an important alternative to traditional sanctions, underscore the dominant focus. Not only is the offender typically viewed as an isolated individual, but the cause of the untoward act is thought to originate in the wrongdoer (Erikson, 1966). Even the reform movement that accompanied the rise of the penitentiary in the last century, which stressed the role of the environment in producing crime, assumed that good wrought in (and by) isolation would carry over into behavior in the outside world (Rothman, 1971). Individual responsibility remains popular among Americans as a lay account of crime and as a moral model of the causes of wrongdoing.

The Japanese appear to view punishment very differently, whether in the family or in practices of incarceration. Restoring role relationships is an important aspect of sanctioning practices. Moreover, to the degree that a contextual actor is defined by as well as tied to social networks, to be isolated or separated from others is a more severe punishment to Japanese in whatever context it occurs (Doi, 1973; Weisz, Rothbaum, & Blackburn, 1984). Japanese reluctance to incarcerate offenders may rest in part on Japan's low crime rate and the generally healthy society it implies (Bayley, 1976; Clifford, 1976; Government of Japan, 1989). This reluctance, however, is also consistent with the view that individual perpetrators are contextual actors and with a legal culture that perceives the law as a less central institution in the resolution of disputes.

Even imprisonment is, at least for some, a more genuine opportunity for rehabilitation or restitution in the Japanese case. Recall from chapter 3 that Naikan therapy was originally used in correctional institutions (e.g., Murase, 1974; Reynolds, 1980). Although Naikan therapy is a type of introspection, it is not individualistic introspection. The goal of the exercise is to activate the patient's guilt vis-à-vis crucial other persons, especially the mother. From our perspective, the enterprise is an intense reminder of one's place in a network of social roles and relationships and of one's debt to it.

In general, across a variety of punishment decisions, American respondents can be expected to advocate punishments that tend to isolate the offender or exact retribution or do both, whereas Japanese respondents will emphasize relationship restoration. Events involving complete strangers are a possible exception to this generalization. Instances of wrongdoing where solidarity is not merely low but nonexistent provide a limiting case for assessing whether Japanese ever adhere to an "American" model in which the actor's deeds overwhelmingly determine responsibility and sanction for wrongdoing. The role of sanctions for wrongdoing by strangers is discussed in chapter 8.

Before turning to the punishment data, two caveats are in order. A theoretical caveat refers to the interpretation of the proposed Japanese emphasis on restoring relations. An emphasis on restoring role relationships does not imply that wrongdoing is taken lightly or "written off" (Braithwaite, 1989). Practices such as Naikan therapy indicate that a concern with rehabilitation of offenders or restoration of relationships between offender and others can coexist with a view of the individual as "responsible" in some moral sense. A concern with restoration also need not mean that punishment is necessarily more lenient. It simply means that the focus of sanctioning differs.

A methodological caveat is also in order about the nature and meaning of these data. This book deals with sanctioning norms rather than sanctioning practices, using survey respondents' attitudes about and judgments of what is right and proper to do in various hypothetical instances of wrongdoing. We assume that norms concerning sanction and actual sanctioning practices are linked and that both are strongly influenced by the nature of social relationships and the nature of a society's legal structure. The differences in the available mechanisms of dispute resolution in Japan and the United States, discussed in chapter 2, lend credence to this assumption. Nevertheless, this chapter does not prove linkages between sanctioning ideology and sanctioning practices. It is more properly seen as raising questions about those linkages for future research to explore.

Punishment Rationales

At the most general level of abstraction, American and Japanese respondents can be expected to differ in their punishment rationales. A list of such rationales would include the following:

Retribution incorporates the idea that individuals should receive as they have given.

Just deserts is similar to retribution. It captures the idea that sanctioning the offender provides justice for victims of crime (e.g., von Hirsch, 1976; Braithwaite & Pettit, 1991).

Incapacitation involves the straightforward idea that a person who is incarcerated or otherwise isolated cannot be in two places at once. Safely put away, the offender can cause no mischief outside (Wilson, 1975).

General deterrence is the sanctioning of one offender as an example to others. Hence it is aimed at other potential perpetrators as well as at the individual offender.

Denunciation is a less instrumental, more expressive cousin of general deterrence. Denunciation expresses society's disapproval of an act of wrong-doing (Braithwaite, 1989; Feinberg, 1970).

The preceding rationales use individuals to social ends but are not aimed directly at the reintegration of the individual. The next three rationales, in contrast, have precisely that aim.

Specific deterrence, like general deterrence, is based on a relatively instrumental or utilitarian view of sanctions. The objective is to alter the individual's cost-benefit calculus so that he or she becomes a rule-abiding citizen.

Rehabilitation pursues a similar objective of reintegrating the offender but from a more normative and more psychological perspective. The goal is to reform the inner person—the individual's motives, values, and sentiments.

Finally, *restoration* attempts directly to restore social relationships. Two related objectives can be present: that of remedying the condition of the party who is harmed or victimized and that of restoring the relationship between parties. Restitution and apology, respectively, characterize these objectives. In the United States, restitution is more often thought of as a remedy in civil or everyday-life cases than as a sanction for intentional wrongdoing.

Americans are expected to favor rationales that are most consistent with an image of the perpetrator as an isolated individual: retribution, just deserts, incapacitation, and general deterrence. Japanese are expected to favor rationales that assume actors are contextual or that prepare actors to return to a social context: specific deterrence, rehabilitation, and restoration (including apology and restitution, where either is an option). We also expect Japanese to be more favorable to denunciation, but as a function of a tightly knit social order rather than as a function of their image of the individual offender (cf. Braithwaite, 1989).

Chapter 5 noted that in the Detroit mailback portion of the survey and in the Yokohama interview, we asked respondents to assess a series of rationales for imprisonment taken from Vidmar (1978).[3] Explanatory phrases (e.g., "makes the criminal suffer for his crime") were presented rather than abstract labels (e.g., "retribution"). A relationship restoration rationale was omitted because the stimuli concerned imprisonment, and both apology and restitution are usually considered alternatives to imprisonment. Assessments were on a 1-to-5 scale (1 = "very good reason" for imprisonment, 5 = "very bad reason").

Table 7.1   Average Agreement with Various Reasons for
Imprisoning People

Concept	Item Sending the criminal to prison	Mean ratings Detroit (N=294)	Yokohama (N=600)
Retribution	A. Makes the criminal suffer for his crime	2.03	2.47
Just deserts	B. Provides justice for the victim of the crime	2.67	2.43
Incapacitation	C. Removes the criminal from society and keeps him from committing another crime while in prison	1.56	2.13
General deterrence	D. Shows other possible crim- inals what will happen to them if they commit the crime	1.91	2.33
Denunciation	E. Shows that society thinks the crime was wrong	2.05	1.67
Specific deterrence	F. Shows the criminal what happens to people who commit crimes; it teaches him a lesson	2.35	1.66
Rehabilitation	G. Reforms or re-educates the criminal while he is imprisoned	2.62	1.54

Note: Score of 1 = very good reason for imprisonment; 5 = very bad reason). In MANOVA, overall F (7, 8,886) = 56.1, $p < .0001$. Country differences for all individual choices are also significantly different with probability at least $p < .01$.

Table 7.1 shows the average evaluations of rationales for imprisonment.[4] Yokohama and Detroit residents differed significantly on all specific punishment rationales. The smallest difference occurred for the rationale labeled "just deserts" (significant at $p < .01$). All other differences were significant at $p < .0001$.

As predicted, reintegration of offenders emerges as a more prevalent objective among Japanese than among American respondents. Detroiters were significantly more likely to advocate retribution, incapacitation, and general deterrence—responses that reflect a view of wrongdoing as committed by isolated actors. Yokohama residents, in contrast, were significantly more likely to favor rehabilitation, specific deterrence, denunciation, and (by a thinner margin) just deserts. The only pattern not consistent with expectations was that for just deserts. It appears that just deserts may be an ambiguous stimulus, at least in the wording used here; it can be interpreted in terms of either retribution to the actor or justice to the victim. Both the direction and the small size of the observed Yokohama-Detroit difference may be a function of this ambiguity.

Overall, these results suggest an American view of the purpose of incarceration in which crime is caused by an isolated individual and is cured by isolating the individual. The hypothesized tendency of Japanese to view actors and action as embedded in communities is compatible with their observed emphases on reintegrating specific offenders (i.e., with specific deterrence and rehabilitation) and on denunciation of offenders in order to restore social order. The greater or lesser support for different punishment rationales in each society can be seen as reflecting differences in the culture's dominant view of the responsible actor. These rationales in turn help to justify different sanctions for specific acts of wrongdoing.

Methods

As noted above, survey respondents in all three cities heard four everyday-life vignettes. In addition, respondents in Detroit and Yokohama heard two vignettes depicting wrongdoing between strangers: the Robbery story, and either the Child or Adult automobile accident story. In both of these cities respondents also assessed the varied rationales for punishment presented in table 7.1.

Across vignettes and across surveys we asked a slightly varying combination of closed- and open-ended punishment questions. The coding of these questions is presented in appendix B. For all stories, respondents were initially asked whether anything should happen to the perpetrator. The respondents who answered "yes" to this first question were asked a follow-up question, usually open-ended, about what specifically should happen to the offender. Open-ended responses were coded into empirically derived categories. The coding categories are themselves evidence of the differences in the kinds of sanctions that typify different role relationships. Certain types of punishments are associated with certain roles or statuses (e.g., juvenile) or with certain relations between offender and victim. One neither spanks an employee nor fires a child. Because of these qualitative differences, comparisons of sanctions across types of ties must be done with care, and some analyses must be done on a story-by-story basis.

Willingness to Intervene

A "yes" response to the question of whether something should "be done to" or "happen to" the actor indicates a willingness to intervene. The data

Table 7.2   Correlation Coefficients between Responsibility Judgments
and Willingness to Punish Wrongdoers

	Detroit	Kanazawa	Yokohama
Family/Equal	.26	.32	.27
Family/Authority	.35	.28	.19
Work/Equal	.25	.37	.29
Work/Authority	.44	.45	.25

Note: Items were scored with 1 = no and 2 = yes to punishment questions; responsibility judgments were scaled 0 = not at all responsible to 10 = fully responsible. All correlations are significant at the .001 level; a perfect positive correlation is 1.0. *N*s range from 489 to 643 responses per vignette (within city).

can answer three questions: Is the decision to intervene affected by the level of responsibility attributed to the actor? Does the willingness to intervene vary between the United States and Japan? And, to the extent that punishment decisions are influenced by the experimental variations in the vignettes, is this influence different in the United States and Japan?

Responsibility and Punishment

Punishment presupposes responsibility. In the area of criminal sanctions, many would argue that punishment requires responsibility (Hart, 1968). The respondents to these surveys were in general agreement with this position. As table 7.2 shows, in every story there is a strong correlation between a respondent's answer as to whether some sanction is called for and the respondent's responsibility judgment. (Chapter 8 will show that a different pattern emerges for automobile accident and crime stories that involve wrongdoing between strangers.)

Does the Japanese contextual view of the actor imply less willingness to punish? Does failure to use deed and context information reflect a live-and-let-live attitude toward wrongdoing? Table 7.3 presents for each city and vignette the percentage of respondents answering that something should happen to the actor (answering "yes" on the dichotomous yes-no punishment item). The few "don't know" responses were excluded from the database to simplify presentation. The percentage of "no" responses can be obtained by subtracting the number shown from 100 percent.

The Japanese view of the responsible actor, however contextual it may be, does not imply an unwillingness to punish (see table 7.3). Japanese are at least as interventionist as their American counterparts in these surveys. Indeed, across the four everyday-life stories, 74 percent of the Japanese respondents recommended some punishment, while only 66 percent of the

Table 7.3   Overall Willingness to Advocate Punishment

Incident type	Detroit (N=678) (%)	Kanazawa (N=640) (%)	Yokohama (N=600) (%)
Family			
equal	85	70	63
authority	26	56	51
Work			
equal	84	85	86
authority	69	89	91
No solidarity[a]			
Child auto accident	52	—	92
Adult auto accident	76	—	100
Crime (robbery)	96	—	99

Note: Cells indicate percentage answering "yes." Aggregating across the first four (everyday life) stories, there is a significant difference among the three cities in this willingness to punish ($X^2 = 54.2$, d.f. $= 2$, $p < .0001$).
[a]Incidents involving strangers were not asked in Kanazawa. Detroit-Yokohama differences in willingness to punish were significant for each accident story; the cities did not differ significantly for the crime story.

Detroit respondents did so. Kanazawa and Yokohama respondents were *more* likely than Detroiters to advocate intervention in the two authority stories, they were less willing to do so in the family/equal story, and no difference was observed in the work/equal story. For all four stories, respondents in the two Japanese cities were not significantly different from one another in expressed willingness to intervene. The Robbery, Child, and Adult stories help tilt the balance in favor of the Japanese. Yokohama respondents were if anything more likely than Detroiters to advocate intervention. On balance the Japanese are more willing to intervene in situations of wrongdoing than are the Detroit respondents.

Deeds, Context, and Punishment

Recall from chapter 6 that whereas both Japanese and Americans used mental state information in judging responsibility, Americans were relatively more sensitive to this type of information. An actor's past pattern of behavior and the presence of an influencing other are each aspects of the context of action, but past pattern is "carried" by the actor and is conceptually closer to deed information, whereas other's influence is closer to role information. Thus, as expected, in judging responsibility Japanese were significantly more likely than Americans to use information about other's influence, while an opposite trend was observed for past pattern information.

We anticipated similar patterns in punishment judgments: Americans, employing an individualistic perspective, should make greater use of mental state and past pattern information, as well as making more use of information about severity of consequences. If Japanese were to be more sensitive to any of this information, they should be more sensitive to the presence of other's influence.

What effects did the experimental variables have on decisions to punish? To address this question we used a model that included the two deed and two context manipulations, plus nation (coded to distinguish Americans from Japanese), as predictors of the decision to punish.[5] In this analysis, the main effect of each independent variable except consequence and nation was significant. The main effects were straightforward. Respondents were more likely to recommend a sanction where mental state was high, a bad past pattern was present, and other's influence was absent. Whatever the specific act of wrongdoing, a perpetrator who meant to do it, who had done it before, and who did it without pressure from others was seen as more worthy of punishment.

In addition, interactions between nation and mental state and between nation and past pattern were statistically significant (see figs. 7.1, 7.2). As expected, when deciding whether to recommend a sanction for the actor, Americans made greater use of mental state and past pattern information than did Japanese. This fact is reflected in the steeper slope of the line from low to high mental state for the Americans in figure 7.1. The same change in mental state had a greater effect on the judgments of Americans. Exactly the same pattern appears in figure 7.2 for the effect of past pattern information. Overall, compared to Detroiters, Japanese were not strongly influenced by these manipulations about deeds when they made sanctioning decisions.

In sum, Japanese and Americans differ little in deciding whether to intervene, but they exhibit more patterned differences in the reasons for intervention. The decisions of Japanese respondents appear to be governed less by deed-related information than the decisions of American respondents. This is consistent with the argument that a more communitarian, contextual view of the social actor underlies sanctioning in the Japanese case.

Type of Punishment

Respondents who answered "yes" to the question of whether something should happen to the actor were asked to specify what should happen. (See appendix B for a list of the final coding categories for this open-ended question.) Like the decision to intervene, the choice of intervention type can

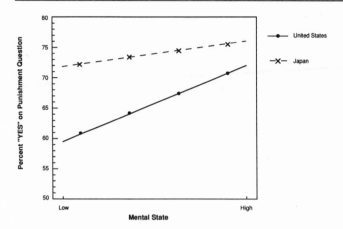

Figure 7.1   Whether to Punish: The Interaction of Nation and Mental State

be analyzed for linkage to responsibility judgments, for cultural differences, and for effects of the experimental variations in deed and context in specific instances of wrongdoing.

The Effect of Responsibility Judgments

Paralleling the preceding analysis, we first examined whether responsibility judgments predicted punishment choices. Unlike the decision about

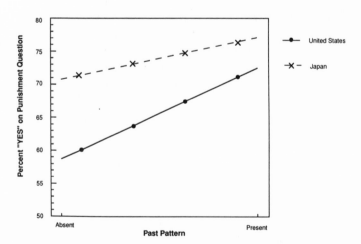

Figure 7.2   Whether to Punish: The Interaction of Nation and Past Pattern

whether to punish, specific punishment choices were only weakly linked to responsibility attributions. Responsibility judgment was a significant predictor of punishment preference in only three out of a possible twelve vignettes (the family/equal and work/authority stories in Detroit and the work/equal story in Yokohama).[6] The lack of linkage reflects two factors. First, outside of criminal sanctions, punishment alternatives are not easily placed on an ordinal scale. How are we to know, for example, that reprimanding one's child should be coded as a harsher punishment than making that child apologize? In response to this problem, our analyses treated the various punishment alternatives as purely nominal choices. Second, the implications of responsibility for punishment or vice versa are not fully clear. Whereas responsibility may be a necessary condition for punishment, it may not be sufficient for choosing the appropriate type of sanction.

Cultural Differences in Types of Punishment

We expected Japanese respondents to concentrate on interventions designed to restore role relations, while we expected Americans to suggest sanctions aimed at isolating or punishing the individual. Table 7.4 presents punishment choices in Detroit, Kanazawa, and Yokohama for the everyday-life vignettes. Coding categories are arranged ordinally within story to reflect our a priori assessment of the degree to which the choices isolate the offender, punishing for a misdeed rather than attempting to achieve reintegration of the offender. The last coding category in each panel, "other," is not ordered with respect to this dimension.[7]

The most dramatic differences are between Detroit and Kanazawa, with Yokohama falling somewhere between them (see table 7.4). The most striking difference between Detroit and the two Japanese cities concerns relationship restoration. This is the most popular category in the Japanese stories, but it is totally absent from the American data. However, a cultural difference in open-ended answers is always a double cultural difference: one between respondents and one between those coding the responses. It is theoretically possible that Detroit respondents' and Kanazawa respondents' answers incorporated the same ideas but that the American coding scheme did not capture this fact. Several considerations suggest that this is not the case. First, Detroit's coding categories were empirically derived (with the exception of a category for a type of restoration, apology, that was included on a priori grounds for the family/equal story but proved to be empty). Second, responses were coded by assistants blind to the study's hypotheses. Third, at the time of this coding the central hypotheses concerned responsibility for wrongdoing. The absence of codes for restorative sanctions in the Detroit

Table 7.4 Types of Punishments Advocated for Everyday Life Incidents

Type of incident	Detroit (%)	Kanazawa (%)	Yokohama (%)	Total (%)
A. Family/Equal				
Restoration	0	51	4	16
Reprimand	16	42	73	40
Deprive of privilege	59	0	8	26
Physical punishment	8	0	6	5
Other	18	7	9	12
(N)	(467)	(339)	(331)	(1,137)
B. Family/Authority				
Restoration	0	45	53	37
Reprimand (counsel)	86	53	34	54
Other	14	3	13	10
(N)	(159)	(232)	(246)	(637)
C. Work/Equal				
Restoration	0	73	0	21
Reprimand	44	18	0	22
Demote	19	1	36	20
Fire	33	2	13	17
Other	4	6	51	20
(N)	(501)	(384)	(443)	(1,328)
D. Work/Authority				
Restoration	0	55	47	34
Reprimand	31	25	15	24
Demote	38	5	18	21
Fire	15	3	5	8
Other	16	11	15	14
(N)	(414)	(388)	(440)	(1,242)

Note: Totals may not equal 100% because of rounding. All comparisons between pairs of cities in the distribution of responses were significant at $p < .0001$.

data is thus unlikely to have resulted from communication of investigators' expectations.

As a control procedure, assuming that restorative Detroit answers might have been assigned to the "other" category, we reanalyzed the data accordingly. However, even when all Detroit responses categorized as "other" were conservatively assigned to a restoration category, a large and significant gulf between American and Japanese answers remained. In short, throughout these data the type of sanction advocated by Japanese and Americans for everyday-life misdeeds differed substantially in expected ways.

In the family/equal vignette in which brothers were fighting, the Detroit and Kanazawa responses differed dramatically for several coding categories (see table 7.4). The relationship restoration difference was striking; no Americans were coded in this fashion in contrast to more than half of the Kanazawa respondents. Here restoration essentially involved apology. Kanazawa residents were also substantially more likely to advocate some form of reprimand (scolding or other verbal punishment). Detroiters tended to advocate more isolative punishments such as spanking or depriving the offender of a privilege. Such responses together made up 67 percent of American answers, in striking contrast to their absence among Kanazawans. "Other" was a larger category among Americans.

Yokohama respondents' answers fell between these groups. Yokohama differed from Detroit in the manner predicted, as there was much less deprivation of privilege and a greater tendency to recommend a reprimand. However, Yokohama respondents differed from those in Kanazawa as well, in that they rarely recommended relationship restoration (4 percent) even though this was an available category. Two factors may contribute to the Yokohama-Kanazawa differences. First, as noted earlier, the punishment question in Yokohama, as in Detroit, asked "what should the punishment be?" In Kanazawa the question was changed to "what should happen to" the actor. Restorative answers are less likely in response to the first version. A second factor is the vignette itself. As discussed in chapter 5, an excusing condition was introduced in Yokohama (but was removed in Kanazawa) as a result of an inadvertent translation error. The Yokohama vignettes implied that the actor's brother was holding onto the bat and refused to let go. Perhaps Yokohama respondents felt an apology would be inappropriate in a situation where, in effect, the other party partly initiated the problem. The degree to which these two methodological factors explain the Yokohama results cannot be determined. It is important to keep in mind, however, that even given these factors the Yokohama respondents are less retributive than the Detroit respondents.

In the family/authority vignette where a mother harmed her child, a substantially smaller proportion of Americans had indicated that anything should happen to the mother (see table 7.3). But when Detroiters did advocate that something be done, they differed predictably from Kanazawa and Yokohama residents. The category "reprimand" was expanded here in both American and Japanese coding schemes to include counseling, psychotherapy, and the like. Detroiters overwhelmingly chose this option, an intervention that focuses on the individual. In the Japanese surveys, in contrast, responses were nearly evenly divided between reprimand (counseling) and relationship restoration. In this context, restoration consisted of such acts as the mother apologizing to her child. The American category for "other" responses was again larger than that for the Japanese, but again conclusions about response patterns would not be affected even if the "other" responses were entirely reassigned to the restoration category.

We have no evidence, of course, regarding how heartfelt the respondent thought the apology would or should be. Practices such as maternal apology may be *kuchisaki,* tip-of-the-tongue remarks to soothe children rather than what an American would interpret as "sincere." But in any case, Japanese respondents could make use of a cultural form—apology to one's child— that may contribute to the restoration of relationship, but which has no counterpart in the American responses. (See Wagatsuma & Rosett, 1986, regarding apology in the law in the United States and Japan.)

In the work/equal vignette involving the used-car salesman, the pattern of responses in the Detroit and Kanazawa surveys repeats the now-familiar pattern: restoration of role ties among Japanese, isolative sanctions among Americans. Detroiters made heavy use of reprimands and distributed a majority of their responses between demoting and firing the salesman. Kanazawa residents, in contrast, were overwhelmingly inclined toward relationship restoration (e.g., apology, paying back money) and almost never advocated either demotion or firing.

The "which punishment" item in the work/equal story was open-ended in Kanazawa and closed-ended in Detroit. In Yokohama the question was also closed-ended, using the Detroit coding categories. Therefore, Yokohama responses provide an indication of how Kanazawa residents might answer the question in closed format. The Yokohama responses were intermediate between those for Detroit and Kanazawa (36 percent in Yokohama advocated demotion, 13 percent firing). In addition, many Yokohama subjects (51 percent) rejected all of the closed-ended categories and chose responses coded as "other."[8]

We do not believe that the inferences from the Detroit-Kanazawa comparison are threatened by these findings. Instead, the Yokohama results probably illustrate that the American investigators' cultural biases produced a less adequate question form in Yokohama. First, open-ended categories are almost certainly a better measure of opinion here. The closed categories based on Detroit pretest data were questioned by the Japanese researchers from the outset. They correctly believed that these were not options Japanese respondents would spontaneously choose, as the large "other" category in Yokohama indicates. Second, these researchers noted that Japanese respondents are often unwilling to challenge survey categories, perhaps more so than their American counterparts. Asked to use predefined choices, Yoko-

Table 7.5 Response to the Question "What Should the Customer
Do?" in the Work/Equal Story

	Detroit (%)	Yokohama (%)	Total (%)
Restoration	48	86	66
Take consumer action	9	0	5
Report salesman to company	11	5	8
Take legal action	18	3	11
Other	14	6	10
(N)	(552)	(513)	(1,065)

Note: $\chi^2 = 194.5$; d.f. $= 4$; $p < .0001$; Cramer's Phi $= .43$

hama respondents often used them. Third, even using preset categories, Yokohama respondents differed significantly from Detroiters in accord with our expectations.

In Detroit and Yokohama we also asked a second question about the salesman story: "What should the customer do?" (see table 7.5). Respondents in both cities frequently called for restoration (e.g., financial compensation for the customer's loss). Note, however, that although 48 percent of Detroit respondents thought the customer should seek restoration, 86 percent of the Yokohama respondents thought so. Conversely, the Japanese respondents were less likely than Americans to say the customer should report the salesman to the company or take legal action. The responses to this question again reflect a Japanese preference for restorative solutions rather than retributive sanctions.

The work/authority vignette about the foreman returns to a comparison of open-ended items in all three surveys. Restoration dominates Kanazawa and Yokohama responses (table 7.4); here it included emotional role restoration (e.g., acts of apology) as well as instrumental restoration (e.g., payment of the injured worker's medical expenses). But the restorative response is absent among Detroiters. Responses to this vignette seemingly tap the spontaneous inclination of Americans, but not Japanese, to advocate demoting or firing as solutions to wrongdoing in the workplace. Detroiters offered these isolative solutions frequently; together they represented 53 percent of American answers. Firing, especially, is a response that is worse than indifferent to role relationships; it actively destroys them. Kanazawa residents were quite disinclined toward either response. Yokohama again stands in the middle, but closer to the Kanazawa results than to those in Detroit.

Overall, these results confirm the basic hypothesis that Japanese respondents are more likely to recommend restorative sanctions whereas American respondents are more likely to recommend isolative ones. If the three surveys are considered separately, the Yokohama respondents stand somewhere between the Detroit and Kanazawa respondents. In several instances methodological factors may explain this result. But we should be open to the possibility that the Yokohama respondents are somewhat more Westernized (individualistic and isolative) in their sanctioning preferences. Part of the reason our Japanese colleagues replicated the survey in Kanazawa was to search for just such differences between the "newer" Japan represented by Yokohama and the "older" Japan that still exists in Kanazawa.

The Effect of Experimental Variables on Punishment Choices

The analysis of the impact of experimental variables on punishment choices is hindered by the difficulty of constructing an ordered scale of punishments across stories and by the failure of the most popular sanction among the Japanese—relationship restoration—to qualify as a coding category among Detroiters. Given these limitations, we chose to construct separate overall summary variables for punishment choices in Detroit and the two Japanese cities. In Detroit the variable distinguishes the reprimand response (e.g., "tell her what she did was wrong") from all other responses (e.g., "fire him" or "send him to his room"). This distinction primarily captures the *harshness* of the recommended sanction. In the Japanese cities, especially Kanazawa, nearly all responses were coded either "restoration" or "reprimand." Thus in these two cities the variable distinguishes restorative responses from all others, including "reprimand." This distinction primarily captures the degree to which the proposed sanction is *isolative*. Because the resulting summary variables are not comparable across countries, we conducted separate analyses for each city. The statistical models assessed the impact of deed and context variables on sanctioning choices. Because the meaning of the various responses can shift across roles, role variables were omitted from this analysis.[9]

The pattern of results is not unlike the findings for the decision regarding whether to punish. In Detroit all variables except consequence severity had a significant impact on the choice of sanction (reprimand/all others). Recall that because Detroit respondents did not offer restoration as a sanction, this result can be interpreted as the effect of deed and context variables on the harshness of the proposed sanction. All effects are as one would expect. Higher mental state, presence of a bad past pattern, and absence of other's influence all led to harsher sanctions: Whatever the act, an actor was more likely to be punished harshly when the actor meant to do it, had done it before, and did it without pressure from others. In Kanazawa only past pattern and other's influence had a significant impact on choice of sanction. The presence of a bad past pattern and the absence of another's influence led to nonrestorative sanctions. Significantly, mental state had no impact on punishment choice in Kanazawa. In Yokohama none of the manipulations had a significant effect on sanctioning choice.

These results once again indicate that Americans make greater use of evidence about an actor's mental state than do Japanese—in this case with regard to how they would choose to punish a wrongdoer. This result must be understood within the context of the decision being made, however. In this analysis the Americans were choosing between harsher and more lenient sanctions. For this choice, mental state information has some relevance. To some extent the Japanese choice was also a choice between harsher or more lenient sanctions. (In both Kanazawa and Yokohama, choosing restorative sanctions was negatively correlated with judged seriousness.) However, the Japanese choice was also between more or less isolative sanctions. Here, it is perhaps not surprising that mental state information appears to be less relevant. It is possible that the fundamental objectives of a sanction, as well as cultural difference in use of information, shape the relevance of various types of information that might be used to make a sanctioning choice.

The Impact of Wrongdoing on Other Roles

Japanese responses to the everyday-life stories indicate that they are less willing to break a person's ties to an employer as a punishment for on-the-job wrongdoing. Japanese employment relationships appear more communal in nature, based on ties that are fundamentally more solidary than is true of most American occupational roles (Lincoln & Kalleberg, 1990; Rohlen, 1974). As any parent of a delinquent teenager can attest, wrongdoing by a member of a highly solidary group affects the entire network by bringing shame and disrepute on other group members. This is part of what Ekland-Olson (1982, 1984) means when he argues that such acts create a disturbance in the relationship. Thus, Japanese occupational roles can affect and be affected by wrongdoing outside of the work setting in a way unfamiliar to Americans. The employer can be thought of as a kind of potential third party to any actor-victim relationship, and this third party's interests may be more salient to Japanese than to Americans. One of the automobile accident vignettes (further discussed in chapter 8) provided an opportunity to explore actor–third party ties.

In the Adult accident vignette, a pair of closed-ended punishment questions probed the linkage between occupational roles and punishments. One question asked whether the driver of a car that hit a female pedestrian should volunteer to resign from his job. The second asked whether his employer should request that he resign.[10] Responses of Detroit and Yokohama residents differed significantly to both questions. Only 4 percent of Detroiters indicated that the employee should volunteer to resign, in contrast to 34 percent of Yokohama residents ($\chi^2 = 90.5$, $p < .0001$). Similarly, only 5 percent of Detroiters, but 26 percent of Yokohama respondents, said that the employer should ask for the driver's resignation ($\chi^2 = 50.8$, $p < .0001$).

These results suggest that because Japanese employment ties are more solidary, the wrongdoer's act may reflect on the employer and fellow employees. Behavior in nonemployment situations is more diffusely relevant to the job relationship. These results teach another lesson as well. Employment may be more like family in Japan, but it is not the same thing. One can be dismissed or resign from employment. In the end, employment is an achieved status and the role of employee is an achieved role. The firm is not family. It is, in Hsu's (1975) useful term, *kin-tract*, somewhere between kinship and contract.

In contrast, the American proclivity to see social actors as isolated individuals may insulate the perpetrator's work life from any impact of outside misdeeds. The actor's behavior does not reflect on these individuals; hence the actor is under no pressure to act to relieve them of the "guilt by association" that flows to those closely tied to a wrongdoer.

To be sure, in the United States extremely high status or visibility may be associated with a "spill-over" from everyday-life wrongdoing into the work context, as is regularly illustrated by the peccadilloes of politicians, but no such tendency emerges within the more ordinary occupational range studied here.[11]

Despite the statistical significance of these results, several caveats are in order. First, the differences were not overpowering, and only a minority of Yokohama residents responded to each item with the "traditional Japanese" reaction stressing reverberation of wrongdoing through a network. Second, contrary to expectations, experimental manipulation of the status of the university employee who had the accident (professor vs. clerk) did not influence Yokohama responses; it had been anticipated that the traditional response would be more frequent when the driver held the higher-status occupation of professor. Third, the occasions in which Japanese actually do resign for such wrongdoing appear to be rare (Rohlen, 1974, pp. 79, 82). Therefore these data provide only limited support for the idea that there is a distinctive, traditional Japanese view of this issue, and responses may reflect this tradition more than they reflect current social practice.[12]

Conclusions

As these survey results indicate, norms about sanctions reflect macrosociological, culturally based variation in conceptions of the social actor as well as microsociological, situationally based differences in how individual actors are viewed. Cross-cultural differences reflect the extent to which the individual is treated as an isolated being or as a member of a community. Correspondingly, within cultures, the key difference between situations concerns the embeddedness of actors, victims, and third parties in a network of social bonds.

Japanese respondents were at least as willing as Americans to advocate that *something* happen to perpetrators, but they had systematically different ideas about what that something should be. In judging an array of everyday-life situations, the modal sanction chosen by Japanese was some form of relationship restoration, whereas sanctions chosen by Americans predominantly served to isolate the individual perpetrator. In addition, American respondents favored more isolative and retributive rationales for imprisonment whereas Japanese respondents favored more restorative, reintegrative rationales. Judgments in one of the automobile accident vignettes served to make the complementary point that to Japanese the solidarity and interweaving of occupational and other roles may make the consequences of wrongdoing spill over from one area into the other in a way that is unusual in the United States. Japanese social ties, though not all-encompassing, are tightly knit and manifold in their effects.

Macrolevel differences between cultures are not the whole story. The relative solidarity of relationships underlies different repertoires of punishment used across incidents within each society. With respect to the most serious sanctions, there is a fundamental difference between our low- and high-solidarity vignettes: between work and family. For work incidents the most severe sanctions destroy or seriously damage the actor's relationship with his employer. Detroit respondents showed greater willingness to disregard role relationships (that is, to fire or demote) in these stories than did Kanazawa respondents. But neither Japanese nor American respondents proposed community-destructive sanctions when family ties were at stake. In spite of Americans' reputation for litigation and conflict (cf. Galanter, 1983), Detroiters also eschewed legal remedies in family relationships.

In our view such choices reflect the point that some social bonds are expected to survive more severe untoward behavior than are others. This expectation applies across cultures as divergent as Japan and the United States, and the repertoires of punitive solutions show comparable situation-based differences. Family relationships, especially, are to be maintained if at all possible. Wherever highly solidary ties exist between parties, informal social control remains workable, and decisions about punishment are likely to emphasize the rebuilding of ties that bind (Black, 1976; Ekland-Olson, 1984). In turn, the existence and strength of informal social controls such as pressures to apologize reduce the need for formal sanction (cf. Haley, 1982b, 1986; Wagatsuma & Rosett, 1986).

This explanation is powerful because it explains differences in sanctioning norms at two levels. Responses both *across* the cultures and *within* each culture varied in a manner consistent with predictions based on solidarity of relationships among the parties. In contrast, an explanation of our findings in terms of "cultural custom" alone would have no a priori basis for anticipating the observed variation within societies. A weaker version of a custom or habit explanation is, of course, always available. The argument would be that responses somehow automatically or blindly follow "custom" and that customs or habits regarding sanction, while varied within each culture, differ between the cultures. Such an argument is not theoretically adequate. It either reduces to an irrationalist conclusion—for example, that Japanese responses are different because of the uniqueness of the Japanese— or it requires a further explanation of why the customs or habits themselves arise (Kidder, 1983).[13]

Thus far, the solidarity of relationships appears to provide a parsimonious account of how norms of sanction come to differ within and across cultures, at least among Americans and Japanese. But we have not yet considered in any depth the limiting case, the incident in which there is no solidarity between the parties. This represents an important piece of the logic of the argument. If we are correct about the dynamics of difference between American and Japanese judgments of wrongdoing—if the dynamics involve different experiences with and sensitivity to social ties—then judgments by Japanese should converge toward those of Americans when social ties are nil. In the next chapter we test this notion.

8

Is Crime Special?
Offenses against
Strangers

Americans who travel to Japan are often
puzzled, envious, or simply relieved by the remarkable safety of Japanese
cities. Consider the following incident that happened to one of us:

> It is late at night on a typical weekend in Roppongi, a "yuppie" area of
> Tokyo with a lot of night life. An American female is returning from a
> party. Around her neck is strung an expensive new camera. The woman
> turns into an alley to take a shortcut to her hotel. Halfway down the alley,
> a scruffy-looking Japanese male emerges from the shadows and ap-
> proaches her. He says, pointing at the camera, *"Nihon-sei no hoo ga ii, des
> ne?"* Immensely relieved at having learned this sentence among her
> rudimentary Japanese, the American woman answers, *"Soo, des ne?"*
> ("Yes, isn't it?") and they part in the night. The man has asked her a
> common question these days: "Japanese-made is better, isn't it?"

Everyday-life incidents like those we have discussed are not the only area of
difference between responsibility Japanese-style and responsibility Amer-
ican-style. Civil suits and criminal trials can be thought of as the tip of the
iceberg of wrongdoing and harmdoing. The acts that inspire them are often a
matter of everyday life gone awry. In chapter 2 we noted the large differences
in civil litigation between the United States and Japan. In this chapter we
address the question of crime[1] and attempt to put it in a familiar theoretical
context: Judgments of crime, like judgments of civil wrongs and everyday-
life disputes, vary as a function of the social relationships of those involved;
further, the responsibility and punishment decisions of Japanese are no
longer special where strangers are involved.

In this chapter we focus on whether Japanese and American respondents
differed systematically in how they judged crime, as in chapter 6 we showed
them to do regarding everyday-life wrongdoing. As an important point of
comparison, results for crime are considered in the context of other incidents
that involve strangers: auto accidents. The data at hand tell us whether

crimes are judged according to rules different from those used to judge everyday-life incidents, as well as whether Japanese and Americans differ in this respect. First, to supplement the data already reviewed concerning civil litigation rates, it is useful to frame the problem statistically by considering just how different the crime rates of the United States and Japan really are. These different rates establish the context within which judgments are made in the two societies.

The Scope of the Problem

Crime Rates

The incidence of crime, particularly serious crime, has long been much lower in Japan than in the United States. Bayley's (1976) work on police in Japan and the United States provides a typical set of crime statistics. In the chapter "Heaven for a Cop," he notes:

> The crime rate in Japan is so low in comparison with that of the United States that Japanese policemen seem hardly to be challenged at all. . . . There were four-and-a-half times as many murders per person in the United States in 1973 as in Japan. . . . The incidence of rape is five times higher in the United States than Japan. . . . In 1973 . . . there were 1,876 robberies in Japan against 382,680 in the United States. . . . To underscore just how different Japan is from the United States with respect to crime, consider this fact: there are four times as many serious crimes committed per person in the United States as there are crimes of all sorts, even the most petty, in Japan. In 1973, for example, there were 8,638,400 serious crimes in the United States; in Japan, there were 1,190,549 crimes of all sorts. (pp. 5–6)

These figures and their implications are virtually unchanged by more than fifteen years of further crime control efforts. The contrast remains stark. For 1983, Japan showed a total of 1,539,782 crimes, for a crime rate of 1,289 per 100,000 persons. For the United States, serious crimes as defined by the FBI Crime Index numbered 12,070,213, for a *serious* crime rate of 5,159 per 100,000 persons, in 1983. And the American crime picture in recent years has been even more grim. As a recent editorial in the *Washington Post* put it: "The fact of the matter is that 1988 was a particularly bad year for law-abiding citizens everywhere in this nation. Violent crime reached an unprecedented level last year, according to the FBI. The number of known serious offenses was 17 percent higher than the figure recorded in 1984. During the same period, violent crime rose by 23 percent" ("Crime in the Cities," 1989, p. A22).

Table 8.1   Trends in Crime Rates, 1960–1987 (Crime rate per 100,000 population)

	United States	Britain	West Germany	Japan
Homicide				
1960	5.1	1.3	2.2	3.0
1970	7.9	1.7	4.0	2.0
1980	10.2	2.6	4.4	1.5
1987	8.3	5.5	4.3	1.3
Larceny				
1960	1,726	1,491	1,538	1,112
1970	3,621	2,749	2,519	1,002
1980	5,353	4,149	3,960	996
1987	4,940	5,803	4,565	1,116

Source: Summary of the White Paper on Crime, 1989 (Government of Japan, Research and Training Institute, Ministry of Justice)

It is not reasonable to argue that differences between the Japanese and American crime rates are somehow an artifact of different rates of reporting. Bayley (1976) notes that crime is more underreported by citizens and records more distorted by police in the United States. These figures are therefore probably a conservative estimate of the profound difference in criminal behavior.

Other cross-cultural data only reinforce the images of Japan as relatively law-abiding and of the United States as a lawless place. Table 8.1 summarizes data from 1960 to 1987 for four countries—Japan, the Federal Republic of Germany (West Germany), Great Britain, and the United States—for homicide and larceny (Government of Japan, 1989). Over the years, the United States shows the highest overall crime rates for these offenses and, for homicide, the sharpest increase over time; Japan shows both the lowest rates and a pattern of stability or *decline* in the crime rate. The two European countries are intermediate with regard to homicide, but closer to the Japanese pattern. For larceny, in contrast, the Germans approach the American crime rate while the Britons have recently exceeded it. Overall, with regard to homicide the United States stands out as particularly violent; with regard to larceny Japan stands out as particularly honest. Japan and the United States occupy the opposite poles in the distribution of violent and property crimes among the major capitalist countries.

Together, these crime rates and the civil statistics reviewed earlier present a picture of Americans as both hasty to do wrong to others and quick to assert that legally actionable harm has been done to themselves. Crime and civil litigation are obviously different in Japan. Is the incidence and judgment of crime really "special" there, some unique outgrowth of an obedient and cohesive culture? Or can it be understood in terms of the same social forces—the same dimensions of solidarity and hierarchy of social ties—that characterize the everyday-life incidents encountered thus far?

Part of the answer to this question involves the issue of possible differences between Japan and the United States in the judgment and punishment of civil and criminal cases. Data reviewed below demonstrate that these differences, surprisingly, do not amount to much. This lends support to the argument that it is not *crime* that is special, it is *strangers* that are special. Life among strangers may generate both the perception and the reality of crime.

American Community: Conciliation and Crime

Small towns and small groups are similar wherever they are. As previously noted, where relationships are more solidary—more "like family"—disputes are less often treated as matters of law and crime rates are lower. Instances of "Japanese" approaches to harmdoing and wrongdoing can also be found in American history. Colonial America was characterized by many solidary groups and towns in which little formal law was needed or sought (Auerbach, 1983; Mann, 1987). The social glue was ethnic and religious, the law often superfluous. Even commerce resisted formal litigation, as the business community found it more congenial to use agreed-upon group norms as standards for settlements. In the United States, law and community began to diverge in the nineteenth century as law became more general and more formal (Mann, 1987). In the face of this formalism, however, some disputants turned from law to find other ways to settle disputes. This is a tendency that has persisted in the business community's preference for "keeping the lawyers out of it" (Macaulay, 1963). In short, wherever there is consensual identity and consensual rules, a group tends to police itself (cf. Braithwaite, 1989). It is important to remember that this self-policing community can restrict personal privacy and some freedom of action. The self in such a time and place is necessarily a contextual self. This may be a price believed to be worth paying, but it is not a trivial correlate of community.

The self-monitoring community fails, as it did in the United States, when it is overwhelmed by strains against cohesion. During the turbulence that closed the nineteenth century, legal controls served as increasingly important instruments of social cohesion. The society struggled to cohere amid the chaos of rapid industrialization, sharp class conflict, severe economic recession, political instability, frontier warfare, and unprecedented immigration. The rule of law provided an alternative means of settling disputes between strangers (Auerbach, 1983, p. 67).

This analysis of the American past suggests two things. First, in a society of strangers the potential for crime, especially property crime, increases. Second, we are more likely to use the law, both civilly and criminally, against strangers than against friends or loved ones. We have argued that Japanese and Americans judge wrongdoing differently in part because Japanese are in general more closely tied to one another. But when disputes are clearly between strangers, the judgments of Japanese and Americans should more closely resemble one another, for the envelope of role obligation and context that so heavily determines Japanese judgments has been stripped away. To test this proposition, incidents involving strangers were included in the Detroit and Yokohama surveys. The two auto accident stories, Child and Adult, were alternated experimentally, so that each respondent heard one of the accidents; all respondents heard the crime (Robbery) story. The general expectation is that the differences observed in chapter 6 regarding responsibility and in chapter 7 regarding punishment will be reduced or eliminated for deeds committed outside the protective envelope of role relationships.

Responsibility: Crime and Auto Accidents

The Vignettes

The crime and auto accident vignettes were presented in detail in chapter 5. The crime (Robbery) was a grocery store robbery in which the store owner was shot. One accident (Adult) involved an adult pedestrian victim crossing the street at a stop sign; the other (Child) involved a child who stepped out from between parked cars. In all three, the mental state of the perpetrator and the severity of the consequences were varied in the same manner as in the everyday-life stories. In contrast to the everyday-life stories, no variations in other's influence were made in any of these vignettes, as none of the situations included actions within established roles or networks of relationships.[2] The actor's past pattern of behavior was varied in the Robbery and Child stories. In the Adult story, the social status of the actor (professor vs. clerk) was varied instead of past pattern. In an accident, where no role hierarchy is involved, social status provides a sort of surrogate for hierarchy. Results involving status will be discussed separately below.

If Japanese and American judgments of accidents and crime do prove to be more similar than their judgments of everyday-life misdeeds, in what ways should judgments converge? Overall, with regard to responsibility or to punishment, Japanese judgments should be as harsh as those of Americans. With regard to the decision models used to make judgments, the Japanese should make relatively greater use of deed information. Recall from chapter 8 that in everyday-life vignettes, Americans made greater use of information

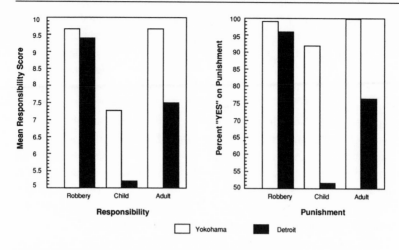

Figure 8.1 Detroit-Yokohama Differences in Responsibility and Punishment for Offenses Involving Strangers

about the actor's mental state than did Japanese. If Japanese judge strangers in the same ways Americans do, this difference may be reduced or eliminated here.

Responsibility: Overall Findings

Figure 8.1 summarizes the average responsibility assigned by Japanese and Americans for each of the vignettes involving strangers. In each case, Yokohama residents assigned significantly more responsibility than Detroiters, in contrast to our earlier finding that residents of both Japanese cities generally assigned *less* responsibility than Detroiters for offenses that involved actors and victims in role relationships. The same Japanese who appeared reluctant to tag the actor with personal responsibility in everyday-life wrongdoing were no longer reluctant where accidents and crime involving strangers were concerned. (Punishment judgments, reproduced from chapter 7, show parallel patterns of greater severity among Japanese; these are discussed below.)

To assess the impact of the experimental variations and of cultural differences in combination, we carried out an ANOVA for each of the three vignettes. As in the analyses described earlier, the dichotomous variables included city, mental state, consequences, and past pattern for the Robbery and Child stories; the actor's social status replaced past pattern in the Adult story. Thus, for all three vignettes, a $2 \times 2 \times 2 \times 2$ experimental design resulted. Note that the high levels of responsibility in figure 8.1 mean that

Table 8.2   Significant Effects of Deed and Context on Responsibility in Offenses Involving Strangers

		Story	
Variations	Robbery	Child accident	Adult accident
Mental state			
Low	9.34	4.95	8.02
High	9.67	7.40	9.37
Consequences			
Low	ns	5.85	ns
High		7.51	
Past pattern*			
Absent	ns	7.09	ns
Present		7.34	

Note: Table entries are mean responsibility scores by experimental manipulations (range, 0–10). *ns* = comparison not significant at $p \leq .05$.
*In the Adult accident, the past pattern manipulation was replaced by actor's status (clerk/professor)

there may be little room for *any* variation in the stories to have an effect. Statistically speaking, responses were always near the "ceiling": a judgment that the actor was fully responsible. Table 8.2 summarizes the overall effects of differences in mental state, consequences, and past pattern (or status) on average responsibility assigned in each story involving strangers.

Robbery

In light of the extraordinarily high levels of responsibility assigned in the Robbery vignette, it is surprising that any of the experimental variations reached significance. However, the actor's mental state still had a significant effect on his responsibility (see table 8.2). In addition, the impact of a bad past pattern nearly reached significance ($p = .06$). When the perpetrator fired gratuitously—rather than in a struggle with the store owner—and when he had a prior record, he was assigned more responsibility.

The only difference between the cities in these judgments of a crime was a relationship among city, consequence severity, and past pattern. There was no evidence of an impact of the actor's past pattern in Yokohama; in Detroit the effect of past pattern was present, but only where consequences were less severe. This subtle difference should not be given too much weight, but it is consistent with our original speculations that Americans might be more sensitive to contextual information about past pattern.

Child Accident

The Child story yielded straightforward effects of each of the experimental variations. More responsibility was assigned when the actor's mental state was high (negligent), when consequences were more severe, and when the actor had a bad past pattern of behavior (see table 8.2). In addition, one interaction among city, mental state, and past pattern emerged. In Detroit, an impact of past pattern was evident regardless of the actor's mental state; in Yokohama, the effect of past pattern was significant only when mental state was high (that is, when the perpetrator was speeding). This result again suggests that Yokohama residents are somewhat less sensitive to contextual information about the actor's past pattern.

Adult Accident

The Adult story was similar to the core everyday-life stories in one respect. An experimental variation in the perpetrator's status—clerk versus professor—was expected to operate as an analog to hierarchy in the everyday-life stories. Just as an authority is judged more severely, all other things being equal, it seemed plausible that the higher-status actor in this accident vignette might be judged by more stringent standards. This speculation is based on the notion that roles, especially professional and prestigious roles, can have a diffuse effect on judgments of an actor even when he or she is not technically "in role." To the extent that Japan represents a culture of hierarchical, contextual selves and social relations, or that roles tend to diffuse across social life more broadly in Japan, sensitivity to the perpetrator's social status should be greater among Japanese.

Table 8.2 indicates that basic effects of the experimental variations in the Adult story were straightforward. Other than the effect of city reported in figure 8.1, the only significant difference occurred for mental state. Much less responsibility was assigned for the low mental state version (a brake failure) than for the high version (failure to see a stop sign). No overall effect appeared for either consequence severity or the actor's status.

However, in contrast to both the Child and Robbery stories, the Adult story revealed numerous complex interrelationships among the variables (see table 8.3). Residents of Yokohama and Detroit differed in the importance of mental state information, in the relation between mental state and the actor's status, and in the relation between consequence severity and status.

Just as the mental state of an authority mattered more than the mental state of an equal in the core role-relationship vignettes, here the mental state of a professor makes a larger difference in his responsibility than does the mental state of a clerk. But this sensitivity to mental state information about a

Table 8.3 Culture and the Impact of Actor's Status: Responsibility Judgments for the Adult Accident

Variations	Detroit		Yokohama	
	Clerk	Professor	Clerk	Professor
Mental state				
Low	6.92	5.81	9.55	9.73
High	8.68	9.22	9.78	9.97
Consequences				
Low	7.46	7.91	9.56	9.77
High	8.17	7.11	9.75	9.89

Note: As in table 8.2, entries are mean responsibility scores by experimental manipulations (range, 0–10)

higher-status actor was concentrated in American respondents. Just as Japanese respondents did not differentiate responsibility allocation on the basis of mental state, neither did they do so on the basis of status or of a status–mental state combination. In part these results reflect the fact that the Japanese were uniformly strict in their judgment of the driver, regardless of his mental state or status; their judgments exhibit very little variance to be explained.

Differences in use of information about consequences are summarized in the bottom half of table 8.3. In Japan, no effects of either status or consequences emerged. In the United States, a higher-status actor was judged to be *less* responsible than a low-status actor when consequences were severe. This result is difficult to explain other than by some sort of vicarious "defensive attribution" (Burger, 1981; Shaver, 1970) or by sympathy for a presumably "responsible" social actor faced with a serious accident.

Three more global findings were related to or based on these patterns. First, Americans were more sensitive to mental state information than were Japanese (averaged across the status of the actor). For this vignette, then, the judgments of Japanese and Americans did not converge with regard to the use of information about the actor's state of mind. Results are instead consistent with earlier evidence that Americans are more sensitive to the actor's mental state. Second, mental state information mattered more where the actor was of high status (averaged across the cities). Third, consequence severity mattered more for the high-status actor (again averaged across the cities). For the last two results, table 8.3 shows that the global finding basically reflects the responses of Americans. Japanese responses can most fairly be characterized as uniformly strict.

Summary: Responsibility among Strangers

The responsibility judgments of Japanese are more like those of Americans where crime and accidents among strangers are concerned than when actor and victim share some social tie or bond. When strangers meet, absolute levels of responsibility assigned are *higher* in Japan, not lower. In addition, the greater sensitivity of Americans to the actor's mental state, so prominent in the earlier findings regarding everyday-life roles, disappears here in two of the stories. It is only evident in the Adult story, where the actor's social status was also introduced. And that vignette *failed* to reveal any differential sensitivity of Japanese to the actor's status itself. It is our interpretation that a Japanese, faced with judging an incident in which a prior relationship does not exist between the parties, begins to make judgments much "like an American": behaving as if the actor were an isolated entity, the deed all-important, and the role its pale backdrop.[3]

These findings may have a competing explanation: that these vignettes are different because they involve more serious wrongdoing. As noted in chapter 5, in both countries the accidents and the crime were seen as having the most serious consequences of all the vignettes. It could therefore be argued that what is really happening is that Japanese judge incidents "like Americans" when the incidents are *serious*. Given this set of vignettes we cannot completely rule out this alternative. There was no story about strangers that had a trivial outcome, nor a family story involving serious criminal activity. Yet the low-seriousness conditions in the accident stories are not, on their face, particularly extreme. Their outcomes were bruises or broken bones. If it were true that Japanese begin to make judgments "like Americans" where consequences are really serious, then it should be possible to observe a difference between the low-seriousness conditions in these stories, where Japanese would be less attentive to mental state information, and the high-seriousness conditions, where they would be more attentive. Statistically, the difference would be reflected in an interaction of mental state and consequences. Yet no difference in the use of mental state information between the low- and high-seriousness experimental conditions was found in either city.

Moreover, the sense of seriousness and the presence of strangers feed on each other. Serious acts of wrongdoing destroy community and make it less likely that a concern for role relationships will exert as strong an influence on judgments. In turn, acts of wrongdoing between strangers are likely to be perceived as more serious. Any linkage between deeds involving strangers and perceived seriousness, therefore, is likely to involve a causal spiral rather than a simple cause and effect. It is reasonable to argue that the greater perceived seriousness in these cases is in part a *product* of the fact that they are offenses between strangers.

Overall, these results indicate that the cultural gulf in the judgment of wrongdoing documented in earlier chapters is a gulf that can be bridged by strangers. A Japanese judging an incident involving strangers, when no contextualizing or hierarchical role information is provided, assigns responsibility much like an American. We next discuss whether this finding extends to the questions of whether to punish and how to do so.

Punishment: Which Kind and How Much?

Whether to Intervene

Yokohama residents in every case were significantly more likely than Detroiters to respond "yes" to the question of whether something should be done to the perpetrator for these offenses involving strangers (see fig. 8.1). This result is particularly noteworthy because of the strong tendency in both cities for respondents to advocate some punishment. That is, significant differences between the Americans and Japanese emerged where there was, statistically speaking, little room for them to do so.

How Much Punishment? The Crime Story

Virtually all Americans and Japanese thought that some punishment was appropriate in the Robbery vignette (see fig. 8.1). Given that the respondent felt some imprisonment was appropriate, it was possible here to generate a more or less metric measure of the amount of punishment, a direct answer to the question, "How much?" Open-ended answers were coded directly into years "plus one," with values ranging from 1 to 51, where 1 = less than one year in prison and 51 = fifty years. Sentences of life in prison and the death penalty were arbitrarily assigned values of 55 and 56. Where a range of years was given (such as "5 to 10"), its midpoint was assigned. The resulting scale of years captured the responses of most Americans and Japanese. In each city, approximately 15 percent of responses consisted of such general answers as "whatever the law says" or "don't know."

The basic differences in punishment assigned between the cities and the significant differences created by each of the experimental variations are summarized in figure 8.2. Again, just as in the yes-no decisions about whether to punish, Yokohama residents were stricter in their punishments for this crime involving strangers.[4] Each experimental variation also had a predictable impact. First, paralleling the assignment of responsibility, both the actor's intent and his past pattern of behavior had an effect. Gratuitous

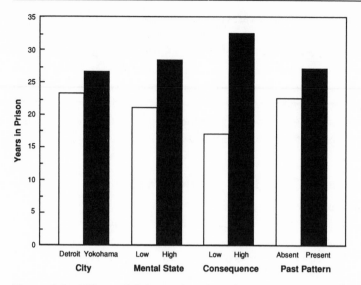

Figure 8.2   Effect of Culture, Deed, and Context on Length of Punishment

shooting and a prior record each led to longer sentences. The greatest difference between the responsibility and punishment decisions appears to involve consequences. Although consequences did not have a significant effect on responsibility, the impact of consequences on punishment was substantial, outweighing all other influences.

The greater impact of consequences at the stage of punishment is understandable for a number of reasons. Perhaps the simplest explanation is that in this crime the differing consequences translate into *different offenses* to be punished. The "low seriousness" variation presented a store owner who is shot and injured in the course of a robbery; in the "high seriousness" version the store owner is killed. In one case, the event depicted is a robbery plus assault with a deadly weapon; in the other case, the event becomes a robbery plus murder. The law itself treats these states of affairs quite differently when it comes to punishment. In our view, then, this vignette serves to illustrate that consequences can play a more crucial role at the stage of punishment than at the stage of responsibility decisions, but this role is in part a matter of defining the crime to be judged.

The effect of the seriousness of consequences was more substantial in Yokohama than in Detroit (see fig. 8.3). (Statistically, this amounts to a significant interaction between city and consequence severity.) As previously outlined, we originally assumed that there would be greater attention to

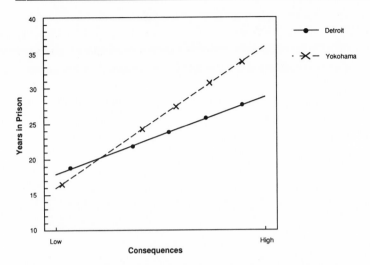

Figure 8.3   Effect of Consequence Severity on Criminal Punishment, by City

consequences in Detroit, because consequence severity is an aspect of the immediate deed rather than of role or context. These findings therefore represent an instance in which Japanese responses were "more American" than those of Americans.

Which Kind of Punishment? Auto Accident Stories

In the automobile accident vignettes, as in the punishment decisions for everyday-life incidents, residents of Detroit and Yokohama were asked whether anything "should be done to the driver," and their open-ended responses were recorded. The one overwhelming feature of open-ended responses for everyday-life wrongdoing was the dominance of restoration of relationships—whether via apology or restitution—in Japan and its absence or near-absence in the United States. We therefore next ask whether the differences between Japanese and American punishment choices remain stark where accidents are concerned. Are the responses of Americans and Japanese regarding auto accidents different as before, or do their decisions converge where incidents between strangers are concerned?

Coding

Overall, four coding categories in Yokohama seemed to represent restoration.[5] In addition to concrete restitution—payment of the victim's *medical expenses*—Yokohama residents also referred to *making an apology, taking the victim to the hospital,* and (rather diffusely) *taking responsibility* for what happened. Unlike the everyday-life stories, in these auto accidents Detroiters did make one response that could fairly be characterized as restitutive: payment of medical expenses. A first indicator of convergence between the cultures was thus in the coding itself. Americans included restorative responses, although their vocabulary of restoration was impoverished and was restricted to its financial aspect.

Codes for more punitive sanctions were almost a mirror image of the restorative codes. Yokohama residents' responses were categorized as including one category for punitive *legal action,* usually described in broad or vague terms. Detroiters, by contrast, provided enough specific references to legal activities to generate three categories: *fine, jail,* and *court* (the third referring to a general "take him to court" response, the first two to specific consequences of court action). Hence in these auto accident stories, unlike the everyday-life vignettes, Japanese respondents sometimes resorted to more stringent and formal legal sanctions, but their vocabulary of legal sanction was more impoverished than that of Americans.

Certain responses were directly comparable across the cultures. In both cities, some mention was made of loss of *driver's license,* of requiring *driver's education,* and "other" responses that did not fit into the preceding categories.

Results

Grouping the restorative answers together into one category, and doing the same with the legal actions, it is possible to compare directly the responses of Detroit and Yokohama residents for both accidents (see table 8.4). In each case the first four categories—restoration, driver's education, loss of license, and legal action—are arranged in what we judge to be an approximate order from least to most isolative. The fifth category, "other," is not ordered.

It is evident in both portions of table 8.4 that Japanese remain more inclined toward relationship restoration than Americans. But responses of Americans are "more Japanese" than was true in the everyday-life vignettes—at least insofar as payment of medical expenses, a concrete and financial form of restitution, is an option that Americans select. What remains lacking in American responses is a more evaluative, emotional side of relationship restoration, as represented in Japanese notions of apology or suggestions that the driver help by taking the victim to a hospital. Such results could be seen as reflecting (badly) on American character and sympathies. However, in each country a legal structure shapes and generates legal culture, and this may be reflected in these sorts of responses about law. Americans involved in auto accidents are warned by their lawyers not to

Table 8.4   Cultural Differences in Type of Punishment Recommended
for Auto Accidents

	Child vignette		Adult vignette	
	Detroit (%)	Yokohama (%)	Detroit (%)	Yokohama (%)
Restoration	10	71	14	65
Driver's ed	3	1	3	1
Lose license	31	6	21	5
Legal action	29	19	33	28
Other	27	4	29	1
(N)	(158)	(249)	(217)	(279)

Note: Columns do not always equal 100% because of rounding error. For each vignette, city differences were highly significant by chi-square tests. The restoration category included both emotional restoration, such as apology, and instrumental or financial restoration, such as monetary restitution.

make such statements as "I'm sorry" so as not to admit fault. And it is almost certainly the case that an American would think twice about taking a victim to the hospital because of the further liability that might be entailed by not waiting for police and ambulance personnel. When law "takes over," when there is a structure of legal actions in place and well-known, it preempts the domain of appropriate responses. In this case, law can have a chilling effect on simple expressions of human feeling and solidarity such as "I'm sorry." Sometimes this is perhaps all a litigant wanted to hear (Bezanson, Cranberg, & Soloski, 1987).

A further message of table 8.4 is that, although Japanese remain strongly inclined toward relationship restoration, their punishment responses for auto accidents are more isolative than are their judgments of everyday-life vignettes. For the first time, Japanese respondents are shown to recommend formal legal punishments. This result is consistent with our expectation that when Japanese are faced with incidents involving strangers, they begin to respond as if the parties were Western-style individuals: isolated entities. As our model has suggested, an individualistic view of the responsible actor entails an emphasis on the actor's immediate deed in attributing responsibility, and it tends to be associated with formal legal means of punishment.

Effects of Experimental Variations on Punishment

WHETHER TO PUNISH. The consensus in both countries was that some punishment is appropriate for each of these stories (see table 8.4). What effect do the experimental variations in the stories have on the punishment

Table 8.5 Effects of Story Variations on Percentage of Respondents Saying That There Should Be a Punishment

	Detroit			Yokohama		
		Accidents			Accidents	
Variations	Robbery (%)	Child (%)	Adult (%)	Robbery (%)	Child (%)	Adult (%)
Mental state						
Low	*ns*	30	61	—	87	—
High		73	92		97	
Consequences						
Low	*ns*	44	*ns*	—	88	—
High		59			97	
Past pattern						
Absent	94	44	*ns*	—	*ns*	—
Present	98	60				

Note: Cells indicate percentage saying "yes." In several cases distributions of responses were so skewed that chi-square tests of effects of the variations were inappropriate or impossible; these are indicated with a dashed line. *ns* = tested but not significant.

decision? Table 8.5 summarizes, for each vignette and each experimental variation, those places where there was a significant effect of the variation on respondents' views of whether to punish the actor. The Child story had the most systematic pattern of effects in both countries: High mental state, severe consequences, and (in Detroit) a bad past pattern were significantly associated with responses of "yes" (that is, something should happen to the actor). In addition, in Detroit mental state had an effect in the Adult story and past pattern had a slight effect in the Robbery. Although Yokohama residents appear less responsive than Detroiters to variations in the story, this is basically because their judgments were so extreme. The overall message of these findings is that the same kinds of factors that govern responsibility judgments also affect punishment decisions. However, Japanese respondents are more broadly inclined to punish than are their American counterparts.

CHOICE OF PUNISHMENT. Punishment choices for the auto accidents were less often affected by the experimental variations than the corresponding responsibility judgments had been. In judging the Child story, both Japanese and American respondents gave punishments that were more geared toward relationship restoration when the actor did not have a bad past pattern of behavior (bad driving). In addition, Japanese respondents more often advocated restoration when the actor's mental state was low (not speeding). For the Adult story, Detroiters gave more restorative responses when the actor's mental state was low (brakes failed), and Yokohama residents were more likely to suggest relationship restoration when consequence severity was low (injury rather than death). In all cases, the restorative American responses were entirely focused on monetary restitution, whereas the Japanese responses also included apologetic behaviors.

These results clarify the implications of relationship restoration for our respondents, both American and Japanese. Overall, restorative answers were more widely proposed when the actor was in some way less blameworthy or when things turned out not so badly. Restoration emerged as a kind of opposite to the isolative, serious option of formal legal sanctions. Whenever restorative answers were less frequent, formal legal alternatives were more often chosen, and vice versa. Logically, if relationship restoration and formal legal action did not represent anchors on a true continuum, it would make as much sense for "driver's education" to go up when restitution went down, or for "other" to go up when legal action went down. It therefore appears reasonable to characterize relationship restoration as a more *lenient* punishment response in comparison to punitive legal actions, as well as one which is less likely to isolate the offender. This interpretation is also consistent with previous results. For example, chapter 7 noted that consequences that were perceived as more serious were associated with less relationship restoration among Japanese respondents.

One important aspect of these effects of experimental variations on punishment is the *lack* of patterned difference between the cities. For example, there was no evidence in these stories that Yokohama residents were less sensitive to information about mental state. If anything, they appeared to be more sensitive to information about seriousness of consequences. Granted, Japanese and American respondents still advocated very different levels of relationship restoration; Japanese chose such options more often, and American restorative choices were entirely focused on financial restitution. However, they appeared to use much the same implicit model in processing information about the deeds they judged.

Conclusions

To grasp the significance of these results, it is helpful to regard them in light of what is known about community and crime in modern Japan. In previous chapters we have documented many ways in which the Japanese have been remarkably successful in maintaining aspects of community from earlier times. For example, the level of involvement of Japanese employees in their enterprises is striking. This involvement is fostered by job stability, by the provision of such amenities as company housing and company-sponsored recreation, and by daily rituals. The employees that do calisthenics together, sing the company song together, work together, and then drink together after hours need not spontaneously like one another. But as in any small town or family, they learn to get along. Likewise, Japanese neighborhoods, even urban neighborhoods, tend to draw people together in a rich set of community ties (Bestor, 1989).

Japanese patterns of policing are consistent with this vision of community. Japanese police stress foot patrols, and police make a notable local presence in small, readily accessible substations (*koban*) opening on the street. From an American point of view, the flavor of Japanese crime prevention is reminiscent of a "return to Mayberry" in which the local police know their community and know that it is unlikely to use deadly force. The community, in turn, knows the police and assumes that police are to be trusted (Bayley, 1976). Just as the firm-as-family metaphor pervades business, the neighborhood-as-home image is part of a legal culture that discourages the use of formal law and leads people to attend to social relationships in processing disputes.

The evidence of the current chapter, however, provides a striking counterexample to the differences previously outlined between Japanese and American legal cultures. When Japanese are asked to judge a situation in which the participants have no prior relationship—in which the solidarity between the parties is essentially zero—their judgments look much like those of Americans. Indeed, in some respects Japanese judge both criminal and civil incidents more stringently than their American counterparts. This suggests that to the extent that urban settings and job conditions become impersonal, these may create pressures for Japanese to converge toward a more individualistic way of judging others. In one sense, it is not crime that is special, but strangers, and Americans and Japanese share this feeling. Therefore, with respect to the overall argument of the book, this chapter provides the "exception that proves the rule."

Although we began by reflecting on the remarkably low Japanese crime rate, this was a chapter about strangers, not about crime. Crime per se was not stressed in the research, for the goal was primarily to test a model of human judgment. But this book's attention to the solidarity and hierarchy of social ties is far from irrelevant to crime and crime rates. Crime and civil offenses, like more trivial everyday wrongs, are linked to social context: to the solidarity of communities and groups and to the nature of the inequalities within them. Relationship solidarity in particular is a key issue that influences whether a citizenry tends to "see no evil," as in the old Buddhist phrase, or locates evil in the offender it beholds. It can be argued that the "Japanese miracle" with regard to both crime and civil litigation reflects the maintenance of a sense, perhaps a myth, of community.[6]

PART THREE   **Law and Society**

_____

9

Empirical Conclusions

What does this research mean? The question can be answered at two very different levels. The straightforward, scientific conclusions about our findings are summarized in this chapter. In the final two chapters we discuss what these findings imply about law, culture, and morality in the United States and Japan.

Chapters 6, 7, and 8 examined the process of attributing responsibility and assigning sanctions in two Japanese cities, Yokohama and Kanazawa, and one American city, Detroit. Throughout, the focus was upon the relative importance of information about the individual (deed information) versus information about the situation (role information) in the attribution process. The findings of the three surveys can be thought of in terms of judgments of everyday-life incidents that vary in their solidarity (how close the parties are) and their hierarchy (whether the relationship is between equals or between authority and subordinate). Two dependent variables, responsibility and punishment, are to be considered. In addition, considerations that come into play when an incident involves strangers deserve special attention. This summary of findings is therefore organized around three issues: responsibility, punishment, and strangers.

Responsibility

Four questions about responsibility have been raised. First, what are the effects of deed and context information on responsibility? Among the elements of deeds, this research concentrated on the actor's mental state and the act's consequences. Among the aspects of context, the research focused on the actor's past pattern of behavior and the presence of another person influencing the actor. Second, what are the effects of roles? We attempted to vary roles along the dimensions of solidarity and hierarchy such that people judged incidents that represented each combination of low versus high solidarity and of relations between equals versus authorities. Third, how do roles serve to modify the ways in which deeds are judged? For example, does information about an actor's mental state have a different meaning or impact when the actor is an authority rather than the equal of the person who is harmed? And fourth, how do the Japanese and American respondents to our surveys differ in their judgments? Is there evidence of a pervasive tendency of Japanese to be more contextual, emphasizing role relations and contexts, or of Americans to be more individualistic, emphasizing aspects of deeds in isolation from their context?

Deeds and Contexts

With respect to the overall effects of deed and context information, all of our expectations were fulfilled. When an actor was more mentally involved in producing an outcome—when what happened was negligent as opposed to accidental, or intentional as opposed to negligent—this actor was held more responsible. When consequences were more severe or when the actor had a bad past pattern of behavior, responsibility was also higher, although the impact of consequence severity was small. Finally, the presence of another person influencing the actor served to lower the actor's responsibility.

Roles

As expected, more responsibility was assigned to actors in less solidary relationships and to authorities.[1]

Role-Deed Interrelationships

Role information affected the use of deed information in three ways:

1. Hierarchy affected the use of information about the actor's mental state. Varying the mental state of the actor had a much greater effect when that actor was an authority. This was especially the case where accidental or negligent rather than intentional acts were concerned. In addition, variations in an authority's mental state had an impact on responsibility over and above implied differences in the actor's purposiveness or the act's avoidability. This residual impact suggests that authorities tend to be held accountable for the unmet obligations of the role. For example, a careless boss is three things: careless, a boss, and a "careless-boss" who should have been more attentive.

2. Solidarity, like hierarchy, affected the use of information about the actor's state of mind. The actor's mental state had a greater impact in stories involving highly solidary ties than when the actor and victim were less closely tied. As was true for authorities, in highly solidary relation-

ships the impact of mental state had a residual component that could not be attributed to an action's sheer purposiveness or an act's avoidability. Perhaps diffuse obligations characterize close ties just as they characterize the role of authority.

3. Hierarchy affected the impact of other's influence. Influence from others who were authorities had a greater impact on reducing an actor's responsibility than influence from others who were equals.

Cultural Differences

Finally, we compared the use of role and deed information in the American and Japanese cities. It is important to emphasize that in both the United States and Japan information about deed, context, and role is used to attribute responsibility. These are basic elements for determining responsibility everywhere. But variations in social structure and in cultural experience can modify the weights that citizens place on these elements. The relative impacts of deeds, contexts, roles, and their interactions were expected to vary cross-culturally.

These expectations were fulfilled. Americans were more sensitive to the immediate aspects of what an actor did, especially that actor's subjective state of mind, than were Japanese. This sensitivity extended to aspects of the context of action that are "actor-carried," such as the past pattern of behavior. Japanese were more sensitive to variation in the social roles of the parties and to the influence of other parties in the social context. These differences were often striking in their magnitude. For example, the sensitivity of Americans to variation in the actor's state of mind was approximately twice the sensitivity shown by Japanese.

These findings are consistent with the two images of the responsible actor to which the anthropological, sociological, and legal literature led us in part I. In the United States this actor appears to be a more isolated, equal individual whose mental state matters greatly. Japanese, in contrast, seem to see the responsible actor as embedded in a web of close and hierarchical ties with others, including victims. The actor exists in a stratified context such that variation in role or context matters greatly.

Punishment

Like wrongdoing itself, sanctions for wrongdoing have consequences for communities as well as for individuals. And like responsibility decisions, sanction decisions may be influenced by the actor's deed and the context within which the act occurred, by the relationship of the parties in dispute, and by the legal culture and conceptions of the social actor that exist in different societies.

Sanctions were examined in two phases: willingness to intervene for some act of wrongdoing, and the kind of sanction to be used if there is an intervention. Willingness to intervene was linked to the level of responsibility attributed to the actor. The greater the responsibility attributed, the more likely it was that a sanction would be imposed. Intervention was also influenced by deed and context information. The actor's state of mind mattered; negligent or intentional acts were more likely to elicit a judgment that there should be a sanction. Similarly, more serious consequences, presence of a past pattern of similar behavior, or the absence of influence from another all increased the willingness to intervene.

The results show interesting and perhaps surprising patterns of cultural difference and similarity. The willingness of Japanese to intervene by imposing a sanction was no less than that of Americans. Indeed, on balance the residents of the two Japanese cities were *more* willing to intervene in situations of wrongdoing than were Detroiters. In both countries, deed and context information also served to moderate these decisions to intervene. Mental state and past pattern information, both of which are attributes carried by the individual actor, had a greater impact on American intervention. This is consistent with the argument that among Americans the responsible actor is more likely to be perceived as an isolated individual, the source of whose deeds lies within the self.

Given a willingness to intervene, the next issue is the choice of sanction. In both Japan and the United States the solidarity of ties between actor and victim seems to be a central determinant of punishment norms. Certain types of punishments are associated with certain roles or statuses (e.g., juvenile) or with certain relations between offender and victim. Punishment practices are most restorative, most sensitive to rebuilding relationships of actor and victim, where relationships are highly solidary. And punishment practices are most isolative and indifferent to relationships where the parties are strangers. Thus the repertoire of punishments that survey respondents suggested in family settings never included the kind of isolation for the perpetrator or total breakage of the relationship that was evidenced in work settings. Respondents in both countries occasionally wanted to fire employees but never children.

Sanctioning decisions are also influenced by legal culture and attendant conceptions of the responsible actor. In these surveys the contrast between Japanese and American decisions was striking. Within each type of role relationship, Japanese respondents were more likely to choose sanctions that restore the relationship between actor and victim and that provide restitution for the victim. If the responsible actor is embedded in a context, such action is likely to restore that context. Americans were more likely to suggest sanctions to isolate the individual. If the responsible actor is initially seen as an independent entity, such an approach to punishment is likely to further isolate this entity.

Rationales for punishment were also examined. As expected, Americans were more favorably disposed than Japanese to retribution, incapacitation, and general deterrence as rationales. These are each consistent with an image of the perpetrator as an isolated individual and a view of punishment as separating the offender from the community. Japanese were more favorably disposed to specific deterrence, rehabilitation, and (in their answers to open-ended questions) restitution. Each of these rationales assumes that actors are contextual or prepares actors to return to a social context.

The punishment results further support the argument that the responsible actor in Japan is a contextual actor, such that the appropriate sanctions are those that reintegrate the wrongdoer and restore relationships, whereas the responsible actor in the United States is an individual to be isolated and punished for wrongdoing. Theoretically, differences in the social structure of relationships in everyday life—especially variations in solidarity—provide a parsimonious account of how sanctioning norms might come to differ both within and across cultures.

Strangers

Judgments of crime and civil wrongs, like judgments of everyday-life disputes, were expected to vary with the social relationships of those involved. If Japanese and Americans assess wrongdoing differently in part because Japanese tend to be more closely tied to one another, then the judgments of Japanese and Americans should more closely resemble one another when disputes are clearly between strangers.

Analysis of the crime and auto accident vignettes supported this argument. Overall, differences in American and Japanese responsibility and punishment decisions were reduced or eliminated when people judged deeds where the actor and victim were strangers. With respect to responsibility judgments, Japanese and American responses converged in two ways. First, Japanese judgments were as harsh as those of Americans. Although in the everyday-life vignettes Japanese respondents routinely assigned less responsibility to the actor than did American respondents, in the stories about strangers the Japanese assigned significantly *more* responsibility. Second, with regard to the factors that came into play in their judgments, Japanese and Americans made similar use of information about deeds. Significantly, the supposed greater sensitivity of Americans to the actor's mental state disappeared in two of the three stories about strangers. We interpret these findings to mean that a Japanese, faced with judging an incident in which a prior relationship does not exist between the parties, makes judgments more like an American.

With respect to punishment, similar patterns emerged in the crime and auto accident cases. Yokohama residents were consistently and significantly more likely than Detroiters to respond "yes" to the question whether something should be done to the perpetrator for these offenses involving strangers. Further, in the crime story, not only did Yokohama residents more frequently wish to impose some sanction, but their average recommended prison term was also longer than that of Detroiters. In each city, sentence lengths were influenced by the actor's mental state, past pattern of behavior, and severity of consequences. The effect of the seriousness of consequences was profound in both cities, but it was more substantial in Yokohama than in Detroit. Thus, for the first time in these data, a story about a crime involving strangers led Japanese to make greater use of information about the actor's deeds than did Americans.

In the automobile accident cases the Japanese remained more inclined toward restorative sanctions than Americans. This is not surprising, given that the repertoire of sanctions with which they are familiar emphasizes such choices. But their punishment responses were more isolative than was true in their judgments of everyday-life vignettes. For the first time, Japanese respondents recommended formal legal punishments, consistent with the expectation that when they are faced with situations involving strangers, Japanese are more likely to respond as if the parties were isolated entities. In these cases Japanese and Americans also converged in their use of mental state and consequence information. They were equally sensitive to information about mental state, and Yokohama residents appeared to be more sensitive to information about consequences.

Conclusions

Taken together, chapters 6, 7, and 8 reveal much about the process of calling people to account. Our model of responsibility has held across cultures in a comparison of Americans and Japanese, and it has helped to predict and to understand differences between the cultures. All responsibility is a function of roles and deeds, of obligations and actions. However, in some roles the weight of obligation is felt more heavily, and in some cultures the texture of differences among roles is felt more sensitively. We have argued that solidary and hierarchical ties evoke judgments based more heavily on the actor's presumed obligations and that the Japanese should exhibit greater sensitivity to the presence of such obligations. The data were consistent with both arguments. Differences between roles constitute the microlevel of variation in judgment that depends on the texture of everyday-life relationships; differences between Japanese and Americans reflect the macrolevel of variation in the overall tenor of these relationships in a society.

At its core, the process of calling a person to account involves conceptions of the responsible actor. American and Japanese conceptions of the responsible actor differ systematically.[2] But these conceptions are not immutable. What do these findings add to our understanding of differences in the two legal systems? Of their potential for change and convergence? The next chapter addresses these questions.

Legal Structure, Legal Culture, and Convergence

> Law . . . contributes to a definition of a style
> of social existence (a culture, shall we say?)
> in the same way that the idea that *virtus* is
> the glory of man, that money makes the
> world go round, or that above the forest of
> parakeets a parakeet of parakeets prevails do.
> They are, such notions, part of what order
> means; visions of community, not echoes of
> it. (Geertz, 1983, p. 218)

This chapter concerns the way legal structure and legal culture interact to create and maintain a legal system. We review a long-running debate about the relative importance of cultural and structural explanations for some observed differences between Japanese and American legal systems; we then discuss how our findings inform this controversy. The chapter concludes with some thoughts as to whether, as some have argued, Japanese and American legal systems—indeed, all capitalist legal systems—tend to converge toward a single model. We begin by telling a story that arises from the facts of a lawsuit.

Martinez v. Santa Clara

Julia Martinez was born and raised in the community of Santa Clara. When she was younger she married an outsider, Myles Martinez. She and her husband stayed in Santa Clara and had several children, including a daughter named Audrey. Before Julia's marriage the community passed a rule saying that only a child whose *father* is from Santa Clara can be considered a Santa Claran. Although Audrey and the other children were raised in Santa Clara and continued to live there as adults, they could not vote nor hold any community office, and in the event of their mother's death they had no right to remain in the community or to inherit her home. Needless to say, both mother and daughter were angry at what they perceived to be the gender discrimination embodied in this rule. Repeatedly, they appealed to the community to change the rule and admit Julia's children into membership. Repeatedly, they were rebuffed. They finally sued, claiming a violation of their civil rights. The court concluded, however, that the interests of the community outweighed the interests of these individual women, and it found for Santa Clara. The court's opinion read in part: "Membership policies . . . are no more or less than a mechanism of social and to an extent psychological and cultural self-definition. The importance of this to Santa Clara . . . cannot be overstressed."

The decision of the trial court was reversed on appeal but was ultimately affirmed by the Supreme Court. The Supreme Court, however, tread less blatantly on individual rights. Its opinion turned on the procedural question of whether Julia and Audrey could bring a suit. The court concluded that a private remedy was not available to the Martinezes. They had no standing.

What is going on here? Have we reported the facts of some Japanese case while changing the names of the parties and the location? After all, the lower court's opinion does reflect an emphasis on community rights over individual claims, and as chapter 2 noted, the Japanese courts use the procedural device of a lack of standing to thwart the assertion of individual rights. Nevertheless, this is an American case, and it is one of recent vintage. Indeed, the Supreme Court opinion was written by Justice Thurgood Marshall, who, before he ascended to the bench, was the chief civil rights attorney for the NAACP, the man who won *Brown v. Board of Education*.

What then? Convergence, perhaps? If so, this would represent not the convergence Americans once had in mind—whereby the Japanese would change their society, eventually developing a legal system and a legal culture like that found in the United States—but convergence in the opposite direction. No, there is no convergence here, for the case *is* about another culture, another culture's ways, and another culture's laws. We have omitted one fact provided by the full name of the lawsuit, *Martinez v. Santa Clara Pueblo*.[1] The case concerns tribal membership rules of the Santa Clara Pueblo in New Mexico. Julia Martinez (whose maiden name is not mentioned) is a member of the Pueblo; her husband Myles, the outsider, is a Navajo.

At least two points can be made from this case. First, the facts as presented here have an emotional effect. Upon reading the case's outcome the average American is likely to be taken aback, if not appalled. There is a sense of unease, even of disbelief, about the accuracy with which the case has been stated. When informed that the case concerns a Native American community, most people to whom we have read the facts report comprehension combined with a sense of relief. These emotions reflect the substantial gulf between the larger American legal culture and legal cultures less committed to individual rights and individualism. Of course, this is not to imply that Pueblo legal culture is necessarily such a culture. We, and perhaps the federal courts as well, know very little about the Pueblo's actual legal values. But the case brings home the degree to which there is such a thing as an American legal culture: a set of assumptions, attitudes, meanings, and ideals concerning the law. It also reveals the degree to which most of us are committed to it (R. J. Smith, 1989).

Second, this case illustrates the potential interweaving of cultural and structural factors in determining behavior in the legal arena. In a few years, faced with *Martinez*-like outcomes, it would not be surprising if the would-be members of the Santa Clara Pueblo become relatively nonlitigious on issues related to gender. We might even find someone willing to assert that their low litigation rates are due to the Pueblo's nonlitigious legal culture. Others could be found to object that the nonuse of the courts is explicable in terms of the lack of legal remedies available (Ramseyer, 1985). In short, the potential consequences of the *Martinez* case might be explained in either cultural or structural terms.

The *Martinez* case presents in microcosm the longstanding debate about the relative importance of structural and cultural explanations for differences in legal systems. The following review of the current status of the structure-culture debate points out what we believe are shortcomings in the way it has traditionally been framed. We argue that a concern with concepts such as the *responsible actor* enriches and expands the debate and gives us better insight into the ways in which culture and structure interact in forming a legal system.

The Legal Structure–Legal Culture Debate

For almost as long as scholars have been comparing Japanese and American societies, debate has persisted about the relative importance of cultural and structural explanations for observed differences. The comparative study of the two legal systems has reflected and continued this debate within the narrower context of legal culture and legal structure.[2] The discussion has ranged over a variety of issues. It is probably fair to say, however, that at its core has been the issue of litigiousness. Various authors have used litigation rates as evidence of cultural values. Kawashima (1963), in probably the first postwar article in English to address the issue directly, noted that Japanese often chose mediation over litigation and sued one another with less frequency than Americans. He attributed this difference primarily to "the social-cultural background of the problem. Traditionally, the Japanese people prefer extra-judicial, informal means of settling a controversy" (p. 43). Although Kawashima attributed difference in litigation rates to cultural factors, he was careful not to label the resulting behavior as irrational. Others, however, were not so cautious (Kim & Lawson, 1979; Noda, 1976). They implied that nonlitigiousness was in some way nonrational.

Kawashima's basic argument went largely unchallenged until Haley's (1978, 1982b) articles. Haley rejected the argument that Japanese litigation rates are lower because the Japanese are reluctant to turn to law. Rather, he argued for an institutional explanation: The Japanese do not litigate because, compared to the alternatives, litigation does not pay. In support of his position Haley mustered several arguments. First, as discussed in chapter 2, he and others have demonstrated various ways in which the Japanese government discouraged litigation and encouraged settlement and mediation in the interwar years. Second, Japanese litigation rates may be low by American standards but are not the lowest in the industrialized world; for example, when compared to European societies they appear to be only slightly lower than average (Sarat & Grossman, 1975). Third, litigation rates since World War II have declined rather than increased, although many had suggested they would rise as Japan became more Westernized. Because litigation rates have been moving in the opposite direction of presumed cultural changes, they must be determined by other factors—that is, by the structure of the legal system.

Unfortunately, as Ramseyer (1988) notes, at the level of individual decisions concerning litigation and settlement, Haley was unable to provide evidence for his thesis. Haley did, however, advance the following argument: The concept of a nonlitigious ethic is useful in explaining Japanese legal behavior only if the disputants reach negotiated or mediated settlements that do not reflect the expected value of a case were it to go to trial. (The expected value of a case is the amount the plaintiff stands to recover if the case goes to trial multiplied by the probability that the plaintiff will prevail.)[3] Note that this is not an argument about why people would choose litigation or settlement, but about what they would settle for. According to Haley's argument, if culture matters they should settle for less. Thus Haley, like some before him, implies that cultural explanations of nonlitigiousness predict economically irrational behavior.

Why this should be so is not clear. Haley's conclusion appears to rest on two assumptions: (1) Preference for settlement versus adjudication entails some type of altruistic commitment to the community that causes one to lessen one's own demand against one's own best interest; and (2) a pattern of settlements that reflected the expected value of suits would be evidence that such altruism did not exist. Both of these assumptions are suspect. Non-litigiousness does not necessarily entail altruism. Nor does a pattern of settlements reflecting the expected value of suits necessarily undermine an altruistic explanation. If both parties to a suit were to behave altruistically in this sense—if they were to look to the good of the community as well as to their own welfare—this would only enlarge the bargaining space within which they could negotiate.[4] Defendants would be willing to settle for more while plaintiffs would be willing to settle for less (Ramseyer & Nakazato, 1989). For Haley to be correct, one side of the dispute must be behaving non-altruistically and in a sense taking advantage of the opponent's altruism (Raiffa, 1982, p. 144).

Haley's arguments did reinforce two ideas, however: that the key component in legal cultural differences is litigiousness and that Japanese legal culture in some way dictates nonrational behavior. Not surprisingly, in an effort to refute his structural explanation, some of Haley's critics agreed with this premise. As Ramseyer (1988) has put it, "They generally respond that most Japanese simply are not the rational wealth-maximizers that he seemed to suggest they were" (p. 112). According to this argument, Japanese legal culture implausibly turns on a requirement that individuals act against their own self-interest, at least insofar as this is defined in utility-maximizing terms. This response also reinforces the idea that litigation decisions—or decisions not to litigate—are at the heart of understanding legal culture, for it is here that the culturally determined, economically irrational behavior can be observed.

Problems of Litigation Rates as the Measure of Legal Culture

Litigation rates, unfortunately, are at best an ambiguous measure of almost anything, including legal culture. The discussion surrounding litigation decisions has often been confusing if not confused because it has failed to be specific about the particular decision under discussion. At times the issue under discussion is the *decision to make a claim* at all, to seek recompense from anyone for some wrongdoing. At other times the discussion is about the *decision to adjudicate* versus the decision to settle out of court. At still other times it is about the *settlement amount*, given a decision to settle (Sanders, 1990). All of these decisions are to some extent contingent on decisions made earlier, yet we often have little data about these previous choices lower down on the "disputing pyramid."

The disputing pyramid is a metaphor to describe the process by which a large number of injuries or other unfortunate outcomes become thought of as acts of wrongdoing, are transformed into claims, and are pursued through legal or nonlegal channels. Some injuries generate no claims, some claims are dropped or not otherwise pursued, some are settled before suit, some suits are settled or dropped before trial, and some decisions are not appealed; the pyramid metaphor reflects the fact that the number of cases constantly decreases as claims move up through the system. Discussions of one part of the disputing pyramid taken out of context may be misleading.[5] For instance, Haley's (1978, 1982b) suggestion that individuals in a nonlitigious culture should settle for less than the expected value of their suits could only be tested by examining those who simply never make a claim as well as those who claim and then settle. Otherwise, a finding that those who make a claim do not settle for less might be explained by a process of adverse selection, insofar as these individuals are the ones who have already overcome cultural compunctions by deciding to claim at all. According to this argument, they would not be representative of the society in question (Hughes, 1989).

Moreover, aggregating litigation rates across all types of disputes often disguises as much as it clarifies. As Haley (1982a) and Tanase (1990) make clear, understanding changes in the litigation rate in specific areas— such as commercial litigation or automobile accidents—requires a longitudinal study of the interactions of courts, litigants, and the legislature.[6]

Even if we are to accept the proposition that an overall litigation rate is informative, Ramseyer and Nakazato (1989, p. 271) note that low rates are consistent with at least three different hypotheses about a legal order: (1) ethical norms discourage recourse to courts or any legal rules; (2) plaintiffs abandon valid legal claims because of large costs and small recoveries; and (3) plaintiffs find that the legal system makes it relatively easy for the parties to a dispute to reach settlements outside the legal system by providing clear guidelines as to the expected value of a claim were it to be litigated.[7]

Most important, to focus on litigation rates causes one to study individual attitudes and decisions at the point at which something has gone wrong rather than at a time when things are going smoothly. This has several significant consequences. First, a focus upon the point of wrongdoing or harmdoing frequently leads to the conclusion that the Japanese legal system is a fragile thing, constantly under attack from individuals wanting to litigate. Second, such a focus reinforces the view that Japanese governmental decisions to structure the law to discourage litigation are an effort by elites to control the populace and are, therefore, less than fully legitimate. Haley concludes his discussion of efforts to emphasize conciliation in the interwar years with the comment: "That conciliation was used extensively even though it was a less satisfactory means for enforcing legal rights than the ideal civil action, underscores the inadequacy of the legal process in Japan" (1982a, p. 145). Viewed from the perspective of the injured claimant, the many steps the Japanese government has taken to suppress litigation take on an air of elite manipulation or even repression. For example, Japan has no civil jury trials, the number of attorneys is restricted, and novel claims are not well received (Haley, 1989).

From this perspective, a legal system that puts few impediments in the way of litigation may appear to be both less fragile and more democratic than that of Japan. It appears less fragile because it does not attempt to thwart individual aggressiveness and individual attempts to gain every possible legal advantage. It appears more democratic in the sense that the state is often willing to respond to the wishes of individual litigants. In the United States, there are no restrictions on the size of the bar, hence there are large numbers of attorneys willing to take claims on a contingent fee. The use of a jury system creates a decision maker whose attention is more likely to be focused on the situation of the litigant and the litigant's individual loss. The courts are more open to creating new obligations and providing large judgments. The aggressive litigant is an individual to be listened to, not suppressed. The result is an attempt to provide what Lawrence Friedman (1985) has called "total justice": the idea that every occasion of misfortune or wrongdoing should have a legal remedy.

These points lead us to conclude that a focus on litigation rates fundamentally biases the legal culture/legal structure debate. Focusing on litigation rates causes us to look at *cultural* values within the narrow context of an individual's decision whether to sue; at the same time, it causes us to look at the court *structure* as the environment within which that decision is made. Hence, the debate has tended to equate cultural explanations with micro processes and structural explanations with macro processes. We argue that this is an error because it misconstrues the role of legal culture in shaping a legal system.

To indicate how this is so, it is useful to consider the legal system from the viewpoint of members of society who are not litigants or potential litigants. These individuals reflect parts of the legal culture that are not dominated by the micro-considerations confronting the litigant. Viewed from their perspective, the Japanese legal system appears less fragile and perhaps more legitimate. In their general attitudes about dispute settlement, as discussed in chapter 2 and as revealed in our data, the Japanese express support for a less adversarial process. For example, Miyazawa (1987, pp. 225–226) reports that in a survey conducted in 1976 asking "Would you consider suing if your rights were violated?" 11 percent of respondents answered "immediately," 24 percent answered "occasionally," and 61 percent answered "no, unless the matter were extremely grave." In response to the question "Which statement most closely reflects your opinion?" 8 percent agreed with the statement "If you think it is better to sue, you may do so"; 43 percent agreed with the statement "Suing is not the most desirable action, but you may use court-sponsored mediation or formal discussion as much as you wish"; and 42 percent agreed with the statement "You should try to avoid bringing suit whenever possible and instead work to resolve the matter through private discussions." When viewed from the perspective of nonlitigants, it is even arguable that a legal system that constantly gives preference to adjudication may be unstable in a different sense: It may be subject to pressures from nonlitigants to restrict litigation (Engel, 1984; Greenhouse, 1986). Recent efforts at tort reform in the United States have enjoyed widespread public support, in part because the public would prefer less litigation (Insurance Information Institute, 1982).

Legal cultural values opposing litigation and emphasizing settlement of disputes in the interest of social harmony are part of *macro* processes: They place external limitations on people's relations (Blau, 1987). Note, however, that such norms are a type of *collective good*. Like street lighting or national defense, their benefits cannot be kept from those who do not share in their creation. Non-taxpayers also have their way lighted and made safer.

In this context, a general willingness to forgo litigation creates a collective benefit, an atmosphere of harmony and compromise, that can be exploited by those who are willing to demand their legal rights (Ramseyer & Nakazato, 1989). A legal culture that discourages litigation and encourages settlement is most vulnerable to the attitudes and actions of actors who are confronted with some injury, contractual dispute, or other problem for which they believe there is someone to blame. The advantage of standing on one's rights and behaving aggressively accrues entirely to the individual, whereas the cost of corroding the atmosphere of harmony is spread throughout the legal order. The litigator is a "free rider" (Olson, 1971).

Those aspects of macrolegal culture that are collective goods are likely to maintain wide support only if people perceive that few are exploiting them for individual advantage (Tanase, 1990). Many Japanese legal reforms can thus be interpreted as a process of constant adjustments to thwart the corrosive impact of litigious free riders on a nonlitigious legal order. The history of reform as reported by such scholars as Haley (1982a) and Tanase (1990) is one of an increase in litigation rates in some areas, which produces legislation designed to deflect disputants from using the courts. Tanase's (1990) discussion of automobile accidents explores the many ways in which the legal process can be structured to minimize the perception among injured individuals that there is substantial discretion in damages one might obtain from an accident, hence that there might be some economic advantage to pursuing a claim aggressively in court. Nevertheless, even in Japan the law is constantly under pressure from some plaintiffs and defendants who attempt to exploit the courts for individual advantage. Tanase (1990, p. 684), for example, notes that behind the formal compensation system lurk "settlement brokers" (*jidanya*) offering to exploit insurance companies' nonassertiveness to obtain a settlement larger than is due.

Once in place, of course, structural factors are an important part of decisions to litigate. As Haley and others have argued, individual views concerning litigation are informed by a belief as to the efficacy or inefficacy of litigation (Haley, 1978). Therefore they are in part the product of earlier efforts to restrict adjudication alternatives (Kidder & Hostetler, 1990). This is reflected in the survey data reported by Miyazawa (1987); 60 percent of the respondents agreed with the statement, "Litigation is expensive and time-consuming, and even when you win, you will usually lose money" (p. 225). If instead 60 percent believed that litigation were cheap, quick, and financially rewarding, we assume that their preference for nonlitigious alternatives would diminish.

Simply because Japanese believe litigation to be inefficacious does not mean, however, that they prefer for litigation to be made easier. A thought experiment in devising justice systems can illustrate this point: Even while reflecting on one's own situation at the time one becomes a potential litigant, one might choose to construct a legal system that thwarts one's efforts to pursue personal ends. For example, it is easy to imagine that one might choose to construct a legal system that thwarts personal desires for vengeance at the time a convicted felon is sentenced for murdering one's spouse. In such cases one may realize that the occasion of personal trouble is not necessarily the best time to choose a set of legal arrangements, for on such occasions people think most about themselves and their individual ends, and less about the implications of those ends for the community. One may prefer to arrange things so that when those occasions do arise the law will thwart one's wishes by, for example, prohibiting testimony concerning the emotional effect of the murder on the victim's family.

At another level, one may wish to arrange things so that certain important areas of life are kept beyond the reach of adjudication. For instance, one may conclude that the slow erosion of family immunities—the prohibitions against spouses suing each other or children suing their parents—may serve the interests of those harmed in the family, but only at the cost of teaching us all that in this important way the family is no different from other role relationships.

In contrast, a society that chooses to focus on citizens' preferences when the citizens are concerned with community values (e.g., harmony, peace) rather than when they are concerned with their individual situations is not basing its choices on less valid or less legitimate components of legal culture. Rather, it is more accurate to say that such a legal order attends to citizens' preferences *when they more nearly reflect the concerns of a contextual self* rather than the concerns of an individual self. To say otherwise is to reflect a particular set of cultural values about the relative importance of the individual and the community; it is to believe that the isolated self is the location of a person's most deeply felt views and that these views are best measured when the person is least sympathetic to the constraints of the social environment. This may be close to the modal self of Americans, but it is a rather far cry from the characteristic self of Japanese. As Kiefer (1976) puts it: "Although Japanese are often acutely aware of discrepancies . . . between inner feelings and outward role demands, they think of the latter . . . as the really important center of the self" (pp. 280–281).

Summary

The discussion of legal culture must move beyond litigation and litigation rates to a larger set of attitudes, beliefs, and values. The boundaries of legal culture are not encompassed by a microprocess concern about whether Japanese litigants behave as economically rational individuals when they litigate. As Miyazawa (1987) notes, "What we must measure is Japanese legal consciousness, separated from such behavior patterns as litigation rate" (p. 223). The research presented in this book has attempted to do just that. The concept of the *responsible actor* is a bridge between general cultural values (such as views of the self) and specific attitudes toward litigation.

The differences in Japanese and American conceptions of the responsible actor reflect the ways in which legal culture is a macro- as well as a microprocess. These conceptions constrain and shape microprocesses in ways that are analogous to the constraints of macrostructural arrangements, such as the nature and availability of courts.

Our findings are powerful because the conceptions of responsibility and sanction embodied in the idea of the responsible actor are not simply attitudes, but are judgments of how acts of wrongdoing should be processed; moreover, these judgments were measured in a context relatively unencumbered by institutional or other structural impediments to alternative conceptions of responsibility and sanction. Differences in Japanese and American judgments discussed in part II cannot be explained by a lack of lawyers or courts or by other institutional constraints. The point, however, is not to pit legal culture against legal structure as a way to produce explanations for differences in Japanese and American legal systems. Rather, it is to show that legal culture legitimizes and supports legal structural arrangements and together these macro processes constrain the alternatives available in the microlevel processing of particular disputes.

Finally, because different conceptions of the responsible actor are closely tied to underlying cultural views of actors, our findings place litigation decisions in a wider context. When responsibility is contingent on role relationships and when sanctions have as their objective the reintegration of the wrongdoer into the social order, the decision to go to court provides an alternative that is flawed in more important ways than the conflict and inharmoniousness it engenders. To the degree that formal adjudication involves rules that generalize rights across roles and situations, to the extent that adjudication forces the responsible actor into the mold of the equal, isolated, contractual individual, it undermines other aspects of Japanese culture. These other aspects in turn support and are supported by general cultural values concerning the nature of the self and the meaning of moral action.

If, in the United States, the culturally consistent legal arrangements are those that emphasize the inward-looking preferences of those who are in trouble, in Japan the culturally consistent arrangements are those that emphasize the outward-looking preferences of those who are not. Hence, such concepts as the responsible actor allow us to begin to see more clearly the sense in which law is more than a tool. It is also an institution that tells us who we are.

Structure, Culture, and the Convergence Hypothesis

We have stressed the impact of social structure on culture and on legal culture. Now it is time to address the possible impact of legal culture on the structure of dispute resolution and punishment of wrongdoers. In the long run, we believe that the relationship between structure and culture is circular: Structural relationships affect cultural values, which in turn affect structural relationships. This mutual causality helps to create stability. Institutions and values tend to reinforce each other. Such stability is not, however, simply the product of natural processes; unlike the orbits of the planets, which are determined by the laws of celestial mechanics, social stability requires constant maintenance. The Japanese work constantly to suppress a legal system that would facilitate litigation and adjudication. Americans expend a good deal of effort to achieve just this type of legal order. The need for these efforts, however, suggests that in both societies, factors are at work that tend to move the law in a different direction: toward more mediative forms in the United States and toward more adjudicative forms in Japan. Over time, are we therefore likely to see the legal systems of Japan and the United States become more like each other? This is part of the larger debate about the likelihood of a convergence of all industrial societies toward one general pattern. We will attempt to explore the possibility of convergence in each direction: Japan becoming more like the United States, and vice versa.

The Cultural Pull toward Change

Immediate, microlevel pressures for convergence come from individuals dissatisfied with current arrangements. For example, this chapter has discussed ways in which the individual interests of litigants in Japan keep pressure on the Japanese system to be more open to litigation. Some academics in Japan have added their support to this goal.[8] However, unlike the early 1960s, when numerous Japanese scholars felt that their legal structure was seriously flawed and that Japan would have to develop a more independent and Western legal system more actively prepared to recognize individual rights (Kawashima, 1963; Maruyama, 1963), many now tend to believe that such a move would be a step backward (Upham, 1987). Turning every rule into a legal rule is not a current Japanese goal (Obuchi, 1987).

Similarly, American legal institutions and substantive law have been under some pressure to become less litigious in order to reflect and support a more contextual view of human relationships. Most writers who support a movement away from litigation in the United States find their philosophical anchor in Michael Sandel's (1982) critique of Western liberalism. Without any referents to cross-cultural comparative literature, Sandel adopts an argument for a type of self that in many ways parallels what we have described in Japan:

> But we cannot regard ourselves as independent . . . without great cost to those loyalties and convictions whose moral force consists partly in the fact that living by them is inseparable from understanding ourselves as the particular persons we are—as members of this family or community or nation or people, as bearers of this history, as sons and daughters of that revolution, as citizens of this republic. Allegiances such as these are

more than values I happen to have or aims I "espouse at any given time." They go beyond the obligations I voluntarily incur and the "natural duties" I owe to human beings as such. They allow that to some I owe more than justice requires or even permits, not by reason of agreements I have made but instead in virtue of those more or less enduring attachments and commitments which taken together partly define the person I am.... To imagine a person incapable of constitutive attachments such as these is not to conceive of an ideally free and rational agent, but to imagine a person wholly without character, without moral depth. (p. 179)

To owe some people more than an individualistic conception of justice "requires or even permits," because of their special relationship to oneself and because one's relationship to them is "constitutive of" one's sense of self, is to be a contextual actor. The fact that this communitarian movement is "home grown" rather than an import from another culture suggests that it does tap a change emerging in American society.

A number of American legal scholars have begun to develop and argue for legal rules and institutions that would further the communitarian goal of what we would term a more contextual society.[9] This line of argument is perhaps most developed in contract law, where, as Presser (1985) notes, there is a "new spirit of contract": "The most forward-looking of today's contracts scholars and an increasing number of judges and legislators are rejecting the old one-shot, amoral, individualistic view of contract, with its principle of *caveat emptor,* and are beginning to recognize that the reality of market conditions today is that most businesses must depend on each other through long-term dealing, that details of contracts cannot be fully spelled out at the beginning, and that performance and success must depend upon continued cooperation and not on continued confrontation" (p. 893).

Other areas may be experiencing the pull of contextualism. Discussing group liability in tort law, Baruch-Bush (1986) professes to see on the part of the judiciary a nascent and largely intuitive reaching for a communitarian view to explain recent decisions creating group liability in such mass tort situations as cases involving asbestos and DES exposure.[10] He suggests that group liability should develop along the following lines: When the members of a putative injurer or victim group are situated so that they either do have, or could have, significant contact and involvement with one another concerning the kind of activity or circumstance that is the subject of the dispute, then group responsibility would foster community formation and development and should be applied (Baruch-Bush, 1986, p. 1554). The express purpose of such an agenda is to alter legal institutions and rules so as to encourage the development of an enhanced sense of community.

Finally, there is the alternative dispute resolution (ADR) movement discussed in chapter 2. Many of its supporters submit that by building institutional alternatives to traditional litigation and adjudication, they are helping to develop a more contextual, communitarian legal order. As Riskin (1982, p. 58) argues, "mediation highlights the inter-connectedness of human beings."

These cultural trends suggest to us that the direction of convergence between legal systems may well find American law becoming more similar to Japanese, rather than the reverse. However, issues dealt with so far are primarily trends in legal culture. Pressures from legal scholars, like pressures from litigants, are unlikely in and of themselves to work fundamental changes in either legal structure or legal culture. As our findings in part II indicate, a more powerful source of change is a shift in the distribution of types of relationships in society. We next consider this alternative.

The Structural Push for Change

One of our central findings is a greater willingness on the part of both Japanese and Americans to engage in legal disputes with strangers and to impose sanctions against them that do not involve reintegration. In the Japanese case this is especially worth emphasizing, as it seems to contradict an otherwise smooth rule of harmony. The finding is not isolated, however. Kawashima (1963, p. 45) noted that when group interests were not at stake, as in disputes between a "usurer and his debtor," litigation is much more common. Miyazawa (1987, p. 228) presents data from a survey in Kyoto indicating that respondents are more willing to consider court action in disputes with strangers (e.g., the seller of a defective new television, the builder of a new house) than in disputes with acquaintances (e.g., a child who injures one's own child, a next-door neighbor). This is especially true when the actual or potential damage is major. Using Japanese insurance company data, Ramseyer and Nakazato (1989, p. 273) find that in the extreme case of wrongful death caused by an automobile accident, the heirs of the victim almost always assert their legal claim against the person who caused the accident.

Changes in characteristic social relationships could change the picture—either in the direction of more individualistic legal solutions in Japan or in the direction of more communitarian solutions in the United States. Were Japanese relationships, especially neighborhood and employment relationships, to become less solidary and more contractual, a drift toward a more individualistic legal culture and toward a legal system more supportive of litigation might well emerge over time.

Some have in fact argued that the type of community organization captured by the idea of *ie*, the traditional family unit, is in decline. For example, R. J. Smith (1978) reports that the number and richness of links between households in a rural community generally declined over a period of twenty-five years. Fukutake (1974) argues: "The era when the members of a village, regardless of occupation, formed a single community and cooperated in all aspects of life, when the village itself controlled and regulated its inhabitants—that era is a thing of the past" (p. 57).

Similar decline is reported in urban areas as well. The traditional Japanese word for the urban community is *kyoodootai*. Fukutake (1982) argues that at least in some urban neighborhoods this type of organization has disintegrated as town dwellers become renters who are mobile. Moreover, these individuals are beyond the control of "men of influence." In place of traditional hierarchical structure, new residents may form estate self-governing associations:

> The disappearance of these communitarian pressures and the undemocratic constraints they implied has meant at the same time that residents become more egotistic in their behavior and less willing to join together in cooperative activity. That is why for the last ten years one has heard people talking of the need to create not *kyoodootai*—the Japanese word that we have translated here as "community"—but *komyuniti*. . . . In modern Japan . . . after the weakening of the solidarity bonds of the old undemocratic community, the feeling that it is necessary to find new ways of evoking a sense of citizen solidarity and cooperation, is expressed by using the borrowed foreign word. The demand for a new *komyuniti* shows just how far the decline of community has gone in Japan's towns and villages. (Fukutake, 1982, p. 137)

New words often mean new social forms, and community in its Western sense—a community of greater individual autonomy and perhaps greater equality—is apparently a growing social form in Japanese neighborhoods.

At the same time, the disintegration of community in Japanese urban areas should not be overstated. Many urban neighborhoods maintain a level of autonomy and sense of identity built around *chokai* or neighborhood organizations. The *chokai* in the Miyamoto-cho neighborhood at Tokyo studied by Bestor (1989) is involved in local crime and fire prevention, disaster preparedness, traffic safety, recycling, distribution of community news on bulletin boards and circulating message boards, promotion of local businesses, social welfare programs such as mutual aid and assistance to the elderly, and organization of recreational activities such as outings and numerous special events—a summer folk-dance festival (*Bon Odori*), a New Year's party, a cherry-blossom-viewing party (*o-hanami*), and the autumn festival (*aki-matsuri*).

In some ways the *chokai* resembles a local chamber of commerce. Much of its leadership and organization is controlled by local business people. But its role in the community and its role in maintaining community are greater than this comparison suggests. At least in theory, every household in Miyamoto-cho is a member of the *chokai*, paying nominal monthly dues of two hundred yen. Most households participate at some level and are involved in the complex hierarchy of the *chokai*.[11] The consequence is that "like hundreds of similar neighborhoods, Miyamoto-cho contains complex configurations of ties and institutions that bind neighbors to one another. . . . The juxtaposition of these tangible social relations with the sense of identity and distinctiveness engendered through these ties and activities (and particularly through events like the *matsuri*) gives life and resiliency to Miyamoto-cho not as a unit of the government's creation or as some primordial 'natural community' somehow isolated from the currents of urban social life around it, but as a response by local residents to the conditions of contemporary urban life as they find it" (Bestor, 1989, pp. 267–268). Even with increased urbanization, many Japanese communities continue to embed their residents in a set of relationships that are both more hierarchical and more enduring than those of their American counterparts. This joint pattern of hierarchy and solidarity is to be found in the community, in the workplace, and in the family. If such relationships continue to dominate Japanese social structure, we should expect relatively little change in Japanese legal culture or in the legal system it helps to maintain.

The distinction between *kyoodootai* and *komyuniti* alerts us to the fact that the greater sense of community sometimes called for in America usually bears little resemblance to the traditional Japanese form: few calls for greater community in America have a vertical as well as a horizontal component (Sandel, 1982, pp. 147–154). Nevertheless, the United States may have begun to move in some small ways toward more solidary and less contractual relationships in vertical as well as horizontal relationships. For example, the decline of primary and secondary industry and the rise of service employment may have altered the nature of interactions in the workplace, both horizontally and vertically. There have also been conscious efforts to change the organization and structure of operations in American enterprises to more nearly conform to Japanese models.[12] Perhaps these changes will nudge the United States toward a less adversarial legal system.

Conclusions

We have argued that legal culture is not solely a microprocess that determines the resolution of a particular dispute; it also influences law at a macroprocess level, constraining possible legal systems as well as specific legal outcomes. The interaction of macrostructure and macroculture creates and maintains legal systems that are more stable than would be expected by looking at either culture or structure alone. This interaction has implications for the possibility of convergence between legal systems. However, neither the Japanese nor the American legal system is so fragile that some type of legal convergence is inevitable.

Although our findings suggest a more important role for legal culture than it has often been given in earlier analyses, ultimately they point to the centrality of social structure in shaping a legal system. If legal change does occur, it will most likely grow out of structural changes in the underlying balance of relationships between people and, over time, changes in a society's cultural conception of what it is to be a responsible actor.

11 The Problem of Justice

Sometimes we do justice to strangers; other times we make justice with friends. This investigation of responsibility and punishment has revealed two images of the responsible actor and hence two faces of everyday justice. In one image, the offender is conceptualized as a stranger, or at best an acquaintance, separate from and equal to the victim. This generates a relatively formal and impersonal justice, with lawyers as its midwives, governed by a set of pervasive, abstract rules appropriate for all occasions. Nothing is beyond the reach of the abstract rule of law. The consequence of a determination of responsibility tends to include the isolation of the offender, whether this determination is official or informal in nature. In another image of the responsible actor, the offender is conceptualized as a loved one or friend: a known entity. In such cases the contributions of offender and victim to the outcome are often intimately known, the impact of the background or context is carefully weighed, and the goal is to reunify or restore bonds between the parties. Disputes tend to be kept beyond the reach of formal adjudicative processes. The consequence of a determination that this actor is responsible tends to include efforts to restore the broken or damaged relationships.

At the microlevel, this book has traced these alternative conceptions of responsibility and justice to the everyday social ties between the parties. At the macrolevel, patterns of judgment of each type have been traced to the distribution of social ties within such larger units as countries. In the case of the United States and Japan, the data suggest that the first pattern, which we will refer to as justice toward strangers, more closely characterizes American responses to wrongdoing; the second pattern, which we will refer to as justice among friends, more closely characterizes Japanese responses. It is obvious, however, that Americans understand and use justice toward friends and intimates, just as Japanese understand and use justice toward strangers. They simply differ, on average, in the extent to which they use one or the other.

Each vision of justice—justice directed at strangers and justice among friends—has limitations. The limitations on doing justice are the focus of this chapter. Like the conceptions of the responsible actor and associated forms of justice, they flow from the nature of social ties: from the hierarchy and solidarity people experience in their dealings with others.

This book has argued that visions of responsibility and justice are shaped by, and in some ways reproduce, variations in the hierarchy and solidarity of everyday social life. Hierarchy and solidarity are logically independent dimensions, such that it is possible to imagine and to find examples of all of their possible configurations. But in the United States and Japan these dimensions have tended toward one of two particular configurations: equality and low solidarity, or authority-subordination and high solidarity. Conceptions of the responsible actor and of justice in the United States are relatively more consistent with relationships of equality and low solidarity, whereas these conceptions in Japan are more consistent with relationships involving hierarchy and high solidarity. Our discussion of the pitfalls of the alternative conceptions of responsibility and justice thus uses American examples for problems of equality and low solidarity and Japanese examples for problems of hierarchy and high solidarity. We also address the macrolevel of general tendencies and general patterns of relationships within the nation rather than the microlevel of specific encounters in everyday life. Theoretically, the problems to be outlined are general limitations on justice—not just in these countries but wherever relationships of the types to be discussed may be found, and at both macro- and microlevels.

Problems of Isolated Equals

Isolation

In terms of the two dimensions of social relationships, it is clear that formal law in the West tends to view disputants as if their relationship were one of equality plus low solidarity, and formal law tends to color—to invade—the premises of everyday life. One clear danger in this is its usual coupling with a vision of the responsible actor as the locus of wrongdoing. The responsible actor in the United States tends to be seen as an (equal) entity acting against a pale background of social forces and obligations.

Many situations arise in which the assumptions of individual control and individual responsibility are incomplete or simply incorrect. Indeed, our legal system recognizes some of these situations by honoring such pleas as the insanity defense. From the point of view of social relationships, perhaps the most interesting case is that of juveniles, whose very existence as a social category implies both their lack of control as independent entities and their reliance on—embeddedness in—the web of social relations in the family. As chapter 7 mentioned, a "family model" of justice in juvenile cases involves treating juveniles in the sort of contextualized way that characterizes justice among friends.

The image of an individual responsible actor, properly punished by isolation, is perhaps most incorrect and most harmful when it is first applied: to youth. The common-sense awareness that this must be true helped form the rationale for the American juvenile court movement at the beginning of this century (Platt, 1969). The new court was idealized as a place of procedural informality pursuing the twin goals of treatment and rehabilitation (Mack, 1909). The American legal system has had a difficult time maintaining this model of justice (Griffiths, 1970).

A series of Supreme Court decisions in the 1960s, in particular *In re Gault*, introduced due process and formalism into the juvenile court and moved it away from the family model captured in the phrase *parens patriae* (the state as parent). Perhaps the key component of the due process revolution in the juvenile court was the creation of a right to counsel. This right responded to a basic problem with pre-*Gault* courts, especially those in large metropolitan areas. The family model was an ideal whose realization had not been attained. No one in the court truly stood in a familial relationship with the children that appeared before it. The court, despite the trappings, was not in a solidary relationship with the child (Lempert & Sanders, 1986). More due process and more formalism appeared to be an appropriate response to this fact. It seemed especially appropriate to provide the juvenile with someone that would represent his or her interests: a lawyer.

As in many legal reforms, the results of the turn toward due process in juvenile cases have been mixed. The percentage of cases in which juveniles are represented varies substantially from jurisdiction to jurisdiction (Sutton, 1988). In Minnesota, for instance, Feld (1984) found some counties where 90 percent of the juveniles were represented and others where only 10 percent were. If one purpose of *Gault* and related cases was to cause the juvenile court to decide cases more as if they were criminal cases, there has been some success. Apparently seriousness of offense and past record are the two most important determinants of sentencing practices (Clarke & Koch, 1980; Fagan, Slaughter, & Hartstone, 1987). However, there is one rather stunning result of this due-process revolution: Children who are represented by counsel are more likely to be found delinquent and more likely to receive harsher sentences than children who are not represented. This result has emerged across a number of studies (Clarke & Koch, 1980; Feld, 1988,

1989). Representation—more due process—leads to harsher results. At least one investigator has responded to this finding by suggesting that the solution is to compel all youths to be represented, or at least to force them to waive their right after consultation with and in the presence of counsel (Feld, 1989, pp. 1325–1328). In this view, the solution to due-process shortcomings is more due process. One is reminded of Grant Gilmore's (1977) comments: "In Heaven there will be no law, and the lion will lie down with the lamb. The values of an unjust society will reflect themselves in an unjust law. The worse the society, the more law there will be. In Hell there will be nothing but law, and due process will be meticulously observed" (p. 111).

The example of the American juvenile court thus exposes one of the problems of justice among strangers. When some of those strangers could be, perhaps should be, treated more in line with the different set of rules applied in family justice, the legal system proves to be unable to resolve the inherent conflicts involved. This inability is not solely a function of problems and contradictions in solidarity, however. It is also related to failure of the legal presumption of equality. Juvenile cases are but one example of this problem.

A Questionable Equality

In addition to its fictitious solidarity, the juvenile court is one of many American legal situations in which the parties are unequal. In the juvenile court an important type of inequality is reflected in judgments of who is believed. A juvenile's accusers—police, teachers, neighbors, sometimes even parents—tend to be believed; children, especially children in trouble, are not (Emerson, 1969). It can also be argued, of course, that the very fact that the accused is a juvenile makes some asymmetry of power inevitable.

Inequality comes in many forms. For example, inequalities of wealth, race, gender, and age play a role in the operation of law. In a sense they distort the legal process from its fictional starting point of equal parties before the law. Here we concentrate on money—economic inequality—and its role in both civil and criminal proceedings.

CIVIL CASES. Inequalities are clearly evident in civil cases. Although devices such as the contingent fee permit poor plaintiffs to pursue causes of action they would otherwise be unable to afford, inequalities disadvantage one party or the other in a number of ways. Most important, perhaps, is the set of advantages that "repeat players," those who repeatedly litigate the same type of case, have over "one-shotters," those who litigate but once (Galanter, 1974). This situation describes many tort suits, landlord-tenant conflicts, and consumer cases where an aggrieved plaintiff confronts a business or insurance company defendant. The defendant is a repeat player; the plaintiff is not. Among the advantages of repeat players are the obvious considerations that they may have better and more experienced counsel. In addition, repeat players enjoy a number of less obvious advantages. They can average gains and losses across a number of cases and are therefore less averse to risk. Moreover, they may sometimes pursue a given case that on its own terms ought to be settled in order to play for a favorable appellate decision that will be of use in future cases.

CRIMINAL CASES. Criminal law is perhaps an even more appropriate example of the impact of economic inequalities on justice because the stakes are so high. The criminal law's fundamental assumption is that all are equally able to obey its precepts. Due-process solutions to economic inequality—the indigent defendant—include right to counsel and other procedural safeguards. These solutions, however, do not pretend to deal with the fact that inequalities of wealth and opportunity help to *generate* criminal behavior in the first place.

Among Western societies the United States has both a high degree of income inequality and a high crime rate. Many would argue that this convergence is no accident (Braithwaite, 1979, 1989; Currie, 1985). Indeed, even within the United States, cities that have a wide income gap between poor and average families have higher crime rates for all types of crime; this difference holds true when the racial composition of the city is taken into account (Braithwaite, 1979, pp. 216–217). It is not race but the lack of money in the face of plenty that is criminogenic. In this regard it seems no accident that Japan, where the crime rate is low, has a less unequal income distribution—one that is similar to such European welfare states as the Netherlands, Sweden, or Norway (Currie, 1985).

Severe income inequality is not merely a vertical slice through society; it often has implications for the horizontal bonds of a community. Currie (1985) argues that a low crime rate is related to "a strong and encompassing community life that offers meaningful work and family roles in the midst of material deprivation. In such a case, even the very poor may have meaningful occupations, as well as close, supportive relations with their families, religious associations, and other local institutions. These relationships provide not only material assistance but also a less tangible but no less important sense of social purpose, cooperation, and mutual responsibility" (pp. 174–175). Currie adds: "It follows that if we wish to mount an effective attack on criminal violence, we cannot be satisfied with simply doling out funds, grudgingly and after the fact, to people who have been stripped of livelihoods and social networks by the dynamics of the private labor market" (p. 178). If a frequent concomitant of inequality is the erosion of community, and if these factors together generate crime, the solution to high crime rates may not lie in more law and more due process. Law is neither the cause nor the cure of such a combination.

In sum, to the extent that a buildup of economic inequalities implies the destruction of solidarity, a society may be left with a kind of worst-case combination. To the extent that equality fosters the preservation of individual rights and solidarity fosters the maintenance of the social fabric, both individual rights and the social fabric may be threatened by inequality.

Summary

In both criminal and civil cases the assumption of equality is frequently violated not by the hierarchies of authority and subordination studied in this research, but by naked differences in the power to be heard, to command resources, and to control one's own fate. This imbalance of power affects the fairness of formal procedures. Even more fundamental, a body of law premised on an *assumption* of equality coupled with a situation that violates this assumption systematically disadvantages some citizens. These include people who are already disadvantaged in status (e.g., juveniles), legal experience (e.g., one-shotters), or income (Calabresi, 1985; Sanders, 1987).

Problems of Solidarity and Hierarchy

"In a highly developed information society and a highly educated society such as Japan, the people require politics that bravely faces problems. In the United States, because there are a considerable number of blacks, Puerto Ricans, and Mexicans, the [intellectual] level is lower" (Chira, 1986). These remarks, made in 1986 by then-prime minister Nakasone of Japan and widely reported by the Japanese and American press, shocked some Americans. Yet this viewpoint about ethnic heterogeneity is not an aberration among Japanese. It is a concomitant of the solidarity and contextualism that lie at the core of justice among friends in the Japanese context. It is part of a more general phenomenon in which "we" are separate from and tend to be superior to "they," thus linking solidarity to the creation of hierarchies between insiders and outsiders. This phenomenon is not unique to Japan, as the American experience with race relations over the centuries indicates.

This discussion of problems in solidarity and hierarchy begins by addressing the general social scientific issue—the fact that solidarity *within* a group seems to imply solidarity *against* some outside or outsiders.

The Problem of Solidarity

Solidarity has boundaries. In part these are group boundaries defined in terms of nation, race, and various forms of respectability. What difference does it make if a person is in "my group" as opposed to "the other group"? Social psychologists have explored this question in laboratory experiments, deliberately creating groups that have rather little basis for existence and then determining whether members behave so as to favor other members of their "minimal groups." A series of experiments by Henri Tajfel and colleagues illustrates the basic finding that people indeed discriminate in favor of members of their own group when allocating resources (Tajfel, 1978, 1981, 1982).

One key experiment (Billig & Tajfel, 1973) assessed whether people favor members of their own group because they are *alike,* as group members often tend to be, or simply because they *are* fellow group members. Not surprisingly, the combination of group identity and similarity created the largest discrimination. But discrimination on the basis of randomly created group identity was significant and was even more powerful than discrimination on the basis of similarity among individuals. In addition, Tajfel, Flament, Billig, and Bundy (1971) explored the patterns of payment of one's own group versus the other group, finding that it is sometimes even more important that the group do *better* in relative terms than that it do well in absolute terms. Group membership per se breeds favoritism in two forms; it can lead to sanctioning or depriving the outgroup as well as rewarding the ingroup.[1]

Several features of the preceding experiments are noteworthy. First, allocations were made to someone other than the self, so that simple self-reward cannot explain ingroup preferences. Second, the experimental design ruled out any explanations involving *real* differences between groups: Nobody was actually more deserving, more needy, or even more noisy about their rights. Third, in this case the artificiality of the experiment was part of its strength. Any preferences for one's own group in such a context, where the meaning and power of "group" is stripped down to its bare essentials, were all the more impressive.

In general, social psychological research on discrimination suggests that solidarity has a price. It is a price usually paid by someone else: by the outgroup, outsider, or deviant. This means that solidarity serves to generate inequalities between those who stand inside and outside the circle of belonging. Let us now look at who is inside, and who outside, the solidary circle of being Japanese.

Protecting the Circle of Solidarity

For many years after the end of the Vietnam war in 1975, [Japan] all but turned away refugees from that war-ravaged country, saying Japan's homogeneity and crowding made it unsuitable for the Vietnamese. While other nations accepted thousands—or in the U.S. case, hundreds of thousands—Japan initially agreed to accept only 500. . . .

In 1985, the government pledged to accept 10,000 Indochinese refugees for permanent resettlement . . . Japan's four government refugee centers are now packed to overflowing with people. . . .

The surge in boat people has . . . created some anxiety here, with at least one municipality objecting to government plans to locate a new refugee camp near it. . . . The government is poised to toughen its policy toward boat people. (Shapiro, 1989b)

What is perhaps most remarkable about Japan's recent acceptance of Vietnamese refugees is the message it provides about what did *not* happen in previous decades.[2] The Japanese stance toward potential immigrants from Vietnam is representative of a traditional extreme reluctance to accept outsiders as citizens or even as long-term residents.

Consistent with the reluctance to allow outsiders in is a negative attitude toward insiders who go out. In recent years one group that has suffered from this attitude are the children of employees who are sent abroad. When these children accompany their parents abroad, they often experience educational and social difficulties on their return (e.g., White, 1987, 1988). These difficulties increase with the number of years spent in other lands. This discrimination takes a number of forms. Japanese education is felt to be more rigorous than that likely to be found abroad; the Japanese language is felt to be too difficult to learn without immersion in it in the home environment. More subtly, it is felt that training in behaving "like a Japanese" is likely to be deficient except at home. The fact that such offspring may return quite fluent in another language and well versed in a foreign culture counts for little, despite the officially acknowledged need for greater internationalism and for understanding of these cultures.

The traditional Japanese stance toward true outsiders—foreign nations and foreign nationals—is also greatly influenced by the boundary of "Japaneseness." There is a general wariness of mixing, at least at its most intimate levels; children of mixed parentage are sometimes targets for discrimination. Each of these boundaries—against immigrants, against Japanese educated abroad, and against children of mixed parentage—represents Japanese acknowledgment of the degree to which their society's harmony, and perhaps its vision of justice, rests on a bedrock of ethnic and cultural homogeneity. Actions that threaten homogeneity are to be avoided. However, Japanese homogeneity is not complete. We turn next to potential internal threats to homogeneity.

Discrimination within the Circle

Membership in any ingroup, including national identities such as "Japanese," is potent to the extent that a clear line can be drawn between "we" and "they" and to the extent that group boundaries cannot be changed (Tajfel, 1981).[3] Japan's island status, its political and geographic isolation over many centuries, and its overall homogeneity in race, language, and culture combine to make a strong group identity. The potency of this identity can be traced in the array of people and groups living in Japan—even indigenous groups—who are seen as *not* fully belonging to the Japanese people. From an American point of view, one of the most interesting features of the discrimination that occurs is the subtlety of the cues that elicit it. At least four major outgroups, some of whom have been mentioned earlier, are minimally distinguishable or physically indistinguishable from "insider" Japanese.

Ainu are the indigenous residents of Japan who were pushed back and northward onto Hokkaido in past millennia. They are, in effect, Japan's Indians. Ainu physically appear at least somewhat Caucasoid; for example, like Caucasians, they are hairier than other Japanese (Befu, 1971, p. 15).

Burakumin (or *eta*), the outcasts from feudal times, are nearly an untouchable caste. They make up perhaps 1 to 3 percent of the population of modern Japan. As Befu (1971) puts it, "The *eta* of Japan are to the Negro of the United States as the Ainu are to the Indians" (p. 125).[4] Burakumin are relatively poor and poorly educated; they are more likely to be absentees, truants, and dropouts from school than are majority-status Japanese; and they are more often delinquent (De Vos, 1973). Burakumin are of special interest to social scientists because they are physically and culturally indistinguishable from other Japanese. Scholars disagree about the underlying causes of the social position of Burakumin, but they were apparently discriminated against on occupational grounds during the Tokugawa era. For example, they worked with hides and leather, which meant that Buddhists considered them unclean. Burakumin were residentially segregated (the name, literally, means village people). Discrimination against Burakumin has persisted into modern times, most notably in marriage practices; sometimes it involves a diligent search through village records to confirm a suspicion that a person has Burakumin ancestors.

Foreign residents in Japan are subject to a variety of restrictions and discriminatory practices. The largest such group, Koreans, represents less than 1 percent of the population of Japan. Resident Koreans often come from families who have spent generations in Japan but have not attained citizenship. The traditional attitude of Japan toward Korea and its people has been one of superior to inferior, and this is reflected in the modern treatment of resident Koreans. Perhaps in reciprocation, Koreans are overrepresented in the statistics on juvenile delinquency and crime (e.g., De Vos, 1973; Yokoyama, 1980).

Victim groups are also discriminated against. Two such groups have been noteworthy in post–World War II Japan: survivors of the atom bombs dropped on Hiroshima and Nagasaki in 1945, and survivors of severe pollution effects such as Minamata disease. Ordinary Japanese have especially feared marriage to bomb survivors on the grounds that radiation exposure may lead to ill health or to mutant offspring (Lifton, 1967). Regarding pollution victims, a fear of such discrimination in fact contributed to victims' reluctance to sue: "[Minamata victims'] initial reaction was to conceal their own and their family members' afflictions. Japanese society, particularly the small-village society characteristic of the Minamata area, is strongly conformist. To be different is difficult, doubly so when the difference is a physical or mental handicap. Because marriage and employment decisions are based on family background as well as individual attributes, the victims' misfortunes implicated their families as well. Even whole communities feared ostracism should the presence of victims in their midst become known to outsiders" (Upham, 1987, p. 37).

As important as the existence of such groups—the Ainu, the Burakumin, the foreigner, the victim—is their response to their disadvantage. Not surprisingly, responses tend toward avoidance of conflict, but even conflictual solutions tend to be extralegal. The reluctance of some pollution victims to use the legal process is an example of the tendency to avoid conflict. The responses of the Burakumin to discrimination exemplify the tendency to avoid legal solutions. The Burakumin have turned away from lawsuits asserting their rights as a way to improve their situation, opting instead for confrontational tactics against people they perceive to have discriminated against them. In part this is a response to the limitations of the Japanese legal process, but it is also the preference of the Buraku liberation movement (Upham, 1987, p. 117).

Confrontational strategies have several drawbacks as vehicles for social change, as Upham notes. Denunciation as a strategy causes individual disputes to remain focused on the particular facts of the case and a particular remedy to those facts. Public law litigation, by contrast, offers the potential of turning specific "grievances into questions of equality, discrimination and social structure that have universal normative appeal" (Upham, 1987, p. 121). The effect of *Brown v. Board of Education* and succeeding cases on the American civil rights movement and the position of African-Americans is a case in point. A legal culture that causes minority groups to eschew litigation alternatives is one that hinders systematic change to improve their situation. The group that stands outside the solidary circle of insiders may fare best if it turns to formal law, even if that law represents a way of forcing strangers to behave themselves.

We turn next to the related question of what happens to Japanese who are not members of a discriminated-against group but who deviate from the group norm in behavior. To ask such questions addresses the problem of expulsion from a solidary circle: the redrawing of the line between ingroup and outgroup.

Harmony, Deviance, and Conflict

Profound harmony among humans requires prodigious effort. When harmony fails in a tightly knit group, the reverberation can be far more shocking than would be the case among a collection of near-strangers. Japan is a prime example of cultures that stress this value, and many observers claim that harmony (*wa*) is the ultimate value in the Japanese cultural palette. Of the initial 338 basic Chinese characters (*kanji*) that are learned by the Japanese child, the first is the character for "one," which is a single simple line. The 338th, the character for *wa*, is more complex. It is a combination of two other *kanji*, one for rice or grain and one for the mouth: "[Wa] . . . Harmony, peace, Japan, to pacify, calm down, soften. [Wa] is having rice or grain in one's mouth or being fed. The rice or grain is softened in the mouth and pacifies or calms down bringing peace and harmony as in Japan" (Dykstra, 1977, p. 169). The primacy of *wa* as a cultural value is usually traced to Prince Shotoku's Seventeen-Article Constitution, circa 604 c.e. As the first article states, when *wa* is present, "what is there which cannot be accomplished?" (Tsunoda et al., cited in R. J. Smith, 1983, p. 50).

Harmony is not simply a matter of togetherness with others in one's group. Earlier chapters characterized Japanese social structure and culture as exemplifying not just contextualism but stratified contextualism: a combination of high solidarity and fine-tuned hierarchies of authority and subordination. Accordingly, *wa* is not simply a matter of group solidarity and conformity to one's equals but is also a matter of compliance with authorities. To be in harmony is to be in one's proper place, with rice in one's mouth. In addition to learning about *wa,* students of Japan learn a proverb: *Deru kui wa utareru* ("the protruding stake is hammered down"; more colloquially, "the nail that sticks up is hammered down" or "stick out and you'll be slammed down").

The dark side of *wa* is found in the extremes to which social control can go when someone becomes a "protruding stake": not just a metaphorical hammering down but full-scale social ostracism. *Mura hatchibu,* village ostracism, is the traditional solution to an unmanageable deviant. Lebra (1976) reports on one famous instance: "The worst crime of a group member, then, is to expose the group shame. . . . In 1952 . . . a case of political scandal involving a violation of law in a village election was exposed by a high school girl through her letter to a newspaper editor. She and her family became victims of *mura hatchibu,* excluded from social interaction with villagers" (p. 36).

Thus village life—and, in modern times, office life—enforces a conformity that can stand in opposition to the rule of law. Deviance means deviation from what the group wants, not deviation from a legal standard. Of course, resorting to ostracism or expulsion is not unique to Japanese culture or Japanese small groups. In many peasant cultures these are the penalties for serious violations of village norms. Nor is potential opposition between conformity to the group and conformity to the law a Japanese monopoly. In the United States, for example, "whistle blowers" are frequently fired. But requirements of conformity are likely to take on an unusual intensity in cultures like that of Japan precisely because of the pull of harmony within group boundaries.

In short, harmony as a central social goal does not produce a conflict-free society. Although tightly knit groups may be more harmonious under ordinary circumstances, they may also be more susceptible to extreme upheaval and factionalism—redrawing of the boundaries between ingroup and outgroup—when conflicts do arise (e.g., Steinhoff, 1984). In the solidary world of the Japanese family, village, or workplace, the cultural value of harmony can in fact exacerbate sensitivity to conflict: "The more harmony-oriented, the more conflict-sensitive. If the Japanese place more value, as I believe they do, upon social interdependence, cooperation, solidarity, or harmony than, say, the Americans, they are more likely to interfere with one another's actions. The norm of harmony may be precisely what makes people more aware of conflicts with others, conflicts between their self-interest and obligations, and so forth. . . . The cultural value of harmony may intensify, instead of mitigate, conflict" (Lebra, 1984, p. 56).[5] Furthermore, when conflict breaks the informal bonds of harmony, it may be more difficult to contain. The birth of the Narita movement and the continuing conflict over

Narita airport construction (Apter & Sawa, 1984) is one example of this difficulty of containment.

As Hanami (1984) points out regarding Japanese labor relations and the student protests of the 1960s, the generally noncontractual and trust-based nature of Japanese relationships (employer-employee, administration-student) can actually impede conflict resolution once overt conflict boils up:

> Disagreements and grievances are supposed to be solved amicably (*nashi-kuzushi*). Patience and forbearance are at a premium. . . . Should disagreements and grievances eventually be made public, the parties defer to each other and settle matters through "emotional understanding" or by "letting the dispute flow to the water." This uniquely Japanese attitude allows disputes to be settled in a natural way with the passage of time, without introducing positive artificial action by a human agency.
>
> An important drawback to this amicable method of settling disputes is that no rules exist to regulate the conduct of both parties except the concept of amicable mutual understanding. Thus when the mutual trust inherent in this emotional relationship is lost, disputes erupt and become difficult to manage. (p. 116)

Again, this pattern is not unique to Japan. It is a problem in conflict resolution found wherever people are closely tied (e.g., Greenhouse, 1986). Why do disputes escalate so dramatically and live on so stubbornly in such controversies? Part of the reason may lie in the self-limiting nature of what we have called justice among friends. When friends are exhausted and become convinced that they are no longer friends, they may lack ways to resolve the conflict on their own. After all, they were previously determined to "keep the lawyers out of it" (Macaulay, 1963, p. 61). Any web of highly solidary relationships is in that sense a web of friends. In Japan, accordingly, not only are legal processes less available than in the United States, but the legal culture of the society does not look to the courts for an acceptable resolution to conflict. The contrast between the Narita controversy and American experience with nuclear power plants offers an instructive comparison. Much of the American controversy over the construction and location of such plants has taken place within the courts, and court decisions are viewed as a legitimate resolution of these conflicts (Useem & Zald, 1982). Particular decisions may or may not be viewed by the participants as correct or even as fully fair; they may or may not be appealed; yet these decisions are makeable, and they exert decisive influence over the behavior of the parties concerned. Lack of such alternatives—essentially, lack of a "court of last resort"—can contribute to endless controversy.

Summary

Japanese social reality is warm and enveloping for those who fit the definition of insider. For outsiders who are not guests—including longtime residents of Japan such as Koreans and outcasts such as Burakumin—social reality can be cold or even hostile. A gap exists between the social presuppositions of justice among friends and the circumstances of outsiders and deviants. As a consequence, something like justice toward strangers is increasingly in demand, even in Japan. The struggle for rights, as seen in recent decades among pollution victims, Burakumin, and others, is played out in the language of equality and low solidarity—and often, ultimately, in the courts (Upham, 1987). These conflicts can be expected to push Japanese law toward a view of the responsible actor as a distinct, equal entity. Change need not be very great or very quick, however. The continuing prevalence of social relations that are both solidary and hierarchical militates against such change; it fosters an opposite conception of social actors as interconnected, contextual members of hierarchies. Insofar as the existence of insiders and ingroups implies the existence—and denigration—of outsiders and outgroups, at some level there will remain an organic connection between the preservation of justice among friends and the preservation of a closed society.

Conclusions

At least two workable alternative visions of responsibility and justice can be discerned, each originating in the nature and boundaries of everyday social relationships between people. The strengths of one vision are the weaknesses of the other. Justice among strangers is demanded by situations—inevitable in modern life—in which the parties have not built up a relationship, a set of common meanings, a life together. Such instances can be as ordinary as an auto accident, as frightening as a crime, or as uplifting of the human spirit as *Brown v. Board of Education*. The United States, for example, has evolved intricate ways for strangers and groups that do not trust one another to deal with—and, when necessary, sue—one another. These strangers are seen as isolated actors against a faintly perceived social background. Even day-to-day wrongdoing tends to be traced to the actions and the character of isolated individuals. In older and more religious terms, we might say that Americans are willing to see evil in the souls of others. The evildoer who is caught is punished, characteristically, by isolation.

One obvious drawback of such an approach to responsibility is that its punishments may be self-perpetuating. Isolation keeps a stranger a stranger and makes a punished stranger into an enemy. Other drawbacks involve the intrusion of solidarity and the fiction of equality. Solidarity intrudes in the judgment process most notably in such events as the judgment of juveniles. There simply are some social identities and relationships for which we cannot forget the existence and power of social ties; "child" is one such identity. The American justice system has handled—or mishandled—this dilemma by vacillating, most recently in the direction of treating children and juveniles like the other strangers caught in the official web. For juveniles and other groups such as the poor, the justice system also fails in its lack of recognition that formal equality before the law may mask profound inequalities of opportunity or resources.

Justice among friends has different characteristics and different weak points. The scope of the justice that characterizes friendship is obviously limited. Although it is more prevalent among Japanese than among Americans in our research, it is not the sort of justice that even Japanese mete out all the time. There are always strangers in this world. Our data show that Japanese judge strangers much as Americans do, and would punish strangers at least as harshly; Japanese simply seem to deal with fewer strangers in their daily routine. The justice arrived at with friends therefore has a certain fragility, depending as it does on a context of familiar faces.

One way of describing the contextual quality of justice among friends is to invoke the old Buddhist prescript popular in Japan: "See no evil, hear no evil, speak no evil." In this vision of justice there appears to be a general reluctance to "see evil" in the wrongdoer—a readiness to acknowledge social, contextual influences and to pursue reconciliation and redemption. Modern Japan, we have seen, represents a superb example of the management of misdeeds within a circle of belonging. Japan has evolved intricate ways for family, friends, and co-workers who must remain in long-term ties to deal with—and, when necessary, extract apology from—one another. A sense of evil is muted or absent, such that day-to-day misdeeds are seen as the actions of a participant in a complex social network of roles, obligations, stresses, and strains. A major goal of sanction is the restoration of social bonds.

However, to "see no evil"—to find responsibility in the situation as well as in the individual, and to strive to bring the individual back into the community—requires knowing what that community is. And knowing who is inside the circle of belonging leads to discrimination against those outside that circle or those who deviate from the circle's rules. In Japan we have also seen a fine-tuned awareness of who is and who is not a full-fledged group member in good standing. Furthermore, the very closeness of the circle militates against finding or developing the kinds of conflict resolution tools that may be needed if situations change from closeness to conflict. In this respect, the informal dispute resolutions that characterize justice among friends are self-limiting.

These limitations of each approach to the judgment of wrongdoing indicate that there is no single correct way to decide about responsibility, no single correct image of the responsible actor, no single correct way to punish. Granted, in many day-to-day settings, we believe that the contextual viewpoint of justice among friends is to be preferred. It creates a self-perpetuating positive feedback loop: apology begets cordiality. In contrast, isolation and retribution beget resentment. But where outsiders are involved or where rights must be demanded, the justice that is meted out among strangers may be both necessary and preferred. We have suggested that the weaknesses of the justice meted out among strangers tend to lie in the ambiguities surrounding equality and in the absence or loss of solidarity. The social "ties that bind" are tied too loosely. Conversely, the weaknesses of justice among friends lie in the potential absence of equality and in the exclusionary consequences of an overpowering solidarity. The ties that bind are tied too tightly.

Each form of justice is admirable in its way. Each has corresponding weaknesses. And each vision of justice exists within and is constrained by a larger social context. The challenge for the future is to draw on the strengths of these admittedly flawed but complementary visions to shape a more adequate and humane response to human frailty.

Appendix A

Summary of the Story Versions

All versions of the stories are reproduced here. A summary of how the versions were coded into the manipulations (intent, consequence, etc.) is presented after the story versions.

Core (Everyday-Life) Stories

Family/Equal Story

1

Ten-year-old Billy and his twin brother were playing baseball with their friend. The brother was at bat when their friend said, "Your turn's over. It's Billy's turn." Billy, a boy who seldom got into fights, grabbed hold of the bat and the brothers began fighting. Billy accidentally hit his brother with the bat. His brother was knocked down and got a large bump on the head.

2

Ten-year-old Billy and his twin brother were playing baseball with their friend. The brother was at bat when their friend said, "Your turn's over. It's Billy's turn." Billy, a boy who seldom got into fights, grabbed hold of the bat and the brothers began fighting. Billy accidentally hit his brother with the bat. His brother was knocked down and had to be taken to the hospital with head injuries.

3

Ten-year-old Billy and his twin brother were playing baseball with their friend. The brother was at bat when Billy said, "Your turn's over. It's my turn." Then Billy, a boy who seldom got into fights, grabbed hold of the bat and the brothers began fighting. Billy accidentally hit his brother with the bat. His brother was knocked down and got a large lump on the head.

4

Ten-year-old Billy and his twin brother were playing baseball with their friend. The brother was at bat when Billy said, "Your turn's over. It's my turn." Then Billy, a boy who seldom got into fights, grabbed hold of the bat and the brothers began fighting. Billy accidentally hit his brother with the bat. His brother was knocked down and had to be taken to the hospital with head injuries.

5

Ten-year-old Billy and his twin brother were playing baseball with their friend. The brother was at bat when their friend said, "Your turn's over. It's Billy's turn." Billy, a boy who often got into fights, grabbed hold of the bat and the brothers began fighting. Billy accidentally hit his brother with the bat. His brother was knocked down and got a large bump on the head.

6

Ten-year-old Billy and his twin brother were playing baseball with their friend. The brother was at bat when their friend said, "Your turn's over. It's Billy's turn." Billy, a boy who often got into fights, grabbed hold of the bat and the brothers began fighting. Billy accidentally hit his brother with the bat. His brother was knocked down and had to be taken to the hospital with head injuries.

7

Ten-year-old Billy and his twin brother were playing baseball with their friend. The brother was at bat when Billy said, "Your turn's over. It's my turn." Then Billy, a boy who often got into fights, grabbed hold of the bat and the brothers began fighting. Billy accidentally hit his brother with the bat. His brother was knocked down and got a large bump on the head.

8

Ten-year-old Billy and his twin brother were playing baseball with their friend. The brother was at bat when Billy said, "Your turn's over. It's my turn." Then Billy, a boy who often got into fights, grabbed hold of the bat and the brothers began fighting. Billy accidentally hit his brother with the bat. His brother was knocked down and had to be taken to the hospital with head injuries.

9

Ten-year-old Billy and his twin brother were playing baseball with their friend. The brother was at bat when their friend said, "Your turn's over. It's Billy's turn." Billy, a boy who seldom got into fights, grabbed hold of the bat and the brothers began fighting. Billy got angry and hit his brother with the bat. His brother was knocked down and got a large bump on the head.

10

Ten-year-old Billy and his twin brother were playing baseball with their friend. The brother was at bat when their friend said, "Your turn's over. It's Billy's turn." Billy, a boy who seldom got into fights, grabbed hold of the bat and the brothers began fighting. Billy got angry and hit his brother with the bat. His brother was knocked down and had to be taken to the hospital with head injuries.

11

Ten-year-old Billy and his twin brother were playing baseball with their friend. The brother was at bat when Billy said, "Your turn's over. It's my turn." Then Billy, a boy who seldom got into fights, grabbed hold of the bat and the brothers began fighting. Billy got angry and hit his brother with the bat. His brother was knocked down and got a large bump on the head.

12

Ten-year-old Billy and his twin brother were playing baseball with their friend. The brother was at bat when Billy said, "Your turn's over. It's my turn." Then Billy, a boy who seldom got into fights, grabbed hold of the bat and the brothers began fighting. Billy got angry and hit his brother with the bat. His brother was knocked down and had to be taken to the hospital with head injuries.

13

Ten-year-old Billy and his twin brother were playing baseball with their friend. The brother was at bat when their friend said, "Your turn's over. It's Billy's turn." Billy, a boy who often got into fights, grabbed hold of the bat and the brothers began fighting. Billy got angry and hit his brother with the bat. His brother was knocked down and got a large bump on the head.

14

Ten-year-old Billy and his twin brother were playing baseball with their friend. The brother was at bat when their friend said, "Your turn's over. It's Billy's turn." Billy, a boy who often got into fights, grabbed hold of the bat and the brothers began fighting. Billy got angry and hit his brother with the bat. His brother was knocked down and had to be taken to the hospital with head injuries.

15

Ten-year-old Billy and his twin brother were playing baseball with their friend. The brother was at bat when Billy said, "Your turn's over. It's my turn." Then Billy, a boy who often got into fights, grabbed hold of the bat and the brothers began fighting. Billy got angry and hit his brother with the bat. His brother was knocked down and got a large bump on the head.

16

Ten-year-old Billy and his twin brother were playing baseball with their friend. The brother was at bat when Billy said, "Your turn's over. It's my turn." Then Billy, a boy who often got into fights, grabbed hold of the bat and the brothers began fighting. Billy got angry and hit his brother with the bat. His brother was knocked down and had to be taken to the hospital with head injuries.

Work/Equal Story

1

A customer went to a used-car lot to buy a car and found one that he liked. Dave, the salesman, thought the car had not been checked over. Dave had been honest with his customers in the past, and he did not think it was a good idea to sell the car without checking it. Another salesman took Dave aside and talked him into selling the car to the customer. The following week, the customer discovered that the car needed fifty dollars' worth of repairs.

2

A customer went to a used-car lot to buy a car and found one that he liked. Dave, the salesman, thought the car had not been checked over. Dave had been honest with his customers in the past, and he did not think it was a good idea to sell the car without checking it. Another salesman took Dave aside and talked him into selling the car to the customer. The following week, the customer discovered that the car needed five hundred dollars' worth of repairs.

3

A customer went to a used-car lot to buy a car and found one that he liked. Dave, the salesman, thought the car had not been checked over. Dave had been honest with his customers in the past, but he thought it would be all right to sell the car without checking it. The following week, the customer discovered that the car needed fifty dollars' worth of repairs.

4

A customer went to a used car lot to buy a car and found one that he liked. Dave, the salesman, thought the car had not been checked over. Dave had been honest with his customers in the past, but he thought it would be all right to sell the car without checking it. The following week, the customer discovered that the car needed five hundred dollars' worth of repairs.

5

A customer went to a used-car lot to buy a car and found one that he liked. Dave, the salesman, thought the car had not been checked over. Dave had sometimes been dishonest with his customers in the past, but he did not think it was a good idea to sell the car without checking it. Another salesman took Dave aside and talked him into selling the car to the customer. The following week, the customer discovered that the car needed fifty dollars' worth of repairs.

6

A customer went to a used car lot to buy a car and found one that he liked. Dave, the salesman, thought the car had not been checked over. Dave had sometimes been dishonest with his customers in the past, but he did not think it was a good idea to sell the car without checking it. Another salesman took Dave aside and talked him into selling the car to the customer. The following week, the customer discovered the car needed five hundred dollars' worth of repairs.

7

A customer went to a used-car lot to buy a car and found one that he liked. Dave, the salesman, thought the car had not been checked over. Dave had sometimes been dishonest with his customers in the past, and he thought it would be all right to sell the car without checking it. The following week, the customer discovered that the car needed fifty dollars' worth of repairs.

8

A customer went to a used-car lot to buy a car and found one that he liked. Dave, the salesman, thought the car had not been checked over. Dave had sometimes been dishonest with his customers in the past, and he thought it would be all right to sell the car without checking it. The following week, the customer discovered that the car needed five hundred dollars' worth of repairs.

9

A customer went to a used-car lot to buy a car and found one that he liked. Dave, the salesman, knew the car had a hidden defect. Dave had been honest with his customers in the past, and he was unwilling to sell the defective car. Another salesman took Dave aside and talked him into selling the car to the customer. The following week, the customer discovered that the car needed fifty dollars' worth of repairs.

10

A customer went to a used-car lot to buy a car and found one that he liked. Dave, the salesman, knew the car had a hidden defect. Dave had been honest with his customers in the past, and he was unwilling to sell the defective car. Another salesman took Dave aside and talked him into selling the car to the customer. The following week, the customer discovered that the car needed five hundred dollars' worth of repairs.

11

A customer went to a used-car lot to buy a car and found one that he liked. Dave, the salesman, knew the car had a hidden defect. Dave had been honest with his customers in the past, but he decided to sell the defective car. The following week, the customer discovered that the car needed fifty dollars' worth of repairs.

12

A customer went to a used-car lot to buy a car and found one that he liked. Dave, the salesman, knew the car had a hidden defect. Dave had been honest with his customers in the past, but he decided to sell the defective car. The following week, the customer discovered that the car needed five hundred dollars' worth of repairs.

13

A customer went to a used-car lot to buy a car and found one that he liked. Dave, the salesman, knew the car had a hidden defect. Dave had sometimes been dishonest with his customers in the past, but he was unwilling to sell the defective car. Another salesman took Dave aside and talked him into selling the car to the customer. The following week, the customer discovered that the car needed fifty dollars' worth of repairs.

14

A customer went to a used-car lot to buy a car and found one that he liked. Dave, the salesman, knew the car had a hidden defect. Dave had sometimes been dishonest with his customers in the past, but he was unwilling to sell the defective car. Another salesman took Dave aside and talked him into selling the car to the customer. The following week, the customer discovered that the car needed five hundred dollars' worth of repairs.

15

A customer went to a used-car lot to buy a car and found one that he liked. Dave, the salesman, knew the car had a hidden defect. Dave had sometimes been dishonest with his customers in the past, and he decided to sell the defective car. The following week, the customer discovered that the car needed fifty dollars' worth of repairs.

16

A customer went to a used-car lot to buy a car and found one that he liked. Dave, the salesman, knew the car had a hidden defect. Dave had sometimes been dishonest with his customers in the past, and he decided to sell the defective car. The following week, the customer discovered that the car needed five hundred dollars' worth of repairs.

Family/Authority Story

1

One evening, Ricky, a four-year-old, threw a tantrum when told it was time to go to bed. Ricky's father became upset and ordered Ricky's mother to go make Ricky behave. His mother often lost her temper when Ricky misbehaved. This night she picked him up, he struggled, and she shoved him into a chair. He struck his head on the back of the chair and had to be taken to the hospital with head injuries.

2

One evening Ricky, a four-year-old, threw a tantrum when told it was time to go to bed. Ricky's father became upset and ordered Ricky's mother to go make Ricky behave. His mother often lost her temper when Ricky misbehaved. This night she picked him up, he struggled, and she shoved him into a chair. He twisted his leg as he fell and had to be taken to the hospital with what turned out to be a sprained ankle.

3

One evening Ricky, a four-year-old, threw a tantrum when told it was time to go to bed. His mother often lost her temper when Ricky misbehaved. This night she picked him up, he struggled, and she shoved him into a chair. He struck his head on the back of the chair and had to be taken to the hospital with head injuries.

4

One evening Ricky, a four-year-old, threw a tantrum when told it was time to go to bed. His mother often lost her temper when Ricky misbehaved. This night she picked him up, he struggled, and she shoved him into a chair. He twisted his leg as he fell and had to be taken to the hospital with what turned out to be a sprained ankle.

5
One evening Ricky, a four-year-old, threw a tantrum when told it was time to go to bed. Ricky's father became upset and ordered Ricky's mother to go make Ricky behave. His mother rarely lost her temper when Ricky misbehaved. This night she picked him up, he struggled, and she shoved him into a chair. He struck his head on the back of the chair and had to be taken to the hospital with head injuries.

6
One evening Ricky, a four-year-old, threw a tantrum when told it was time to go to bed. Ricky's father became upset and ordered Ricky's mother to go make Ricky behave. His mother rarely lost her temper when Ricky misbehaved. This night she picked him up, he struggled, and she shoved him into a chair. He twisted his leg as he fell and had to be taken to the hospital with what turned out to be a sprained ankle.

7
One evening Ricky, a four-year-old, threw a tantrum when told it was time to go to bed. His mother rarely lost her temper when Ricky misbehaved. This night she picked him up, he struggled, and she shoved him into a chair. He struck his head on the back of the chair and had to be taken to the hospital with head injuries.

8
One evening Ricky, a four-year-old, threw a tantrum when told it was time to go to bed. His mother rarely lost her temper when Ricky misbehaved. This night she picked him up, he struggled, and she shoved him into a chair. He twisted his leg as he fell and had to be taken to the hospital with what turned out to be a sprained ankle.

9
One evening Ricky, a four-year-old, threw a tantrum when told it was time to go to bed. Ricky's father became upset and ordered Ricky's mother to go make Ricky behave. His mother often lost her temper when Ricky misbehaved. This night she picked him up, he struggled, and slipped from her hands. He hit his head on the floor and had to be taken to the hospital with head injuries.

10
One evening Ricky, a four-year-old, threw a tantrum when told it was time to go to bed. Ricky's father became upset and ordered Ricky's mother to go make Ricky behave. His mother often lost her temper when Ricky misbehaved. This night she picked him up, he struggled, and slipped from her hands. He twisted his leg as he fell and had to be taken to the hospital with what turned out to be a sprained ankle.

11

One evening Ricky, a four-year-old, threw a tantrum when told it was time to go to bed. His mother often lost her temper when Ricky misbehaved. This night she picked him up, he struggled, and slipped from her hands. He hit his head on the floor and had to be taken to the hospital with head injuries.

12

One evening Ricky, a four-year-old, threw a tantrum when told it was time to go to bed. His mother often lost her temper when Ricky misbehaved. This night she picked him up, he struggled, and slipped from her hands. He twisted his leg as he fell and had to be taken to the hospital with what turned out to be a sprained ankle.

13

One evening Ricky, a four-year-old, threw a tantrum when told it was time to go to bed. Ricky's father became upset and ordered Ricky's mother to go make Ricky behave. His mother rarely lost her temper when Ricky misbehaved. This night she picked him up, he struggled, and slipped from her hands. He hit his head on the floor and had to be taken to the hospital with head injuries.

14

One evening Ricky, a four-year-old, threw a tantrum when told it was time to go to bed. Ricky's father became upset and ordered Ricky's mother to go make Ricky behave. His mother rarely lost her temper when Ricky misbehaved. This night she picked him up, he struggled, and slipped from her hands. He twisted his leg as he fell and had to be taken to the hospital with what turned out to be a sprained ankle.

15

One evening Ricky, a four-year-old, threw a tantrum when told it was time to go to bed. His mother rarely lost her temper when Ricky misbehaved. This night she picked him up, he struggled, and slipped from her hands. He hit his head on the floor and had to be taken to the hospital with head injuries.

16

One evening Ricky, a four-year-old, threw a tantrum when told it was time to go to bed. His mother rarely lost her temper when Ricky misbehaved. This night she picked him up, he struggled, and slipped from her hands. He twisted his leg as he fell and had to be taken to the hospital with what turned out to be a sprained ankle.

Work/Authority Story

1

Joe is the foreman on a factory assembly line. The line was stopped for repairs during the week. Since the company was trying to fill a big order, this day Joe's boss told him not to let the line stop. Joe had always been careful about safety procedures before, but during the day he was very busy keeping the line running. He did not notice that the safety guard on one of the machines had not been attached properly. Just before quitting time a worker caught his hand in the machine and lost two fingers.

2

Joe is the foreman on a factory assembly line. The line was stopped for repairs during the week. Since the company was trying to fill a big order, this day Joe's boss told him not to let the line stop. During the day Joe noticed that the safety guard on one of the machines had not been attached properly. Joe had always been careful about safety procedures before, but he decided to do nothing until that day's run was finished. Just before quitting time a worker caught his hand in the machine and lost two fingers.

3

Joe is the foreman on a factory assembly line. The line was stopped for repairs during the week. Since the company was trying to fill a big order, this day Joe's boss told him not to let the line stop. Joe had sometimes been careless about safety procedures before, and during the day he was very busy keeping the line running. He did not notice that the safety guard on one of the machines had not been attached properly. Just before quitting time a worker caught his hand in the machine and lost two fingers.

4

Joe is the foreman on a factory assembly line. The line was stopped for repairs during the week. Since the company was trying to fill a big order, this day Joe's boss told him not to let the line stop. During the day Joe noticed that the safety guard on one of the machines had not been attached properly. Joe had sometimes been careless about safety procedures before, and he decided to do nothing until that day's run was finished. Just before quitting time a worker caught his hand in the machine and lost two fingers.

5

Joe is the foreman on a factory assembly line. The line was stopped for repairs during the week. Since the company was trying to fill a big order, this day Joe decided not to let the line stop. Joe had always been careful about safety procedures before, but during the day he was very busy keeping the line running. He did not notice that the safety guard on one of the machines had not been attached properly. Just before quitting time a worker caught his hand in the machine and lost two fingers.

6

Joe is the foreman on a factory assembly line. The line was stopped for repairs during the week. Since the company was trying to fill a big order, this day Joe decided not to let the line stop. During the day Joe noticed that the safety guard on one of the machines had not been attached properly. Joe had always been careful about safety procedures before, but he decided to do nothing until that day's run was finished. Just before quitting time a worker caught his hand in the machine and lost two fingers.

7

Joe is the foreman on a factory assembly line. The line was stopped for repairs during the week. Since the company was trying to fill a big order, this day Joe decided not to let the line stop. Joe had sometimes been careless about safety procedures before, and during the day he was very busy keeping the line running. He did not notice that the safety guard on one of the machines had not been attached properly. Just before quitting time a worker caught his hand in the machine and lost two fingers.

8

Joe is the foreman on a factory assembly line. The line was stopped for repairs during the week. Since the company was trying to fill a big order, this day Joe decided not to let the line stop. During the day Joe noticed that the safety guard on one of the machines had not been attached properly. Joe had sometimes been careless about safety procedures before, and he decided to do nothing until that day's run was finished. Just before quitting time a worker caught his hand in the machine and lost two fingers.

9

Joe is the foreman on a factory assembly line. The line was stopped for repairs during the week. Since the company was trying to fill a big order, this day Joe's boss told him not to let the line stop. Joe had always been careful about safety procedures before, but during the day he was very busy keeping the line running. He did not notice that the safety guard on one of the machines had not been attached properly. Just before quitting time a worker caught his hand in the machine and suffered bad bruises.

10

Joe is the foreman on a factory assembly line. The line was stopped for repairs during the week. Since the company was trying to fill a big order, this day Joe's boss told him not to let the line stop. During the day Joe noticed that the safety guard on one of the machines had not been attached properly. Joe had always been careful about safety procedures before, but he decided to do nothing until that day's run was finished. Just before quitting time a worker caught his hand in the machine and suffered bad bruises.

11

Joe is the foreman on a factory assembly line. The line was stopped for repairs during the week. Since the company was trying to fill a big order, this day Joe's boss told him not to let the line stop. Joe had sometimes been careless about safety procedures before, and during the day he was very busy keeping the line running. He did not notice that the safety guard on one of the machines had not been attached properly. Just before quitting time a worker caught his hand in the machine and suffered bad bruises.

12

Joe is the foreman on a factory assembly line. The line was stopped for repairs during the week. Since the company was trying to fill a big order, this day Joe's boss told him not to let the line stop. During the day Joe noticed that the safety guard on one of the machines had not been attached properly. Joe had sometimes been careless about safety procedures before, and he decided to do nothing until that day's run was finished. Just before quitting time a worker caught his hand in the machine and suffered bad bruises.

13

Joe is the foreman on a factory assembly line. The line was stopped for repairs during the week. Since the company was trying to fill a big order, this day Joe decided not to let the line stop. Joe had always been careful about safety procedures before, but during the day he was very busy keeping the line running. He did not notice that the safety guard on one of the machines had not been attached properly. Just before quitting time a worker caught his hand in the machine and suffered bad bruises.

14

Joe is the foreman on a factory assembly line. The line was stopped for repairs during the week. Since the company was trying to fill a big order, this day Joe decided not to let the line stop. During the day Joe noticed that the safety guard on one of the machines had not been attached properly. Joe had always been careful about safety procedures before, but he decided to do nothing until that day's run was finished. Just before quitting time a worker caught his hand in the machine and suffered bad bruises.

15

Joe is the foreman on a factory assembly line. The line was stopped for repairs during the week. Since the company was trying to fill a big order, this day Joe decided not to let the line stop. Joe had sometimes been careless about safety procedures before, and during the day he was very busy keeping the line running. He did not notice that the safety guard on one of the machines had not been attached properly. Just before quitting time a worker caught his hand in the machine and suffered bad bruises.

16

Joe is the foreman on a factory assembly line. The line was stopped for repairs during the week. Since the company was trying to fill a big order, this day Joe decided not to let the line stop. During the day Joe noticed that the safety guard on one of the machines had not been attached properly. Joe had sometimes been careless about safety procedures before, and he decided to do nothing until that day's run was finished. Just before quitting time a worker caught his hand in the machine and suffered bad bruises.

Stories Involving Strangers

Child Accident Story

1

A man was driving down a narrow one-way street when a child about eight years old stepped out from between two parked cars. The man's car hit the child. The child received only a few bruises from the accident. Witnesses stated that the man was driving below the speed limit. This was the man's first accident in his twelve years of driving.

2

A man was driving down a narrow one-way street when a child about eight years old stepped out from between two parked cars. The man's car hit the child. The child received only a few bruises from the accident. Witnesses stated that the man was driving below the speed limit. This was the man's fourth accident in his twelve years of driving.

3

A man was driving down a narrow one-way street when a child about eight years old stepped out from between two parked cars. The man's car hit the child. The child received only a few bruises from the accident. Witnesses stated that the man was driving above the speed limit. This was the man's first accident in his twelve years of driving.

4

A man was driving down a narrow one-way street when a child about eight years old stepped out from between two parked cars. The man's car hit the child. The child received only a few bruises from the accident. Witnesses stated that the man was driving above the speed limit. This was the man's fourth accident in his twelve years of driving.

5

A man was driving down a narrow one-way street when a child about eight years old stepped out from between two parked cars. The man's car hit the child. The child received several broken bones from the accident. Witnesses stated that the man was driving below the speed limit. This was the man's first accident in his twelve years of driving.

6

A man was driving down a narrow one-way street when a child about eight years old stepped out from between two parked cars. The man's car hit the child. The child received several broken bones from the accident. Witnesses stated that the man was driving below the speed limit. This was the man's fourth accident in his twelve years of driving.

7

A man was driving down a narrow one-way street when a child about eight years old stepped out from between two parked cars. The man's car hit the child. The child received several broken bones from the accident. Witnesses stated that the man was driving above the speed limit. This was the man's first accident in his twelve years of driving.

8

A man was driving down a narrow one-way street when a child about eight years old stepped out from between two parked cars. The man's car hit the child. The child received several broken bones from the accident. Witnesses stated that the man was driving above the speed limit. This was the man's fourth accident in his twelve years of driving.

Adult Accident Story

1

A housewife who was walking across the street at a stop sign was hit by a car and received a broken leg. The driver of the car was a clerk at the university who was going out for lunch. The driver failed to see the stop sign at the intersection and hit the woman.

2

A housewife who was walking across the street at a stop sign was hit by a car and received a broken leg. The driver of the car was a clerk at the university who was going out for lunch. The driver saw the woman crossing the street, but his brakes failed and he could not stop in time.

3

A housewife who was walking across the street at a stop sign was hit by a car and received a broken leg. The driver of the car was a professor at the university who was going out for lunch. The driver failed to see the stop sign at the intersection and hit the woman.

4

A housewife who was walking across the street at a stop sign was hit by a car and received a broken leg. The driver of the car was a professor at the university who was going out for lunch. The driver saw the woman crossing the street, but his brakes failed and he could not stop in time.

5

A housewife who was walking across the street at a stop sign was hit by a car and killed. The driver of the car was a clerk at the university who was going out for lunch. The driver failed to see the stop sign at the intersection and hit the woman.

6

A housewife who was walking across the street at a stop sign was hit by a car and killed. The driver of the car was a clerk at the university who was going out for lunch. The driver saw the woman crossing the street, but his brakes failed and he could not stop in time.

7

A housewife who was walking across the street at a stop sign was hit by a car and killed. The driver of the car was a professor at the university who was going out for lunch. The driver failed to see the stop sign at the intersection and hit the woman.

8

A housewife who was walking across the street at a stop sign was hit by a car and killed. The driver of the car was a professor at the university who was going out for lunch. The driver saw the woman crossing the street, but his brakes failed and he could not stop in time.

Robbery Story

1

Thomas Wilson was robbing a store, and as he was leaving with the money, he shot and killed the store owner. Thomas had no prior criminal record.

2

Thomas Wilson was robbing a store, and as he was leaving with the money, he shot and wounded the store owner. Thomas had no prior criminal record.

3

Thomas Wilson was robbing a store, and as he was leaving with the money, he shot and killed the store owner. Thomas had been in jail before for assault with a deadly weapon.

4

Thomas Wilson was robbing a store, and as he was leaving with the money, he shot and wounded the store owner. Thomas had been in jail before for assault with a deadly weapon.

5

Thomas Wilson was robbing a store, and as he was leaving with the money, the store owner tried to overpower him and take the gun. There was a brief struggle, and the gun accidentally fired. The store owner was killed. Thomas had no prior criminal record.

6

Thomas Wilson was robbing a store, and as he was leaving with the money, the store owner tried to overpower him and take the gun. There was a brief struggle, and the gun accidentally fired. The store owner was killed. Thomas had no prior criminal record.

7

Thomas Wilson was robbing a store, and as he was leaving with the money, the store owner tried to overpower him and take the gun. There was a brief struggle, and the gun accidentally fired. The store owner was killed. Thomas had been in jail before for assault with a deadly weapon.

8

Thomas Wilson was robbing a store, and as he was leaving with the money, the store owner tried to overpower him and take the gun. There was a brief struggle, and the gun accidentally fired. The store owner was wounded. Thomas had been in jail before for assault with a deadly weapon.

Coding of Versions into Variables

Family/Equal Story

Mental State	Low	= versions 1–8
	High	= 9–16
Consequences	Low	= 1, 3, 5, 7, 9, 11, 13, 15
	High	= 2, 4, 6, 8, 10, 12, 14, 16
Past Pattern	Absent	= 1–4, 9–12
	Present	= 5–8, 13–16
Other's Influence	Absent	= 3, 4, 7, 8, 11, 12, 15, 16
	Present	= 1, 2, 5, 6, 9, 10, 13, 14

Work/Equal Story

Mental State	Low	= 1–8
	High	= 9–16
Consequences	Low	= 1, 3, 5, 7, 9, 11, 13, 15
	High	= 2, 4, 6, 8, 10, 12, 14, 16
Past Pattern	Absent	= 1–4, 9–12
	Present	= 5–8, 13–16

Other's Influence   Absent = 3, 4, 7, 8, 11, 12, 15, 16
                        Present = 1, 2, 5, 6, 9, 10, 13, 14

Family/Authority Story

Mental State   Low   = 9–16
                       High   = 1–8
Consequences   Low   = 2, 4, 6, 8, 10, 12, 14, 16
                       High   = 1, 3, 5, 7, 9, 11, 13, 15
Past Pattern   Absent = 5–8, 13–16
                       Present = 1–4, 9–12
Other's Influence Absent = 3, 4, 7, 8, 11, 12, 15, 16
                       Present = 1, 2, 5, 6, 9, 10, 13, 14

Work/Authority Story

Mental State   Low   = 1, 3, 5, 7, 9, 11, 13, 15
                       High   = 2, 4, 6, 8, 10, 12, 14, 16
Consequences   Low   = 9–16
                       High   = 1–8
Past Pattern   Absent = 1, 2, 5, 6, 9, 10, 13, 14
                       Present = 3, 4, 7, 8, 11, 12, 15, 16
Other's Influence Absent = 5–8, 13–16
                       Present = 1–4, 9–12

Child Accident Story

Mental State   Low   = 1, 2, 5, 6
                       High   = 3, 4, 7, 8
Consequences   Low   = 1–4
                       High   = 5–8
Past Pattern   Absent = 1, 3, 5, 7
                       Present = 2, 4, 6, 8

Adult Accident Story

Mental State   Low   = 2, 4, 6, 8
                       High   = 1, 3, 5, 7
Consequences   Low   = 1–4
                       High   = 5–8
Actor Status   Low   = 1, 2, 5, 6
                       High   = 3, 4, 7, 8

Robbery Story

Mental State	Low	= 5–8
	High	= 1–4
Consequences	Low	= 2, 4, 6, 8
	High	= 1, 3, 5, 7
Past Pattern	Absent	= 1, 2, 5, 6
	Present	= 3, 4, 7, 8

Appendix B

Punishment Questions

As noted in the text, across vignettes and across surveys we asked a slightly varying combination of closed- and open-ended punishment questions. In all stories an initial question asked respondents whether anything should happen to the perpetrator. Its wording varied somewhat by context. The item referred to a prison term in the criminal case, to punishment for the offending child in the family/equal case, and to whether something should "be done to" or "happen to" the actor in the other vignettes. In Japanese, where the passive voice is an odd construction, an active form was used instead. Questions therefore asked whether anyone should "do something to" or "punish" the offending party in places where the American version asked if something "should be done to" the offender or the offender "should be punished."

The respondents who answered "yes" to this first question were asked a follow-up question, usually open-ended, about what specifically should happen to the offender. Exceptions to this format included the work/equal story about the salesman and the street crime story. The Detroit and Yokohama salesman vignettes used Detroit pretest data to form closed-ended choices among steps the owner should take against the salesman. The Japanese researchers altered Kanazawa's work/equal items to follow the open-ended form of the other vignettes. In the text (chapter 7) we examine the effects of closed- versus open-ended format on punishment responses for this story. In the crime vignette, once incarceration had been indicated as appropriate, the issue became length of sentence. This was essentially a "guided open" item.

In the Detroit survey's high-solidarity (family) stories, the follow-up question asked, "What should the punishment be?" Yokohama's family vignettes had the same wording as Detroit's, although our collaborators advised against this literal translation because they felt that in Japanese the word *punishment* (*batsu*) is legalistic, hence odd to use for sanctions within the family. In the Kanazawa survey they did change the question to "what should happen to" the perpetrator, which was the wording used in the work stories in both countries. Analyses are performed on respondents' first answers to this open-ended query.

Empirically based codes for the open-ended Detroit and Yokohama responses were initially developed separately by each research team. Coding of the Yokohama data was carried out by a bilingual Japanese graduate student at the

University of Michigan under our direction, using the Japanese categories, because the Japanese researchers were unable to complete this task. Later the Japanese researchers produced a more general seventeen-category scale of sanctions for the Kanazawa data. But the number of categories was unwieldy, and some categories were rarely or never used or applied to only one setting. For the final set of codes presented here, we collapsed the seventeen abstract codes from the Kanazawa coding scheme into a more manageable number and superimposed them on the Detroit and Yokohama codes. In nearly every case there was a Kanazawa counterpart for Detroit and Yokohama codes.

In only one situation was an appropriate Kanazawa category lacking. The Detroit data originally contained infrequently used codes for certain combination answers. For example, Detroiters occasionally recommended such actions as "paddle his behind and send him to his room" for the family/equal boy's punishment. We constructed a code that paired two responses (spanking and deprivation of privilege) for such answers rather than making assumptions about conceptual priority among punishments when the order might be simply temporal. There were no comparable Kanazawa codes. American combination responses were combined into the category "other."

In contrast, Japanese categories that involved variations of restoration had no American counterparts. In only one Detroit story was there a coding category for restoration; unlike the other empirically derived categories, it was included on the basis of our a priori expectations, and the category proved to be empty. A coding memo used by the American and Japanese investigators that presents the final coding categories for the open-ended punishment questions follows.

Open-ended Codes for Detroit, Kanazawa, and Yokohama Studies

For each vignette, original codes that were applied in each separate survey are presented first, followed by the variables that were created for use in data analyses of that vignette across cities. Recodes were necessary for a number of reasons. A large number of original categories (especially in Kanazawa) did not have any corresponding answers. Original categories were not always comparable across cities, and even when the same categories were present, they were not always in the same order. The recoded variables have the same categories, in the same order, in each city where a question was asked.

All categories refer to the *first response* to open-ended queries except where noted.

Work/Equal (Salesman) Story

What do you think the owner of the used car lot should do to Dave?

Detroit Codes	Kanazawa Codes*	Yokohama Codes
1 = do nothing	1 = ABSTAN	1 = do nothing
2 = lower pay	2 = VERBAL	2 = lower pay
3 = fire	3 = INFPRE	3 = fire

4 = other
5 = reprimand[a]
6 = depends on information[a]
    not in story
8 = DK
9 = NA

4 = INFCOR
5 = DOCUMT
6 = SFINC
7 = SFPUNL
8 = SFPUNH
9 = FINC
10 = FPUNL
11 = FPUNH
12 = APOLGY
13 = COMPEN
14 = ALSANC
15 = OTHERS
17 = ABSPUN
88 = UNSUIT

4 = other
8 = DK, NA

[a]These Detroit codes were made up after examining the responses originally categorized as "other" (4). The remaining category 4 consists of all answers that could not be categorized anywhere else (including in 5 and 6).

*Kanazawa abbreviations (computer file labels for the following categories of response): ABSTAN = abstract, general apology; VERBAL = reprimand, scolding; INFPRE = informal punishment, deprive of privilege; INFCOR = informal punishment, corporal (spanking); DOCUMT = written apology; SFINC = semi-formal punishment, financial (includes lower pay); SFPUNL = semi-formal punishment, light (includes demotion); SFPUNH = semi-formal punishment, heavy (includes firing); FINC = formal incapacitation (includes loss of license or certificate); FPUNL = formal punishment, light (includes fines); FPUNH = formal punishment, heavy (includes jail terms); APOLGY = repayment (apology); COMPEN = formal restitution (compensation); ALSANC = abstract (nonspecific) legal sanctions; OTHERS = other (uncodable) responses; ABSPUN = unspecified abstract punishment; UNSUIT = not applicable

Work/Equal (Salesman) Story

What should the customer do?
(Asked in Detroit and Yokohama)

Detroit Codes	Yokohama Codes
1 = have used car lot fix car	1 = get compensation or repair
2 = get money back	2 = report to company what salesman did
3 = take consumer action	
4 = inform car company about what salesman did	3 = take consumer action
	4 = take civil action (sue)
5 = sue the used car lot	5 = other
7 = other	9 = DK, NA
8 = DK	
9 = NA	
0 = INAP	

Combined Codes Used in Detroit-Yokohama-Kanazawa Large File Analyses

We adopted the same approach used for the Kanazawa original codes. The same code numbers apply across all stories. As was true in Kanazawa, some categories apply only to particular stories. For example, "deprive of privilege" and "spank" apply only to family/equal, and "demote" or "fire" apply only to the work stories.

Work/Equal Story

What should the owner do to Dave?

(Category 1, "do nothing," in original Detroit and Yokohama codes was treated as if it were the answer to the question, "Should anything happen to Dave?" and all other categories were treated as if they were responses to the follow-up, "What should happen to Dave?" This makes the data structure of Dave the same across cities and the same as the other core vignettes.

1 = restoration

> (Detroit original codes lacked this category)
> (Kanazawa original categories 1, 5, 12, 13)
> (Yokohama original codes lacked this category)

2 = reprimand

> (Detroit category 5)
> (Kanazawa category 2)
> (Yokohama codes lacked this category)

3 = deprive of privilege

> empty category in all cities

4 = spank

> empty category in all cities

5 = demote, lower pay

> (Detroit category 2)
> (Kanazawa categories 6 and 7)
> (Yokohama category 2)

6 = fire

> (Detroit category 3)
> (Kanazawa categories 8 and 9)
> (Yokohama category 3)

7 = other

> (Detroit categories 4 and 6)
> (Kanazawa categories 14, 15, 17, 88)
> (Yokohama category 4)

What should the customer do? (Detroit and Yokohama data)

1 = restoration

> (Detroit categories 1 and 2)

(Yokohama category 1)
2 = consumer action
    (Detroit category 3)
    (Yokohama category 3)
3 = report to company
    (Detroit category 4)
    (Yokohama category 2)
4 = take legal action
    (Detroit category 5)
    (Yokohama category 4)
7 = other
    (Detroit category 7)
    (Yokohama category 5)

Family/Equal (Twins) Story

Detroit Codes	Kanazawa Codes	Yokohama Codes
1 = not pay any attention to Billy	1 = ABSTAN	1 = scold
2 = scold or tell child to behave	2 = VERBAL	2 = reason, warning
	3 = INFPRE	3 = deprive privilege
	4 = INFCOR	4 = spank or other physical punish-ment
3 = take away privilege	5 = DOCUMT	
	6 = SFINC	
4 = spank or other physical punishment	7 = SFPUNL	5 = apology, restitution
	8 = SFPUNH	6 = other
	9 = FINC	9 = DK, NA
5 = reason with child	10 = FPUNL	
6 = make child apologize	11 = FPUNH	
	12 = APOLGY	
7 = depends on circumstances	13 = COMPEN	
	14 = ALSANC	
8 = multiple mention of 3 and 4	15 = OTHERS	
	17 = ABSPUN	
96 = other single mention	88 = UNSUIT	
97 = other multiple mention		
98 = DK		
99 = NA		
00 = INAP		

Combined Codes Used in Detroit-Yokohama-Kanazawa Large File Analyses

Family/Equal (Twins) Story

Note that in Detroit and Yokohama these answers came in response to the question, "What should the punishment be?" In Kanazawa, the wording was changed to "What should happen [to Yasuhiko]?" This means that the Kanazawa question is now parallel to those for other vignettes but differs from its counterparts for this particular vignette.

1 = restoration
  (Detroit original category 6)
  (Kanazawa original categories 1, 5, 12, 13)
  (Yokohama original category 5)
2 = reprimand
  (Detroit categories 2 and 5)
  (Kanazawa category 2)
  (Yokohama categories 1 and 2)
3 = deprive of privilege
  Category 3 in all three cities
4 = spank
  Category 4 in all three cities
5 = demote, lower pay
  empty category in all cities
6 = fire
  empty category in all cities
7 = other
  (Detroit categories 7, 8, 96, and 97)
  (Kanazawa categories 14, 15, 17, 88)
  (Yokohama category 6)

Family/Authority (Mother) Story

Detroit Codes	Kanazawa Codes	Yokohama Codes
1 = counseling, reprimand	1 = ABSTAN	1 = counseling, reprimand
2 = nothing	2 = VERBAL	2 = compensation,
7 = other	3 = INFPRE	apology
8 = DK	4 = INFCOR	3 = treat child better
9 = NA	5 = DOCUMT	4 = other
0 = INAP	6 = SFINC	9 = DK, NA
	7 = SFPUNL	

$$8 = \text{SFPUNH}$$
$$9 = \text{FINC}$$
$$10 = \text{FPUNL}$$
$$11 = \text{FPUNH}$$
$$12 = \text{APOLGY}$$
$$13 = \text{COMPEN}$$
$$14 = \text{ALSANC}$$
$$15 = \text{OTHERS}$$
$$17 = \text{ABSPUN}$$
$$88 = \text{UNSUIT}$$

Combined Codes Used in Detroit-Yokohama-Kanazawa Large File Analyses

Family/Authority (Mother) Story

Note that in Yokohama, the Japanese translation of "What should happen to Ricky's mother" resulted in a wording that was ambiguous regarding whether something was being done to her or she was doing something. This was changed in Kanazawa so that the question is basically the same as Detroit's.

1 = restoration
    (Detroit original codes lacked this category)
    (Kanazawa original categories 1, 5, 12, 13)
    (Yokohama original categories 2 and 3)
2 = reprimand (includes counseling)
    (Detroit category 1)
    (Kanazawa category 2)
    (Yokohama category 1)
3 = deprive of privilege
    empty category in all cities
4 = spank
    empty category in all cities
5 = demote, lower pay
    empty category in all cities
6 = fire
    empty category in all cities
7 = other
    (Detroit category 7)
    (Kanazawa categories 14, 15, 17, 88)
    (Yokohama category 4)

Note that respondents who were originally coded under category 2 in Detroit ("nothing") were treated as if they had answered "no" to the preceding question ("Should anything happen to Ricky's mother for what she did?")

Work/Authority (Foreman) Story

Detroit Codes	Kanazawa Codes	Yokohama Codes
1 = do nothing	1 = ABSTAN	1 = warning, repri-
2 = lower pay	2 = VERBAL	mand
3 = fire	3 = INFPRE	2 = lower pay
4 = demote	4 = INFCOR	3 = demote
5 = verbal reprimand	5 = DOCUMT	4 = fire
6 = depends on information	6 = SFINC	5 = compensation,
7 = multiple mention	7 = SFPUNL	apology, take
97 = other	8 = SFPUNH	responsibility
98 = DK	9 = FINC	6 = other
99 = NA	10 = FPUNL	9 = DK, NA
	11 = FPUNH	
	12 = APOLGY	
	13 = COMPEN	
	14 = ALSANC	
	15 = OTHERS	
	17 = ABSPUN	
	88 = UNSUIT	

Combined Codes Used in Detroit-Yokohama-Kanazawa Large File Analyses

Work/Authority (Foreman) Story

1 = restoration
(Detroit original codes lacked this category)
(Kanazawa original categories 1, 5, 12, 13)
(Yokohama original category 5)
2 = reprimand
(Detroit category 5)
(Kanazawa category 2)
(Yokohama category 1)
3 = deprive of privilege
empty category in all cities
4 = spank
empty category in all cities
5 = demote, lower pay
(Detroit categories 2 and 4)
(Kanazawa categories 6 and 7)

(Yokohama categories 2 and 3)
6 = fire
(Detroit category 3)
(Kanazawa categories 8 and 9)
(Yokohama category 4)
7 = other
(Detroit categories 6, 7, and 97)
(Kanazawa categories 14, 15, 17, 88)
(Yokohama category 6)

Stories Involving Strangers*

Auto Accident (Child Victim)

(Vignette presented only in Detroit and Yokohama)

Detroit Codes	Yokohama Codes
1 = take license away	1 = take license away
2 = fine	2 = take driver's education
3 = jail term	3 = pay medical fees
4 = pay medical expenses	4 = let him apologize
5 = tried, prosecuted, taken to court, probation	5 = take victim to hospital
6 = take driver's education	6 = take responsibility
7 = other	7 = legal punishment
8 = DK	8 = other
9 = NA	9 = DK, NA
0 = INAP	

*Auto accidents only; coding of punishment for crime story (robbery) is explained in text of chapter 8

Auto Accident (Adult Victim)

(Vignette presented only in Detroit and Yokohama)

Detroit Codes	Yokohama Codes
1 = take license away	1 = take license away
2 = fine	2 = take driver's education
3 = jail term	3 = pay medical fees
4 = pay medical expenses	4 = let him apologize
5 = tried, prosecuted, taken to court, probation	5 = take victim to hospital
6 = take driver's education	6 = take responsibility
7 = other	7 = legal punishment

8 = DK	8 = other
9 = NA	9 = DK, NA
0 = INAP	

Combined Codes Used in Detroit-Yokohama Large File Analyses

Both Auto Accident Stories

1 = restoration
    (Detroit original category 4)
    (Yokohama original categories 3, 4, 5, and 6)
2 = require driver's education
    (Detroit category 6)
    (Yokohama category 2)
3 = lose license
    (Detroit category 1)
    (Yokohama category 1)
4 = legal sanction
    (Detroit categories 2, 3, and 5)
    (Yokohama category 7)
5 = other
    (Detroit category 7)
    (Yokohama category 8)

Notes

Chapter 1: The Problem of Responsibility

1. Munch and Smelser (1987) list the following definitions of *micro* and *macro*: Micro as dealing with individuals and macro as dealing with populations; micro as the focus on small social units and macro on large social units; micro as individual interactions with limited scope and macro with societal scope (e.g., value-systems); micro as interaction (encounters and exchanges) and macro as repeated experiences of large numbers of persons in time and space; micro as psychological propositions, on the basis of which statements and laws about larger-scale social processes and structures (macro) are made.

2. The research reported here comes from surveys in three cities: Yokohama, Kanazawa, and Detroit. As noted in the preface, the Japanese research was carried out in collaboration with a team of lawyers and social scientists headed by Dr. Zensuke Ishimura and including (in alphabetical order) Professors Yoko Hosoi and Noburo Matsubara, Dr. Haruo Nishimura, and Professors Kazuhiko Tokoro and Nobuho Tomita. Recently this team published a report of this and related research on responsibility (Ishimura, Tokoro, & Nishimura, 1986).

3. In this regard the beliefs of the Baptists of Hopewell are similar to those of the Amish (Kidder & Hostetler, 1990).

4. Susan Pharr (1990) has recently proposed a similar typology in discussing conflict and conflict resolution in Japanese politics. She proposes one dimension of the *social rank* of protesters relative to authorities, essentially parallel to our dimension of hierarchy. Protesters who in her terms are distant from the authorities in social rank would stand in a relation of subordination; protesters who are similar would stand in a relation of equality (or near equality). Similarly, her second dimension of the *density of social relations* (ranging from low to high) directly parallels our dimension of solidarity of ties.

5. In contrast to our two dimensions of social relations, psychologist Alan Fiske (in press) proposes four qualitatively distinct types, "elementary forms," of social interaction. He calls these forms, ordered from least to most cognitively complex, *communal sharing, authority ranking, equality matching,* and *market pricing.* (Logically, these involve calculations at the nominal, ordinal, interval, and ratio levels, respectively; see Fiske, 1990, in press.) Fiske's scheme is more ambitious than our own, in that he is attempting a general theory of social life; we seek more specifically to enunciate principles of responsibility and justice. However, his model is theoretically more restrictive than our own in two senses. It posits discontinuities and links them to cognitive development, whereas we postulate dimensions and make no claims about cognitive prerequisites. More important, his model does not incorporate interactive combinations of solidarity and hierarchy.

6. For a contemporary discussion of causation in psychology, see Shaver (1985).

7. Adherents of some types of determinism would argue that people can never do otherwise and that focusing on issues of agency and purpose is misguided (Skinner, 1971). Some writers in the area of attribution theory in social psychology have attacked the deterministic position and have argued that psychological theories can and should be based on a free-will model (Shaver, 1985). We do not wish to engage in this debate. It is sufficient to our purpose to show that concepts of agency and purpose help us to understand similarities and differences in the attribution processes in Japan and the United States.

8. One empirical issue that we have investigated before (Sanders & Hamilton, 1987) is not addressed in this book: the question of group cleavages within societies in judging wrongdoing. Our earlier analyses have convinced us that such cleavages are few. For example, in both countries men and women, older and younger, less and more educated, and richer and poorer respondents tended to judge responsibility and punishment in similar ways. There appears to be a sort of "common law" for judging wrongdoing that is remarkably consistent across various demographic groups *within* these countries, even though judgments differ dramatically both between the United States and Japan and between different types of role relationships within these countries.

Chapter 2: Social Structure and Legal Structure

1. Other obligations—*giri*—also held a major place in the value system of Japan during its modernization process, as they do today. But *giri* can be experienced between equals as well as hierarchical unequals.

2. Theoretical and experimental work in game theory supports this argument. It suggests that as future moves, such as decisions whether to cooperate, become more important relative to a current move (measured as the "discount parameter"), the likelihood of cooperation increases (Axelrod, 1984; Scholz, 1984).

3. Hsu (1983) argues that primogeniture was an important difference between otherwise similar Japanese and Chinese social structures. Primogeniture accentuated the hierarchical nature of family life and pushed younger sons out of the kin group and into other groups where they reproduced the family pattern of organization.

4. The interpretation of Japanese firm and family as historically intertwined is also supported linguistically. In modern usage, *uchi* (inside) often refers to one's in-group, including those at one's place of work; its opposite is *soto* (outside), used to refer to those who are excluded or are non-members. *Uchi* originally meant "my home." By contrast, in modern usage *oya* refers to "parent" and *ko* to "child." In the workplace the ubiquitous superior-subordinate relationships of mentoring and obligation are referred to as *oyabun-kobun* (parent role–child role) relations. Americans hearing these terms often conclude that the family analogy has been applied to the firm once more. But linguistically, the reverse is closer to the truth. *Oya* originally referred to the leader of a work group in a Japanese village, and *ko* referred to a follower (Tsurumi, 1979b). Thus "family" language invaded firm in the case of *uchi*, and "firm" language invaded family in the case of *oya-ko*. Each concept evokes one aspect of the close and hierarchical ties that pervade Japanese work life.

5. Friedman (1988) questions the common interpretation of the Japanese "dual labor market" that depicts workers in smaller supplier firms as being inevitably disadvantaged (see Johnson, 1982). Many workers in smaller firms effectively trade job security for a higher possibility of self-employment or managerial promotion. Lifetime earnings are roughly equivalent for employees of large and small firms (Friedman, 1988, p. 140).

6. Of course, not all law is a reinstitutionalization of rules generated in other institutions. Some laws (e.g., tax laws) are, from their inception, generated for governmental purposes. Other rules are put into legal form because institutions know they will be unable to enforce their own rules. Still other rules are designed to govern relationships between institutions.

7. These differences are reflected in the training given lawyers in the two societies. American law students are given what Riskin (1982) calls a standard philosophical map. This map is dominated by "two assumptions about matters that lawyers handle: (1) that disputants are adversaries—i.e., if one wins, the others must lose—and (2) that disputes may be resolved through application, by a third party, of some general rule of law" (p. 45). In Japan, as in most of the world, a law degree is an undergraduate degree. Instruction is conducted not through case analysis but rather through the study of legislative texts. The result is that "in America students become more problem oriented, while in Japan they become more 'theory-consistency' oriented" (M. Kato, 1987, p. 631). To be oriented to the problems of one's client is an important step toward an adversarial structure and ideology.

8. As Danzig and Lowy (1975) note, when avoidance or "lumping it" is the result of the real or perceived costs of disputing, there may be hidden social costs and distributional consequences attached to this way of resolving disputes. More accessible forums for disputing may help people who cannot truly avoid others with whom they are locked into relationships. They may also help the relatively poor members of the community who cannot afford to litigate over relatively small sums. The small-claims court movement in the United States originally was proposed precisely to handle small claims of poor litigants because it was felt that otherwise these people could only "lump it" when injured (Scott, 1923).

Chapter 3: Culture and the Socialization Process

1. For discussions of American individualism see Baruch-Bush, 1986; Bellah, Madsen, Sullivan, Swidler, & Tipton, 1985; Frolock, 1987; F. Johnson, 1985; Lasch, 1979; Macneil, 1985; Presser, 1985; Sandel, 1982. For discussions of Japanese contextualism see Azuma, 1984; Barnlund, 1975; Caudill, 1973; Cousins, 1989; De Vos, 1973, 1985; Doi, 1973, 1986; Hamaguchi, 1985; Kawashima, 1968; Kojima, 1984; Lebra, 1976; Murakami, 1985; Nakamura, 1964; Nakane, 1970; Pascale & Athos, 1981; R. J. Smith, 1983, 1985; Weisz, Rothbaum, & Blackburn, 1984.

Other recent cross-cultural research has used slightly different terminology from our own, arguing that various non-Western cultures tend to be "collectivistic" or "holistic" or even "dividual" as opposed to individualistic. (See, e.g., Bharati, 1985; Dumont, 1970; Hofstede, 1980; Leung & Lind, 1986; Shweder & Bourne, 1982; see also Hui & Triandis, 1986, for a general discussion of the meaning of collectivism.) We adopted the term *contextual* to describe the alternative to individual because the individualism/collectivism distinction embeds Western assumptions about the unit of analysis, to the extent that a collectivity is a collection of individual elements (Hamaguchi, 1985).

Much of the popular and academic writing about individualism in America can be understood as a reaction to the perceived sins of "collectivism" in socialist and communist societies. Collectivism should not be confused with contextualism. In this regard we agree with Dumont (1977) that Marxist economics rests on a conception of actors as individuals, and with Polanyi (1944) that modern socialism evolved from a reaction to the nineteenth century's unbridled market economy. This concept of the collectivity is not the contextualism of Japan nor of the less industrialized world (Dumont, 1970; Hamaguchi, 1985; Hoover, 1922/1979).

2. The patterns described here are *Japanese* patterns and are not necessarily shared throughout the languages of the Asian mainland and island groups. The Japanese language is unusual in the richness of its hierarchical distinctions (Brown, 1965). Contrasting examples include the language of the Ifaluk of Micronesia, discussed above (Lutz, 1985).

3. See, e.g., Harré, 1977; Nakamura, 1964, 1968; Passin, 1980; Suzuki, 1978.

4. In figure 3.1 we focus on typical conceptions of the self. In figure 1.1 we focused on the nature of social relationships. Dominant types of social relationships in a society create typical conceptions of the self.

5. This fluidity across situations is, of course, the theoretical position of many Western social scientists about the nature of *any* self. However, it appears that most citizens in the West do not see one another in so contextual a fashion, but instead overattribute actions, especially the actions of others, to personal stable traits (e.g., Ross, 1977).

6. In addition to references cited below, we are indebted to the following sources: Befu (1971), Hendry (1987), Lebra (1976), and Lebra and Lebra (1974) on early childhood socialization; the 1989 special issue of the *Journal of Japanese Studies* on early childhood, edited by Thomas Rohlen, especially Rohlen's paper on the nature of authority in Japan; Cummings (1980), Rohlen (1983), and White (1987) on Japanese education; Stevenson, Azuma, and Hakuta (1986) on child development and education; and the overview of Japanese education by the Task Force of the U.S. Department of Education (1987).

7. For a review of the literature on Japanese versus American senses of control that adopts this dichotomy between internal and external control, see Weisz et al. (1984). For examples of research challenging this dichotomy, see Ryan and Connell (1989); Hamilton, Blumenfeld, Akoh, and Miura (1989b).

8. Other terms suffer the same fate of untranslatability in the reverse direction. One of us once spent half an hour trying to convey the meaning of *nerd* to a Japanese. This person's English skills were quite good. The cultural category—a word that placed a negative connotation on intelligence and high achievement—was the problem.

9. A recent partial replication of Caudill and Weinstein by Otaki, Durrett, Richards, Nyquist, and Pennebaker (1986) suggests that differences between Japanese and American mothers' handling of infants may be getting smaller. This study of thirty American and fifty-two Japanese mother-infant dyads replicated the Caudill and Weinstein patterns for maternal presence with the child and for active positioning of the baby; however, Japanese mothers did not lull the baby more and the American mothers' tendency to chat with the baby more did not attain significance.

10. High school is exacting intellectually as well. Extensive preparation for national college entrance exams dominates the lives of many high school students. The race to college is a major national preoccupation. A large percentage of students do not only their required homework, but also the work of special after-school "cram schools" known as *juku*. There is a slang term for the period of exams: "examination hell." It is national news when the names of successful applicants to prestigious Tokyo University (Todai) are publicly posted. Students who fail to gain admission to the college of their choice often spend an additional year of study and try again. During that period they are known as *ronin*. In feudal days, *ronin* were samurai who had no master. Access to college education in modern Japan is a sort of morality play that revolves around samurai virtues. (See Thomas Rohlen's 1983 book *Japan's High Schools*.)

11. Relatively less research attention has been paid to socialization in colleges, perhaps because the role of college in Japanese adult socialization is less central than it

is in the United States. As Kitamura (1986, pp. 165–166) notes, the university curriculum is but weakly relevant to "the needs of the business world and the employment practices of Japanese society. . . . employers in Japan usually prefer to recruit 'generalists' rather than narrowly focused 'specialists,' as they themselves provide intensive courses to train employees for their particular needs." As a result, Japanese university life serves as what Kitamura (1986, p. 166) terms a "buffer zone" between the pressures of secondary education and the process of absorption into adult work roles.

12. See Clifford, 1976, for a description of adult corrections and handling of delinquency in Japan.

Chapter 4: Responsibility: A Research Agenda

1. Perhaps because of Heider's acknowledged debt to Piaget, his levels have frequently been interpreted by later researchers as cognitive developmental in nature. The developmental trend that Heider suggested was that children are more likely to attribute more responsibility at lower levels, whereas adults are more likely to require that a perpetrator be intentional before attributing responsibility and are more likely to take justifications and excuses into account. (For recent research on this topic see Fincham, 1983, 1985; Fincham & Jaspars, 1979, 1980; Fishbein & Ajzen, 1973; Hamilton, Blumenfeld, & Kushler, 1988; Harris, 1977; Shaw & Sulzer, 1964; Vidmar & Crinklaw, 1974.) Other research has used Heider's levels to explore such topics as attribution to self versus other (Fincham & Jaspars, 1979); cultural differences in attribution (Garcia-Esteve & Shaw, 1968; Shaw & Iwawaki, 1972); and intelligence (Shaw & Schneider, 1969).

2. It may be relevant that neither the Anglo-American nor the German-Japanese legal tradition regards consequence severity per se as determining responsibility.

3. It is logically possible to envision other combinations. One way of describing the defense of insanity, for example, might be to argue that the person lacked control but had (insane) intent (Lempert & Sanders, 1986). Self-defense as a justification essentially refers to an action that is non-negligent (such that the individual behaved reasonably under the circumstances) yet intentional as to producing harmful consequences. In our society individuals are rarely held criminally responsible for such excused or justified behaviors. This research does not explore any such situations, and thus Heider's categories of Causality, Foreseeability, and Intentionality may be thought of as being on a continuum for our purposes.

4. Logically, there are three possible combinations of harmdoing: authority harming subordinate, equal harming equal, and subordinate harming authority. Our research concerned the first two of these.

5. In the terms of Fuller's (1969) distinction, a morality of aspiration as well as a morality of duty attaches to superiors. A morality of aspiration focuses upon achieving good deeds and striving for good performance, whereas a morality of duty refers to punishments after the fact for failures to meet a "bottom line" of performance. Superiors in hierarchies are held liable for their obligations as well as their actions.

6. In earlier publications we explored other interactions less central to the theoretical argument, such as a three-way interaction of other's influence with solidarity and hierarchy and an interaction of past pattern with nation (Hamilton & Sanders, 1981, 1983). (We expected other's influence to be greatest for the low solidarity–authority story, second greatest for the high solidarity–authority story, and least for the two equal actors; we expected past pattern information to be used more by Americans than by Japanese.) Although results tended in the predicted directions, they failed to reach conventional levels of statistical significance ($p < .05$).

Chapter 5: Methods: Experiments in Surveys

1. In earlier publications, we used an alternative strategy (Hamilton & Sanders, 1981, 1983). This alternative approach uses the full (saturated) model—here, a 2^7 design—but tests it repeatedly by creating a series of randomly generated subsets of the person-story pieces of data. This strategy amounts to creating and testing quasi-independent replications of the design. Repeated testing of subsets of data is conservative in the sense that it does not inflate the number of observations by using multiple observations from each person. This is, however, a relatively trivial gain with datasets as large as these. Repeated testing is less conservative in other respects. The numerous higher-order effects may generate some results that appear to be significant simply on a random basis, and the error term may be a less stable estimate because it is less inclusive. In this case the two methods of dealing with a factorial survey design yielded closely comparable conclusions, and the method we have chosen to highlight in this book is simpler to present.

2. The Detroit Area Study is an annual study of the Detroit Metropolitan Area conducted by faculty and students at the University of Michigan.

3. Robert Groves conducted a comparison of responses given face-to-face and those given over the phone in this and other surveys; he found phone interviews to yield results closely comparable to the traditional face-to-face method (Groves, personal communication, 1977; see also Groves & Kahn, 1979). Here the two forms of interview are combined in analyses.

4. The choice of father to represent influence from the other might be disputed. However, if there is asymmetry between husbands and wives with regard to marital power, dominance is most often found to lie with the husband. Therefore in our view this choice of "other" represented a relatively weak, but still realistic, difference in hierarchy.

5. Certain problems were created by timing constraints; the Yokohama translation into Japanese could not be fully backtranslated and checked by the American investigators until after the survey had gone into the field. Although the Japanese team carried out its own backtranslation operations, a small number of problems were not caught; these are discussed in the text, and the Kanazawa instrument corrects them.

6. As noted in chapter 4, this trichotomy does not exhaust the logical possibilities in the relation of avoidability and purpose. It is possible for a person to do something on purpose but for us to conclude that the person could not have avoided what happened. This category—unavoidable purposive acts—was the smallest category of responses among the four possible combinations of the two questions, purposiveness and avoidability. This was the case in all three cities and for all stories. In most cases the category was small enough that a survey researcher would reasonably conclude that the respondents who gave those answers had misunderstood the question. We therefore dropped this category, restricting the analysis to judgments that an act was accidental, negligent, or intentional.

7. The table excludes the "inconsistent" response that an action, although unavoidable, was also intentional (see note 6). As the Ns indicate, more Japanese respondents made this sort of response, hence more missing data appear in the Yokohama and Kanazawa surveys. These differences are not overwhelming and appear to reflect the cultural nuances of translating and/or understanding avoidability. For example, Japanese who responded that the action in the family/equal story could not be avoided (literally, in Japanese, "helped") but was nonetheless intentional were essentially making a judgment that children can't help themselves or control their impulses given what they may intend.

Chapter 6: Responsibility: The Evidence

1. A difference of such magnitude would occur less than one in ten thousand times by chance. Recall that N in these analyses is the number of persons times the number of vignettes judged. With samples of this size, the substantive conclusions would be the same if the analyses were carried out based on the number of persons. (See note 1, chapter 5.)

2. The metric for this table's information, the unstandardized regression coefficient, was chosen because it can be readily interpreted: The unstandardized coefficient is the amount of difference created in the dependent variable (here, responsibility) if the independent variable is changed by one unit. Therefore purposiveness, which is measured on a 0-to-10 scale, has much smaller unstandardized coefficients than does avoidability, which is an either-or (avoidable–not avoidable) dichotomy.

3. Here and in later figures, the ANOVA described in chapter 5 showed that these slope differences were significant (here, there was a significant interaction of solidarity and mental state).

4. A small interaction of the two role dimensions, the hierarchy and solidarity of relations, and an interaction among hierarchy, solidarity, and city were also observed. These were not significant after we controlled for the perceived state of mind of the actor. This latter result resolves one issue raised in chapter 5 regarding whether the family/equal story stood out statistically from the others. Controlling for the actor's mental state, it did not. Finally, there was also a small three-way interaction of mental state, consequences, and solidarity. With low solidarity, the impact of mental state was greater where consequences were of *low* severity; with high solidarity, the impact of mental state was greater where consequences were of *high* severity ($p = .04$).

5. Analyses also showed that Japanese and American respondents differed in their use of other's influence information in low- versus high-solidarity stories (that is, an interaction of city, other's influence, and solidarity was observed). The effect of other's influence was always larger among Japanese respondents, but the difference between low- and high-solidarity incidents was also greater for Japanese. This result is consistent with the general picture of Japanese sensitivity to this issue. Other's influence matters more overall to Japanese respondents, and they are more sensitive to its nuances.

6. Haidt (personal communication) reports that his follow-up research shows similar trends when a fully between-respondents design is used.

7. Some American decisions have been truly shocking. See, for example, *Yania v. Bigan* (1959), where the plaintiff's husband had been a business visitor on the defendant's land. The defendant enticed the victim to jump into an old coal strip-mining ditch filled with water and let him drown. The court held that there was no duty to rescue.

Chapter 7: Punishment

1. This chapter draws heavily on Hamilton & Sanders (1988).

2. Because Braithwaite (1989) is concerned with criminal activity, his distinction between *reintegrative shaming* and *stigmatizing shaming* concentrates on affective rather than financial aspects of sanction. Our concept of relationship *restoration* incorporates the former and our concept of *isolation* of the offender incorporates the latter. The more emotionally neutral terms "restoration" versus "isolation" better incorporate the array of financial restitution options and other forms of civil and everyday sanction that do not appear to carry strong elements of shame but that nevertheless can be arrayed on a dimension from restoration of the relationship to isolation of the offender.

3. The questions about rationales were relegated to the Detroit mailback because of time constraints. The N for the mailback was 339, or 50 percent of the overall sample. This raises questions of comparability between the Detroit subsample and the Yokohama sample. Comparing Detroit's mailback subsample with the full Detroit sample suggests that sample differences cannot account for the observed results. Detroit respondents who filled out and returned mailback questionnaires were significantly more educated and more likely to be female than the sample as a whole (Adams, 1977). However, more educated and female respondents are, if anything, somewhat less likely to advocate retributive punishment rationales, both within our mailback sample and in other studies (e.g., Vidmar & Ellsworth, 1974). Therefore, if anything, the Detroit mailback's biased sample worked against our hypotheses.

4. Data for the multiple non-independent responses were first analyzed via multiple analysis of variance (MANOVA). The overall difference between Japanese and American respondents was substantial [$F(7,886) = 56.1, p < .0001$], justifying further analysis.

5. We calculated maximum likelihood estimates of each parameter in a logistic regression analysis in which the dependent variable was willingness to punish wrongdoers (where $0 = $ yes, $1 = $ no to the punishment question and in which each independent variable was coded as a dummy variable with $1 = $ high mental state, high consequence, the presence of a past pattern of bad behavior, the presence of influence from another, and Japanese respondents). This model did not include the role variables, solidarity and hierarchy, for two reasons. First, punishment decisions, more than responsibility decisions, are unique to each situation. The decision to punish can be influenced in part by the available repertoire of sanctions. (If the only sanction were the death penalty, for example, fewer people would be punished for robberies.) Second, the repertoire of sanctions varies not only across role relations, but also between nations. Thus each story in each country is in some ways unique with regard to the issue of sanctions, meaning that role effects or role-nation interaction effects can be misleading.

6. In the family/equal story, respondents who preferred that the brother be reprimanded had significantly lower responsibility scores than those who preferred each of the other punishments (deprive of a privilege, spank, other). In the work/authority story, respondents who preferred that the foreman be fired had significantly higher responsibility scores than those who preferred to reprimand or demote the foreman. In the Yokohama work/equal story, respondents who felt that the salesman should be demoted or fired had significantly higher responsibility scores than those who chose the "other" category. For convenience these descriptive statistics were calculated by running a series of one-way ANOVAs where responsibility judgments were predicted by punishment choices.

7. Separate statistical tests were also conducted excluding this category from the analysis. Excluding "other" had only a small effect on the results except for comparisons including the work/equal story in Yokohama; in this case there was no precoded category for relationship restoration, hence more than half of all responses were coded "other." The relative strength of association between pairs of cities remained unchanged, and for every story the Detroit-Kanazawa and Detroit-Yokohama differences were greater than the Kanazawa-Yokohama difference.

8. Unfortunately, we were not able to arrange to have these "other" codes recoded to see what portion are restorative of the relationship.

9. Maximum likelihood estimates were calculated for each parameter in a logistic regression analysis similar to that described in note 5 of this chapter. In the Detroit analysis the dependent variable was type of sanction, where $0 = $ reprimand and $1 = $ all other responses. In Kanazawa and Yokohama the dependent variable was type of

sanction, where 0 = restoration and 1 = all other responses (including reprimand). Each independent variable was coded as a dummy variable with 1 = high mental state, high consequence, presence of a past pattern of bad behavior, and presence of influence from another.

10. The question, introduced by our Japanese colleagues, asked whether the employer should request that the employee resign. This is not identical to a question asking whether the employer should fire the employee. Whether a refusal to acquiesce to a resign request would lead to involuntary discharge cannot be answered in these data.

11. The impact of offender–third party relationships on sanctioning is quite complex. This is especially true when the wrongdoer is of high status. While the "well-connected" offender with many solidary and diffuse ties may be initially well protected or buffered from punishment, an incontrovertible offense may have more deep and longstanding consequences. The literature on white-collar and corporate crime, for example, shows that highly placed executives often are punished lightly or not at all (e.g., Reiman, 1979). On the other hand, the executive who is caught faces an array of informal and extralegal penalties—such as loss of job, reputation, and powerful friends—that may be quite serious and permanent. This study does not directly explore the issues of the extensiveness of actor networks and the implications of third-party ties.

12. This interpretation gains some support from the fact that these questions were virtually the only ones that showed effects of respondents' age. Japanese over age fifty were significantly more likely than those aged twenty to thirty-four or thirty-five to fifty to link the driver's occupational future to his nonwork-related auto accident (voluntary resignation, $\chi^2 = 7.98$, $p = .02$; university request, $\chi^2 = 8.1$, $p = .02$). For a discussion of the role of gender, education, and age differences in these data, see Sanders and Hamilton (1987).

13. See also Mouer and Sugimoto (1986) regarding assumptions of uniqueness among Japanese.

Chapter 8: Is Crime Special?

1. Because our vignette concerns a robbery, in this chapter our discussion is restricted to "street crime." In future research we hope to explore responsibility judgments for other types of crime (Grabosky, Braithwaite, & Wilson, 1987).

2. As Braithwaite (personal communication, 1991) notes, the brevity of our vignettes insures that the crime and accident stories present a decontextualized encounter between strangers. In fact, crimes and torts do have contexts and many times are not encounters between complete strangers. When people are provided with more contextual information about a crime, as is the case with jurors hearing an actual case, they become less punitive (see Roberts & Doob, 1989). If Japanese respondents are more likely to use contextual and role information when it is present, in actual criminal cases differences between the countries in responsibility and punishment decisions may be greater than our vignette data suggest.

3. This is consistent with Braithwaite's (1989) argument that the punishment practice of reintegrative shaming is less possible, and less of a goal, among strangers. These data help to suggest *why* reintegrative shaming tends to be concentrated in circles of prior acquaintance; it is in these circles that a misdeed is more often seen as occurring in a context, against a social background, rather than as a product of the will of an isolated wrongdoer.

4. The harshness of Japanese sanctions in the crime story must be tempered by our findings reported in chapter 7 that the Japanese envision imprisonment to be less

isolative (e.g., Naikan therapy) and less punitive than do Americans. However, Japanese sentences are so lengthy that it is difficult to explain them solely as a product of different perceptions of the purpose and effect of imprisonment.

5. As indicated in chapter 7, our category of restoration subsumes Braithwaite's (1989) concept of reintegrative shaming and our category of isolation subsumes his concept of stigmatizing shaming.

6. Certain Japanese crime control practices such as local foot patrols are obviously transferrable to the American scene. However, this sense—or myth—of community may be impossible to import. For example, virtually all discussions of the American crime rate make some reference to America's great ethnic and racial heterogeneity, substantial economic stratification, or both. Each of these factors can undermine a sense of community, and each contributes to crime (Currie, 1985).

Chapter 9: Empirical Conclusions

1. This effect for authorities required that we control for differences in the perceived mental state of the actor, as described in chapters 5 and 6.

2. In this research, the concept of the responsible actor is an intervening variable or sensitizing concept rather than a directly observable outcome. The ideas that the survey respondents had about the offenders they were judging were not directly measured, but rather were inferred from the patterns of responses about responsibility and punishment.

Chapter 10: Legal Structure, Legal Culture, and Convergence

1. For a discussion of this and similar cases, see Garet (1983).

2. See Haley (1978, 1982b); Henderson (1965); Kato (1987); Kawashima (1963); Kidder and Hostetler (1990); Kim and Lawson (1979); Miyazawa (1987); Noda (1976); Ramseyer (1985, 1988); Ramseyer and Nakazato (1989); Rosch (1987); Upham (1987); Wagatsuma and Rosett (1986).

3. For example, if the plaintiff has a 50 percent chance of winning a suit and if he stands to recover $10,000, the case has an expected value of $5,000. Of course, no one can be certain about either the probability of victory or the size of the recovery given victory. Hence the parties may disagree about the expected value of a suit. For further discussion see Lempert and Sanders (1986).

4. Recall from note 3 that the expected value of the hypothetical case is $5,000. If, however, the plaintiff, not wanting to appear greedy nor to unnecessarily offend the defendant, were willing to settle for $4,000, while the defendant, not wanting to appear to be a cheapskate nor to unnecessarily offend the plaintiff, were willing to pay $6,000, any settlement between $4,000 and $6,000 would be acceptable. The "bargaining space" would be $2,000 in this case.

5. See Miller and Sarat (1980–1981); Felstiner, Abel, and Sarat (1980–1981); Sanders and Joyce (1990).

6. The literature on the study of litigation rates in the United States is formidable. On the limitations of aggregating litigation rates across subject matter areas, see Daniels (1985); L. M. Friedman (1983); Munger (1988).

7. Ramseyer (1988) and Tanase (1990) note that many aspects of the Japanese legal system make it relatively easy to agree on the expected value of a suit. This, in turn, facilitates the possibility of settlement (see Lempert & Sanders, 1986, chap. 6).

8. See Ramseyer and Nakazato (1989, p. 267, n. 16) for a list of citations.

9. See Schuck (1984); Presser (1985); Sherry (1986); Macneil (1980, 1985); Yeazell (1977).

10. See, for instance, *Sindell v. Abbott Laboratories* (1980).

11. This hierarchical structure exists side-by-side with an ideology of egalitarianism within the neighborhood. Bestor (1989) comments: "Residents point out examples of highly placed government bureaucrats, teachers, and symphony orchestra members cooperating in community affairs with carpenters, retail merchants, and day laborers; status in the outside world, they insist, does not intrude into local affairs. Yet against the backdrop of this ethos of communal egalitarianism, neighborhood activities are planned and carried out in organizations that are elaborately structured hierarchies" (pp. 164–165).

12. See Vogel (1979); Ouchi (1980, 1981); Lincoln and Kalleberg (1990).

Chapter 11: The Problem of Justice

1. For a recent example of the research in this tradition, see Gaertner, Mann, Murrell, and Dovido (1989); for recent reviews, see Hogg and Abrams (1988), Messick and Mackie (1989), Stephan (1985), and Wilder (1986), in addition to the works cited in the text.

2. To be sure, the United States had a special obligation to Vietnamese refugees given its role in the Vietnam War. Vietnamese immigration to such nations as Canada, however, has vastly exceeded immigration to Japan.

3. Patterns of discrimination described in the rest of the book are widely reported in standard sources on Japan. For examples, see Befu (1971), De Vos (1973), Lebra (1976), R. J. Smith (1983), and White (1987). In the text we give citations only where a specific point of information is to be attributed to a particular source. Most of these targets of discrimination and forms of discrimination are openly discussed by Japanese citizens in casual conversations.

4. The social role of Burakumin has been intensively analyzed in such works as De Vos and Wagatsuma's classic *Japan's Invisible Race* (1966) and Yoshino and Murakoshi's *The Invisible Visible Minority* (1977).

5. Similarly, political scientist John Campbell (1988, p. 7) concludes: "I would go so far as to argue that Japan is a profoundly conflict-oriented society, one that assumes that any human endeavor is likely to be fatally disrupted by clashes of interest or individual temperament, so that extraordinary care must be taken to preserve a semblance of 'harmony' by manipulating social relationships."

References

Adams, A. (1977). *Assessment of mailback nonresponse to a two-phase study.* Unpublished manuscript, University of Michigan, Sociology Department.

Ajzen, I., & Fishbein, M. (1973). Attitudinal and normative variables as predictors of specific behaviors. *Journal of Personality and Social Psychology, 27,* 41–57.

Alexander, J., Giesen, B., Munch, R., & Smelser, N. (Eds.) (1987). *The micromacro link.* Berkeley: University of California Press.

Allston, J. P. (1986). *The American samurai: Blending American and Japanese managerial practices.* New York: DeGruyter.

Alves, W., & Rossi, P. (1978). Who should get what? Fairness judgments of the distribution of earnings. *American Journal of Sociology, 84,* 541–564.

Apter, D., & Sawa, N. (1984). *Against the state.* Cambridge, Mass.: Harvard University Press.

Argyle, M., Shimoda, K., & Little, B. (1978). Variance due to persons and situations in England and Japan. *British Journal of Social and Clinical Psychology, 17,* 335–337.

Aries, P. (1962). *Centuries of childhood.* New York: Vintage Books.

Aron, A., Aron, E. N., Tudor, M., & Nelson, C. Close relationships as including other in the self. *Journal of Personality and Social Psychology, 60,* 241–253.

Atsumi, R. (1979). Tsukiai—Obligatory personal relationships of Japanese white-collar company employees. *Human Organization, 38,* 63–70.

Auerbach, J. S. (1983). *Justice without law? Resolving disputes without lawyers.* New York: Oxford University Press.

Austin, J. L. (1961). A plea for excuses. In H. Morris (Ed.), *Freedom and responsibility* (pp. 6–19). Stanford, Calif.: Stanford University Press.

Axelrod, R. M. (1984). *The evolution of cooperation.* New York: Basic Books.

Azuma, H. (1984). Secondary control as a heterogeneous category. *American Psychologist, 39,* 970–971.

Barnlund, D. C. (1975). *Public and private self in Japan and the United States.* Tokyo: Simul Press.

Baruch-Bush, R. A. (1986). Between two worlds: The shift from individual to group responsibility in the law of causation of injury. *UCLA Law Review, 33,* 1473–1563.

Baumgartner, M. P. (1988). *The moral order of a suburb*. New York: Oxford University Press.

Bayley, D. H. (1976). *Forces of order*. Berkeley: University of California Press.

Befu, H. (1971). *Japan: An anthropological introduction*. New York: Harper and Row.

Bellah, R. (1985). *Tokugawa religion*. New York: Free Press. (Original work published 1957.)

Bellah, R., Madsen, R., Sullivan, W. M., Swidler, A., & Tipton, S. M. (1985). *Habits of the heart*. Berkeley: University of California Press.

Benedict, R. (1946). *The chrysanthemum and the sword*. Boston: Houghton Mifflin.

Bestor, T. (1989). *Neighborhood Tokyo*. Stanford, Calif.: Stanford University Press.

Bezanson, R., Cranberg, G., & Soloski, J. (1987). *Libel law and the free press: Myth and reality*. New York: Free Press.

Bharati, A. (1985). The self in Hindu thought and action. In A. J. Marsella, G. De Vos, & F. L. K. Hsu (Eds.), *Culture and self: Asian and Western perspectives* (pp. 185–230). New York: Tavistock.

Biddle, B. J. (1979). *Role theory: Expectations, identities and behaviors*. New York: Academic Press.

Biddle, B. J., & Thomas, E. J. (Eds.) (1966). *Role theory: Concepts and research*. New York: Wiley.

Bies, R. J. (1987). The predicament of injustice: The management of moral outrage. In B. Staw & L. Cummings (Eds.), *Research in organizational behavior* (Vol. 9, pp. 289–319). Greenwich, Conn.: JAI Press.

Billig, M., & Tajfel, H. (1973). Social categorization and similarity in intergroup behavior. *European Journal of Social Psychology, 3*, 27–52.

Black, D. (1976). *The behavior of law*. New York: Academic Press.

Blau, P. M. (1955). *The dynamics of bureaucracy*. Chicago: University of Chicago Press.

Blau, P. M. (1964). *Exchange and power in social life*. New York: Wiley.

Blau, P. M. (1987). Contrasting theoretical perspectives. In J. Alexander, B. Giesen, R. Munch, & N. Smelser (Eds.), *The micro-macro link* (pp. 71–85). Berkeley: University of California Press.

Bohannan, P. (1965). The differing realms of the law. *American Anthropologist* Special Publication: *The Ethnography of Law*, Laura Nader (Ed.), *67* (6), pt. 2, 33–42.

Braithwaite, J. (1979). *Inequality, crime, and public policy*. London: Routledge & Kegan Paul.

Braithwaite, J. (1989). *Crime, shame and reintegration*. Cambridge: Cambridge University Press.

Braithwaite, J., Fisse, B., & Geis, G. (1987). Covert facilitation and crime: Restoring balance to the entrapment debate. *Journal of Social Issues, 43*, 5–41.

Braithwaite, J., & Pettit, P. (1991). *Not just deserts: A republican theory of criminal justice*. New York: Oxford University Press.

Brand, M. (1984). *Intending and acting: Toward a naturalized action theory*. Cambridge, Mass.: MIT Press.

Brickman, P. (1977). Crime and punishment in sports and society. *Journal of Social Issues, 33,* 140–164.

Brown, R. (1965). *Social psychology.* New York: Free Press.

Bryant, T. (1984). Marital dissolution in Japan: Legal obstacles and their impact. *Law in Japan, 17,* 73–97.

Burger, J. M. (1981). Motivational biases in the attribution of responsibility for an accident: A meta-analysis of the defensive attribution hypothesis. *Psychological Bulletin, 90,* 496–512.

Calabresi, G. (1985). *Ideals, beliefs, attitudes, and the law: Private law perspectives on a public law problem.* Syracuse, N.Y.: Syracuse University Press.

Campbell, J. C. (1988). *Politics and culture in Japan.* Ann Arbor, Mich.: Institute for Social Research.

Caudill, W. A. (1973). The influence of social structure and culture on human behavior in modern Japan. *Journal of Nervous and Mental Disease, 157,* 240–257.

Caudill, W. A., & Plath, D. W. (1974). Who sleeps by whom? Parent-child involvement in urban Japanese families. In T. S. Lebra & W. P. Lebra (Eds.), *Japanese culture and behavior* (pp. 277–312). Honolulu: University of Hawaii Press. (Reprinted from *Psychiatry, 29,* 344–366.)

Caudill, W. A., & Weinstein, H. (1969). Maternal care and infant behavior in Japan and America. *Psychiatry, 32,* 12–43.

Chira, S. (1985, October 25). Japan Air Lines' heavy burden: 520 deaths. *New York Times,* p. A6.

Chira, S. (1986, September 24). 2 papers quote Japanese leader on abilities of minorities in U.S. *New York Times,* p. A12.

City of Yokohama, 1985. (1985). Yokohama, Japan: City of Yokohama.

Clark, M. S., & Mills, J. (1979). Interpersonal attraction in exchange and communal relationships. *Journal of Personality and Social Psychology, 37,* 12–24.

Clark, M. S., Quellette, R., Powell, M., & Milberg, S. (1987). Relationship type, recipient mood, and helping. *Journal of Personality and Social Psychology, 53,* 94–103.

Clarke, S., & Koch, G. (1980). Juvenile court: Therapy or crime control, and do lawyers make a difference? *Law and Society Review, 14,* 263–308.

Clifford, W. (1976). *Crime control in Japan.* Toronto: Lexington Books.

Cohen, J., & Cohen, P. (1983). *Applied multiple regression/correlation analysis for the behavioral sciences* (2nd ed.). Hillsdale, N.J.: Erlbaum.

Cole, R. E. (1971). *Japanese blue collar: The changing tradition.* Berkeley: University of California Press.

Cole, R. E. (1972). Permanent employment in Japan: Facts and fantasies. *Industrial Labor Relations Review, 26,* 612–630.

Cole, R. E. (1979). *Work, mobility, and participation: A comparative study of American and Japanese industry.* Berkeley: University of California Press.

Coleman, J. S. (1986). Social theory, social research and a theory of action. *American Journal of Sociology, 91,* 1309–1335.

Coleman, J. S. (1990). *Foundations of social theory.* Cambridge, Mass.: Belknap.

Collingwood, R. G. (1940). *An essay on metaphysics.* Oxford: Clarendon Press.

Comber, L. C., & Keeves, J. (1973). *Science achievement in nineteen countries.* New York: Wiley.

Cook, T. D., & Campbell, D. T. (1979). *Quasi-experimentation: Design and analysis issues for field settings.* Boston: Houghton Mifflin.

Cooley, C. H. (1962). *Social organization.* New York: Scribner. (Original work published 1909.)

Coons, J. (1987). Consistency. *California Law Review, 75,* 59–113.

Cousins, S. (1989). Culture and self-perception in Japan and the United States. *Journal of Personality and Social Psychology, 56,* 124–131.

Crash survivors say Delta "digging up dirt" to force settlements. (1986, November 3). *Houston Post,* p. A10.

Crime in the cities. (1989, September 7). *Washington Post,* p. A22.

Cummings, W. K. (1980). *Education and equality in Japan.* Princeton, N.J.: Princeton University Press.

Currie, E. (1985). *Confronting crime.* New York: Pantheon.

Dahrendorf, R. (1959). *Class and class conflict in industrial society.* Stanford, Calif.: University of California Press.

Daniels, S. (1985). Continuity and change in patterns of case handling: A case study of two rural counties. *Law and Society Review, 19,* 381–420.

Danzig, R. (1973). Toward the creation of a complementary, decentralized system of criminal justice. *Stanford Law Review, 26,* 1–54.

Danzig, R., & Lowy, M. (1975). Everyday disputes and mediation in the United States: A reply to Professor Felstiner. *Law and Society Review, 9,* 675–694.

Davis, L. H. (1979). *Theory of action.* Englewood Cliffs, N.J.: Prentice-Hall.

De Jong, W., Morris, W. N., & Hastorf, A. H. (1976). Effects of an escaped accomplice on the punishment assigned to a criminal defendant. *Journal of Personality and Social Psychology, 33,* 192–198.

DeLorean, J. Z., & Wright, J. P. (1979). *On a clear day you can see General Motors.* Grosse Pointe, Mich.: Wright Enterprises.

deMause, L. (Ed.) (1974). *The history of childhood.* New York: Harper Torchbooks.

de Tocqueville, A. (1981). *Democracy in America.* New York: Modern Library. (Original work published 1835.)

De Vos, G. (1973). *Socialization for achievement: Essays on the cultural psychology of the Japanese.* Berkeley: University of California Press.

De Vos, G. (1985). Dimensions of the self in Japanese culture. In A. J. Marsella, G. De Vos, & F. L. K. Hsu (Eds.), *Culture and self: Asian and Western perspectives* (pp. 141–184). New York: Tavistock.

De Vos, G., & Wagatsuma, N. (1966). *Japan's invisible race: Caste in culture and personality.* Berkeley: University of California Press.

Doi, T. (1973). *The anatomy of dependence.* New York: Kodansha.

Doi, T. (1986). *The anatomy of self.* New York: Kodansha.

Dore, R. P. (1967). Mobility, equality, and individuation in modern Japan. In R. P.

Dore (Ed.), *Aspects of social change in modern Japan* (pp. 113–150). Princeton, N.J.: Princeton University Press.

Dore, R. P. (1973). *British factory, Japanese factory: The origins of diversity in industrial relations.* Berkeley: University of California Press.

Dumont, L. (1970). *Homo hierarchicus: An essay on the caste system.* Chicago: University of Chicago Press.

Dumont, L. (1977). *From Mandeville to Marx: The genesis and triumph of economic ideology.* Chicago: University of Chicago Press.

Durkheim, E. (1933). *The division of labor in society* (J. W. Swain, Trans.). New York: Macmillan. (Original work published 1893.)

Dykstra, A. (1977). *The kanji ABC.* Los Altos, Calif.: William Kaufman.

Eisuke, D. (1984). Seniority wages and labour management. In T. Shigeyoshi & J. Bergmann (Eds.), *Industrial relations in transition* (pp. 119–130). Tokyo: University of Tokyo Press.

Ekland-Olson, S. (1982). Deviance, social control, and social networks. In S. Spitzer & R. Simon (Eds.), *Research in law, deviance, and social control* (Vol. 4, pp. 271–299). Greenwich, Conn.: JAI Press.

Ekland-Olson, S. (1984). Social control and relational disturbance: A microstructural paradigm. In D. Black (Ed.), *Toward a general theory of social control* (Vol. 2, pp. 209–233). New York: Academic Press.

Emerson, R. (1969). *Judging delinquents.* Chicago: Aldine.

Engel, D. (1984). The oven bird's song: Insiders, outsiders, and personal injuries in an American community. *Law and Society Review, 18,* 551–582.

Erikson, K. T. (1966). *Wayward Puritans.* New York: Wiley.

Erikson, K. T. (1976). *Everything in its path: Destruction of community in the Buffalo Creek flood.* New York: Simon and Schuster.

Fagan, J., Slaughter, E., & Hartstone, E. (1987). Blind justice? The impact of race on the juvenile justice process. *Crime and Delinquency, 33,* 224–258.

Fajans, J. (1985). The person in social context: The social character of Baining "psychology". In G. M. White & J. Kirkpatrick (Eds.), *Person, self, and experience: Exploring Pacific ethnopsychologies* (pp. 367–397). Berkeley: University of California Press.

Farley, R., Schuman, H., Bianchi, S., Colasanto, D. L., & Hatchett, S. (1978). Chocolate city, vanilla suburbs: Will the trend toward racially separate communities continue? *Social Science Research, 7,* 319–344.

Federal Rules of Civil Procedure. (1987). Mineola, N.Y.: Foundation Press.

Feinberg, J. (1970). *Doing and deserving: Essays in the theory of responsibility.* Princeton, N.J.: Princeton University Press.

Feinberg, J. (1980). The nature and value of rights. In J. Feinberg (Ed.), *Rights, justice and the bounds of liberty* (pp. 143–150). Princeton, N.J.: Princeton University Press.

Feld, B. (1984). Criminalizing juvenile justice: Rules of procedure for juvenile court. *Minnesota Law Review, 69,* 141–276.

Feld, B. (1988). *In re Gault* revisited: A cross-state comparison of the right to counsel in juvenile court. *Crime and Delinquency, 34,* 393–424.

Feld, B. (1989). The right to counsel in juvenile court: An empirical study of when lawyers appear and the difference they make. *Journal of Criminal Law and Criminology, 79,* 1184–1346.

Felsteiner, W. (1974). Influences of social organization on dispute governance of rail freight contracting. *Journal of Legal Studies, 13,* 63–94.

Felstiner, W., Abel, R., & Sarat, A. (1980–81). The emergence and transformation of disputes: Naming, blaming, claiming . . . . *Law and Society Review, 15,* 631–654.

Fincham, F. D. (1983). Developmental dimensions of attribution theory. In J. M. Jaspars, F. D. Fincham, & M. Hewstone (Eds.), *Attribution theory and research: Conceptual, developmental and social dimensions* (pp. 117–164). New York: Academic Press.

Fincham, F. D. (1985). Outcome valence and situational constraints in the responsibility attributions of children and adults. *Social Cognition, 3,* 218–233.

Fincham, F. D., & Jaspars, J. M. (1979). Attribution of responsibility to the self and other in children and adults. *Journal of Personality and Social Psychology, 37,* 51–56.

Fincham, F. D., & Jaspars, J. M. (1980). Attribution of responsibility: From man-the-scientist to man-as-lawyer. In L. Berkowitz (Ed.), *Advances in experimental social psychology* (Vol. 13, pp. 82–138). New York: Academic Press.

Fishbein, M., & Ajzen, I. (1973). Attribution of responsibility: A theoretical note. *Journal of Experimental Social Psychology, 9,* 148–153.

Fiske, A. P. (1990). Relativity within Moose ("Mossi") culture: Four incommensurable models for social relationships. *Ethos, 18,* 180–204.

Fiske, A. P. (in press). *Structures of social life: The four elementary forms of human relations.* New York: Free Press.

French, J., & Raven, B. (1959). The bases of social power. In D. Cartwright (Ed.), *Studies in social power* (pp. 150–167). Ann Arbor, Mich.: Institute for Social Research.

Friedman, D. (1988). *The misunderstood miracle: Industrial development and political change in Japan.* Ithaca, N.Y.: Cornell University Press.

Friedman, L. M. (1977). *Law and society: An introduction.* Englewood Cliffs, N.J.: Prentice-Hall.

Friedman, L. M. (1983). Courts over time: A survey of theories and research. In K. Boyum & L. Mather (Eds.), *Empirical theories about courts* (pp. 9–50). New York: Longman.

Friedman, L. M. (1985). *Total justice.* New York: Russell Sage Foundation.

Friedman, M. (1982). *Capitalism and freedom.* Chicago: University of Chicago Press.

Frolock, F. (1987). *Rational association.* Syracuse, N.Y.: Syracuse University Press.

Fruin, W. M. (1980). The family as firm and the firm as family in Japan: The case of the Kikkoman Shoyu Company Limited. *Journal of Family History, 5,* 432–449.

Fukutake, T. (1974). *Japanese rural society.* London: Oxford University Press.

Fukutake, T. (1982). *The Japanese social structure: Its evolution in the modern century* (R. Dore, Trans.). Tokyo: University of Tokyo Press.

Fuller, L. (1969). *The morality of law* (rev. ed.). New Haven and London: Yale University Press.

Gaertner, S. L., Mann, J., Murrell, A., & Dovido, J. F. (1989). Reducing intergroup bias: The benefits of recategorization. *Journal of Personality and Social Psychology, 57,* 239–249.

Galanter, M. (1974). Why the "haves" come out ahead: Speculations on the limits of legal change. *Law and Society Review, 9,* 95–160.

Galanter, M. (1983). Reading the landscape of disputes: What we know and don't know (and think we know) about our allegedly contentious and litigious society. *UCLA Law Review, 31,* 4–71.

Garcia-Esteve, J., & Shaw, M. E. (1968). Rural and urban patterns of responsibility attribution in Puerto Rico. *Journal of Social Psychology, 77,* 143–149.

Garet, R. (1983). Communality and existence: The rights of groups. *Southern California Law Review, 56,* 1001–1075.

Geertz, C. (1973). *Interpretation of cultures.* New York: Basic Books.

Geertz, C. (1975). On the nature of anthropological understanding. *American Scientist, 63,* 47–53.

Geertz, C. (1983). *Local knowledge: Further essays in interpretive anthropology.* New York: Basic Books.

Gellhorn, W. (1966). Settling disagreements with officials in Japan. *Harvard Law Review, 79,* 685–732.

Gergen, K. (1984). Theory of the self: Impasse and evolution. In L. Berkowitz (Ed.), *Advances in experimental social psychology* (Vol. 17, pp. 49–115). Orlando, Fla.: Academic Press.

Gilmore, G. (1977). *The ages of American law.* New Haven and London: Yale University Press.

Gluckman, M. (1967). *The judicial process among the Barotse of northern Rhodesia.* Manchester: Manchester University Press.

Goffman, E. (1971). *Relations in public: Microstudies of the public order.* New York: Basic Books.

Goldberg, S., Green, E., & Sander, F. (1985). *Dispute resolution.* Boston: Little, Brown.

Gottfredson, M. R., & Hindelang, M. J. (1979). A study of the behavior of law. *American Sociological Review, 44,* 3–17.

Government of Japan. (1989). *Summary of the White Paper on Crime 1989.* Tokyo: Research and Training Institute, Ministry of Justice.

Grabosky, P., Braithwaite, J., & Wilson, P. (1987). The myth of community tolernace toward white-collar crime. *Australian and New Zealand Journal of Criminology, 20,* 33–44.

Green, L. (1930). *Judge and jury.* Kansas City, Mo.: Vernon Law Book.

Greenhouse, C. J. (1986). *Praying for justice.* Ithaca, N.Y.: Cornell University Press.

Griffiths, J. (1970). Ideology in criminal procedure, or a third model of the criminal process. *Yale Law Journal, 79,* 359–417.

Groves, R. M., & Kahn, R. L. (1979). *Surveys by telephone.* New York: Academic Press.

Haidt, J. (1988). *Social frames of moral judgment.* Unpublished manuscript, University of Pennsylvania, Psychology Department.

Haley, J. O. (1978). The myth of the reluctant litigant. *Journal of Japanese Studies, 4,* 359–390.

Haley, J. O. (1982a). The politics of informal justice: The Japanese experience, 1922–1942. In R. Abel (Ed.), *The politics of informal justice* (Vol. 2, pp. 125–147). New York: Academic Press.

Haley, J. O. (1982b). Sheathing the sword of justice in Japan: An essay on law without sanctions. *Journal of Japanese Studies, 8,* 265–281.

Haley, J. O. (1986). Comment: The implications of apology. *Law and Society Review, 20,* 499–507.

Haley, J. O. (1989). Luck, law, culture and trade: The intractability of United States-Japan trade conflict. *Cornell International Law Journal, 22,* 103–123.

Hamaguchi, E. (1985). A contextual model of the Japanese: Toward a methodological innovation in Japanese studies. *Journal of Japanese Studies, 11,* 289–321.

Hamilton, V. L. (1978a). Obedience and responsibility: A jury simulation. *Journal of Personality and Social Psychology, 36,* 126–146.

Hamilton, V. L. (1978b). Who is responsible? Toward a social psychology of responsibility attribution. *Social Psychology, 41,* 316–328.

Hamilton, V. L. (1986). Chains of command: Responsibility attribution in hierarchies. *Journal of Applied Social Psychology, 16,* 118–138.

Hamilton, V. L., Blumenfeld, P. C., Akoh, H., & Miura, K. (1989a). Citizenship and scholarship in Japanese and American fifth grades. *American Educational Research Journal, 26,* 44–72.

Hamilton, V. L., Blumenfeld, P. C., Akoh, H., & Miura, K. (1989b). Japanese and American children's reasons for the things they do in school. *American Educational Research Journal, 26,* 545–571.

Hamilton, V. L., Blumenfeld, P. C., & Kushler, R. H. (1988). A question of standards: Attributions of blame and credit for classroom acts. *Journal of Personality and Social Psychology, 54,* 34–48.

Hamilton, V. L., & Sanders, J. (1981). Effects of roles and deeds on responsibility judgments: The normative structure of wrongdoing. *Social Psychology Quarterly, 44,* 237–254.

Hamilton, V. L., & Sanders, J. (with Y. Hosoi, Z. Ishimura, N. Matsubara, H.

Nishimura, N. Tomita, & K. Tokoro). (1983). Universals in judging wrongdoing: Japanese and Americans compared. *American Sociological Review, 48,* 199–211.

Hamilton, V. L., & Sanders, J. (with Y. Hosoi, Z. Ishimura, N. Matsubara, H. Nishimura, N. Tomita, & K. Tokoro). (1988). Punishment and the individual in the United States and Japan. *Law and Society Review, 22,* 301–328.

Hanami, T. (1984). Conflict and its resolution in industrial relations and labor law. In E. S. Krauss, T. P. Rohlen, and P. G. Steinhoff (Eds.), *Conflict in Japan* (pp. 107–135). Honolulu: University of Hawaii Press.

Harré, R. (1977). The self in monodrama. In T. Mischel (Ed.), *The self: Psychological and philosophical issues* (pp. 318–348). Totowa, N.J.: Rowan and Littlefield.

Harris, B. (1977). Developmental differences in the attribution of responsibility. *Developmental Psychology, 13,* 257–265.

Hart, H. L. A. (1968). *Punishment and responsibility.* New York: Oxford University Press.

Hart, H. L. A., & Honoré, H. M. (1959). *Causation and the law.* Oxford: Clarendon Press.

Hashimoto, M., & Raisian, J. (1985). Employment tenure and earnings profiles in Japan and the United States. *American Economic Review, 75,* 721–735.

Hattori, T., & Henderson, D. F. (1985). *Civil procedure in Japan.* New York: Matthew Bender.

Heider, F. (1958). *The psychology of interpersonal relations.* New York: Wiley.

Heilbroner, R. L. (1970). *The making of economic man* (3rd ed.). Englewood Cliffs, N.J.: Prentice-Hall.

Heiss, J. (1981). Social roles. In M. Rosenberg & R. H. Turner (Eds.), *Social psychology: Sociological perspectives* (pp. 94–129). New York: Basic Books.

Henderson, D. F. (1965). *Conciliation in Japanese law: Tokugawa and modern.* (2 vols.) Seattle: University of Washington Press.

Hendry, J. (1986). *Becoming Japanese: The world of the pre-school child.* Honolulu: University of Hawaii Press.

Hendry, J. (1987). *Understanding Japanese society.* London: Croom Helm.

Hiatt, F. (1990, July 15). Girl's death sparks debate on discipline in Japan's schools. *Washington Post,* p. A22.

Hill, S. (1981). *Competition and control at work.* Cambridge, Mass.: MIT Press.

Hofstede, G. (1980). *Culture's consequences.* Beverly Hills, Calif.: Sage.

Hogg, M. A., & Abrams, D. (1988). *Social identifications: A social psychology of intergroup relations and group processes.* London: Routledge & Kegan Paul.

Hoover, H. (1979). *American individualism.* New York: Garland. (Original work published 1922.)

Hornsby, J. (1980). *Actions.* London: Routledge & Kegan Paul.

Hsu, F. (1975). *Iemoto: The heart of Japan.* New York: Wiley.

Hsu, F. (1983). *Rugged individualism reconsidered.* Knoxville: University of Tennessee Press.

Hughes, J. (1989). The effect of medical malpractice reform laws on claim disposition. *International Review of Law and Economics, 9,* 57–78.

Hui, C. H., & Triandis, H. C. (1986). Individualism-collectivism: A study of cross-cultural researchers. *Journal of Cross-Cultural Psychology, 17,* 225–248.

Husen, T. (1967). *International study of achievement in mathematics: A comparison of twelve countries.* New York: Wiley.

Insurance Information Institute. (1982). *Attitudes toward the liability and litigation system.* New York: Author.

Introducing Kanazawa Japan. (1983). Kanazawa, Japan: Commerce, Industry, and Tourism Division, Department of Economics, City of Kanazawa.

Ishimura, Z., Tokoro, K., & Nishimura, H. (1986). *Sekinin to batsu no ishiki kozo* [The cognitive structure of responsibility and punishment]. Tokyo: Taga Press.

Ishimura, Z., & Wada, Y. (1984, June). *Dispute processing among citizens in Tokyo, Japan.* Paper presented at the annual meeting of the Law and Society Association, Boston.

James, W. (1981). *The principles of psychology.* Cambridge, Mass.: Harvard University Press. (Original work published 1890.)

Jasso, G., & Rossi, P. H. (1977). Distributive justice and earned income. *American Sociological Review, 42,* 639–651.

Johnson, C. (1982). *MITI and the Japanese miracle.* Stanford, Calif.: Stanford University Press.

Johnson, F. (1985). The Western concept of self. In A. J. Marsella, G. De Vos, & F. L. K. Hsu (Eds.), *Culture and self: Asian and Western perspectives* (pp. 91–138). New York: Tavistock.

Jones, E. E., & McGillis, D. (1976). Correspondent inferences and the attribution cube: A comparative appraisal. In J. H. Harvey, W. J. Ickes, & R. F. Kidd (Eds.), *New directions in attribution research* (Vol. 1, pp. 389–420). Hillsdale, N.J.: Erlbaum.

Jones, E. E., & Nisbett, R. (1971). The actor and the observer: Divergent perceptions of behavior. In E. E. Jones, D. E. Kanouse, H. H. Kelley, N. E. Nisbett, S. Valins, & B. Weiner (Eds.), *Attribution: Perceiving the causes of behavior* (pp. 79–94). Morristown, N.J.: General Learning Press.

Kalleberg, A. L., & Lincoln, J. R. (1988). The structure of earnings inequality in the United States and Japan. *American Journal of Sociology, 94,* S121–S153.

Kato, H. (1979). Development nineteenth-century style: Some historical parallels between the United States and Japan. In H. J. Gans, N. Glazer, J. R. Gusfield, & C. Jencks (Eds.), *On the making of Americans: Essays in honor of David Riesman* (pp. 173–190). Camden, N.J.: University of Pennsylvania Press.

Kato, M. (1987). The role of law and lawyers in Japan and the United States. *Brigham Young University Law Review,* 627–698.

Kawashima, T. (1963). Dispute resolution in contemporary Japan. In A. von

Mehren (Ed.), *Law in Japan* (pp. 41–72). Cambridge, Mass.: Harvard University Press.

Kawashima, T. (1968). The status of the individual in the notion of law, right, and social order in Japan. In C. A. Moore (Ed.), *The status of the individual in East and West* (pp. 429–448). Honolulu: University of Hawaii Press.

Keeton, P., Dobbs, D., Keeton, R., & Owen, D. (1984). *Prosser and Keeton on the law of torts* (5th ed.). St. Paul: West.

Kelley, H. H. (1967). Attribution theory in social psychology. In D. Levine (Ed.), *Nebraska Symposium on Motivation* (Vol. 15, pp. 192–238). Lincoln: University of Nebraska Press.

Kelley, H. H. (1971). Causal schemata and the attribution process. In E. E. Jones, D. E. Kanouse, H. H. Kelley, R. E. Nisbett, S. Valins, & B. Weiner (Eds.), *Attribution: Perceiving the causes of behavior* (pp. 151–174). Morristown, N.J.: General Learning Press.

Kelley, H. H. (1973). The process of causal attribution. *American Psychologist, 28,* 107–128.

Kelman, H. C., & Hamilton, V. L. (1989). *Crimes of obedience: Toward a social psychology of authority and responsibility.* New Haven and London: Yale University Press.

Kidder, R. L. (1983). *Connecting law and society.* Englewood Cliffs, N.J.: Prentice-Hall.

Kidder, R. L., & Hostetler, J. A. (1990). Managing ideologies: Harmony as ideology in Amish and Japanese societies. *Law and Society Review, 24,* 895–922.

Kiefer, C. (1976). The *danchi zoko* and the evolution of metropolitan mind. In L. Austin (Ed.), *Japan: The paradox of progress* (pp. 279–300). New Haven and London: Yale University Press.

Kim, C., & Lawson, C. (1979). The law of the subtle mind: The traditional Japanese conception of law. *International and Comparative Law Quarterly, 28,* 491–513.

Kinmonth, E. H. (1981). *The self-made man in Meiji Japanese thought: From samurai to salary man.* Berkeley: University of California Press.

Kitamura, K. (1986). The decline and reform of education in Japan: A comparative perspective. In W. K. Cummings, E. R. Beauchamp, S. Ichikawa, V. N. Kobayashi, & M. Ushiogi (Eds.), *Educational policies in crisis* (pp. 153–170). New York: Praeger.

Kohlberg, L. (1969). Stage and sequence: The cognitive-developmental approach to socialization. In D. A. Goslin (Ed.), *Handbook of socialization theory and research* (pp. 347–480). Chicago: Rand-McNally.

Kohlberg, L. (1981). *The philosophy of moral development: Moral stages and the idea of justice.* San Francisco: Harper and Row.

Kohlberg, L. (1984). *The psychology of moral development: The nature and validity of moral stages.* San Francisco: Harper and Row.

Koike, K. (1983). Internal labor markets: Workers in large firms. In T. Shirai

(Ed.), *Contemporary industrial relations in Japan* (pp. 29–62). Madison: University of Wisconsin Press.

Kojima, H. (1984). A significant stride toward the comparative study of control. *American Psychologist, 39,* 972–973.

Kozol, J. (1985). *Illiterate America.* New York: New American Library.

Krauss, E. S., Rohlen, T. P., & Steinhoff, P. G. (Eds.) (1984). *Conflict in Japan.* Honolulu: University of Hawaii Press.

Lasch, C. (1979). *The culture of narcissism.* New York: Warner Books.

Lebra, T. S. (1976). *Japanese patterns of behavior.* Honolulu: University of Hawaii Press.

Lebra, T. S. (1984). Nonconfrontational strategies for management of interpersonal conflicts. In E. S. Krauss, T. P. Rohlen, & P. G. Steinhoff (Eds.), *Conflict in Japan* (pp. 41–60). Honolulu: University of Hawaii Press.

Lebra, T. S., & Lebra, W. P. (Eds.) (1974). *Japanese culture and behavior.* Honolulu: University of Hawaii Press.

Lempert, R., & Sanders, J. (1986). *An invitation to law and social science.* Philadelphia: University of Pennsylvania Press.

Leung, K., & Lind, E. A. (1986). Procedural justice and culture: Effects of culture, gender, and investigator status on procedural preference. *Journal of Personality and Social Psychology, 50,* 1134–1140.

Levy, R. I. (1973). *Tahitians: Mind and experience in the Society Islands.* Chicago: University of Chicago Press.

Lifton, R. J. (1967). *Death in life: Survivors of Hiroshima.* New York: Simon and Schuster.

Lincoln, J. R., & Kalleberg, A. L. (1985). Work organization and workforce commitment: A study of plants and employees in the U.S. and Japan. *American Sociological Review, 50,* 738–760.

Lincoln, J. R., & Kalleberg, A. L. (1990). *Culture, control, and commitment: A study of work organization and work attitudes in the United States and Japan.* Cambridge: Cambridge University Press.

Lincoln, J. R., & McBride, K. (1987). Japanese industrial organization in comparative perspective. *Annual Review of Sociology, 13,* 289–312.

Lind, E. A., & Tyler, T. R. (1988). *The social psychology of procedural justice.* New York: Plenum Press.

Lloyd-Bostock, S. (1983). Attributions of cause and responsibility as social phenomena. In J. M. Jaspars, F. D. Fincham, & M. Hewstone (Eds.), *Attribution theory and research: Conceptual, developmental and social dimensions* (pp. 261–289). New York: Academic Press.

Lukes, S. (1973). *Individualism.* Oxford: Basil Blackwell.

Lutz, C. (1985). Ethnopsychology compared to what? Explaining behavior and consciousness among the Ifaluk. In G. M. White & J. Kirkpatrick (Eds.), *Person, self, and experience* (pp. 35–79). Berkeley: University of California Press.

Macaulay, S. (1963). Non-contractual relations in business: A preliminary study. *American Sociological Review, 28,* 55–67.

Mack, J. (1909). The juvenile court. *Harvard Law Review, 23,* 104–122.

Mackie, J. L. (1965). Causes and conditions. *American Philosophical Quarterly, 2,* 245–264.

Macneil, I. (1980). *The new social contract: An inquiry into modern contractual relations.* New Haven and London: Yale University Press.

Macneil, I. (1985). Bureaucracy, liberalism, and community—American style. *Northwestern University Law Review, 79,* 900–948.

Maine, H. (1963). *Ancient law.* Boston: Beacon Press. (Orig. published 1906.)

Mann, B. (1987). *Neighbors and strangers: Law and community in early Connecticut.* Chapel Hill: University of North Carolina Press.

Marshall, R. C. (1984). *Collective decision making in rural Japan* (Michigan Papers in Japanese Studies No. 11). Ann Arbor: University of Michigan, Center for Japanese Studies.

Maruyama, M. (1963). *Thought and behavior in modern Japanese politics* (I. Morris, Trans.). Oxford: Oxford University Press.

Maruyama, M. (1974). *Studies in the intellectual history of Tokugawa Japan* (M. Hane, Trans.). Princeton, N.J.: Princeton University Press.

Mauss, M. (1985). A category of the human mind: The notion of person; the notion of self. In M. Carrithers, S. Collins, & S. Lukes (Eds.), *The category of the person* (pp. 1–25). Cambridge: Cambridge University Press. (Reprinted from *Journal of the Royal Anthropological Institute,* 1938, *68* [W. D. Halls, Trans.]).

McClain, J. L. (1982). *Kanazawa: A seventeenth-century Japanese castle town.* New Haven and London: Yale University Press.

Mead, G. H. (1934). *Mind, self, and society.* Chicago: University of Chicago Press.

Messick, D. M., & Mackie, D. M. (1989). Intergroup relations. *Annual Review of Psychology, 40,* 45–81.

Miller, J. G. (1984). Culture and the development of everyday social explanations. *Journal of Personality and Social Personality, 46,* 961–978.

Miller, J. G., Bersoff, D. M., & Harwood, R. L. (1990). Perceptions of social responsibilities in India and in the United States: Moral imperatives or personal decisions? *Journal of Personality and Social Psychology, 58,* 33–47.

Miller, R., & Sarat, A. (1980–1981). Grievances, claims and disputes: Assessing the adversary culture. *Law and Society Review, 15,* 525–566.

Mills, J., & Clark, M. S. (1982). Exchange and communal relationships. In L. Wheeler (Ed.), *Review of personality and social psychology* (Vol. 3, pp. 121–144). Beverly Hills, Calif.: Sage.

Miyazawa, S. (1987). Taking Kawashima seriously: A review of Japanese research on Japanese legal consciousness and disputing behavior. *Law and Society Review, 21,* 219–241.

Monson, T. C. (1983). Implications of the traits v. situations controversy for differences in the attributions of actors and observers. In J. M. Jaspars, F. D. Fincham, & M. Hewstone (Eds.), *Attribution theory and research: Conceptual, developmental and social dimensions* (pp. 293–314). New York: Academic Press.

Mouer, R., & Sugimoto, Y. (1986). *Images of Japanese society.* London: Kegan Paul International.

Munch, R., & Smelser, N. J. (1987). Relating the micro and macro. In J. C. Alexander, B. Giesen, R. Munch, & N. J. Smelser (Eds.), *The micro-macro link* (pp. 356–388). Berkeley: University of California Press.

Munger, F. (1988). Law, change and litigation: A critical examination of an empirical research tradition. *Law and Society Review, 22,* 57–101.

Murakami, Y. (1985). *Ie* society as a pattern of civilization: Response to criticism. *Journal of Japanese Studies, 11,* 401–421.

Murase, T. (1974). Naikan therapy. In T. S. Lebra & W. P. Lebra (Eds.), *Japanese culture and behavior* (pp. 431–442). Honolulu: University of Hawaii Press.

Murase, T. (1982). Sunao: A central value in Japanese psychotherapy. In A. J. Marsella & G. M. White (Eds.), *Cultural conceptions of mental health and therapy* (pp. 317–329). Dordrecht, The Netherlands: D. Reidel.

Nader, L. (1969). *Law in culture and society.* Chicago: Aldine.

Nakamura, H. (1964). *Ways of thinking of Eastern peoples: India, China, Tibet, Japan* (P. P. Wiener, Ed. and Trans.). (Revised translation.) Honolulu: University of Hawaii Press.

Nakamura, H. (1968). Consciousness of the individual and the universal among the Japanese. In C. A. Moore (Ed.), *The status of the individual in East and West* (pp. 141–160). Honolulu: University of Hawaii Press.

Nakane, C. (1970). *Japanese society.* Berkeley: University of California Press.

Narain, K. V. (1985). Yokohama. In D. Jurkowitz (Ed.), *Fodor's Japan* (pp. 235–249). New York: Fodor's Travel Guides.

Nisbett, R. E., & Ross, L. (1980). *Human inference: Strategies and shortcomings of social judgment.* Englewood Cliffs, N.J.: Prentice-Hall.

Nock, S., & Rossi, P. H. (1978). Ascription versus achievement in the attribution of family social status. *American Journal of Sociology, 84,* 565–590.

Noda, Y. (1976). *Introduction to Japanese law* (A. H. Angels, Ed. and Trans.). Tokyo: University of Tokyo Press.

Obuchi, T. (1987). Role of the court in the process of informal dispute resolution in Japan: Traditional and modern aspects, with special emphasis on in-court compromise. *Law in Japan, 20,* 74–101.

Ochs, E. (1982). Talking to children in Western Samoa. *Language and Society, 11,* 77–104.

Olson, M. (1971). *The logic of collective action: Public goods and the theory of groups.* New York: Schocken.

Otaki, M., Durrett, M. E., Richards, P., Nyquist, L., & Pennebaker, J. W. (1986). Maternal and infant behavior in Japan and America: A partial replication. *Journal of Cross-Cultural Psychology, 17,* 251–268.

Ouchi, W. G. (1980). Markets, bureaucracies, and clans. *Administrative Science Quarterly, 25,* 129–141.

Ouchi, W. G. (1981). *Theory Z.* New York: Avon.

Ouchi, W. G., & Johnson, J. B. (1978). Types of organizational control and their relationship to emotional well being. *Administrative Science Quarterly, 23,* 293–317.

Packer, H. (1968). *The limits of the criminal sanction.* Palo Alto, Calif.: Stanford University Press.

Palay, T. 1984. Comparative institutional economics: The governance of rail freight contracting. *Journal of Legal Studies, 13,* 265–287.

Parsons, T. (1951). *The social system.* New York: Free Press.

Pascale, R. T., & Athos, A. G. (1981). *The art of Japanese management.* New York: Simon and Schuster.

Passin, H. (1980). *Japanese and the Japanese: Language and culture change.* Tokyo: Kinseido.

Pharr, S. J. (1990). *Losing face: Status politics in Japan.* Berkeley: University of California Press.

Phillips, D. C. (1976). *Holistic thought in social science.* Stanford, Calif.: Stanford University Press.

Piaget, J. (1965). *The moral judgment of the child.* New York: Free Press. (Original work published 1932.)

Platt, A. (1969). *The child savers: The invention of delinquency.* Chicago: University of Chicago Press.

Polanyi, K. (1944). *The great transformation.* Boston: Beacon Press.

Presser, S. (1985). Some realism about Orphism, or the critical legal studies movement and the new great chain of being: An English legal academic's guide to the current state of American law. *Northwestern University Law Review, 79,* 869–899.

Przeworski, A., & Teune, H. (1970). *The logic of comparative social inquiry.* New York: Wiley.

Raab, F. (1968). History, freedom and responsibility. In M. Broadbeck (Ed.), *Readings in the philosophy of the social sciences* (pp. 694–704). New York: Macmillan.

Raiffa, H. (1982). *The art and science of negotiation.* Cambridge, Mass.: Harvard University Press.

Ramseyer, J. M. (1985). The costs of the consensual myth: Antitrust enforcement and institutional barriers to litigation in Japan. *Yale Law Journal, 94,* 604–645.

Ramseyer, J. M. (1988). Reluctant litigant revisited: Rationality and disputes in Japan. *Journal of Japanese Studies, 14,* 111–123.

Ramseyer, J. M., & Nakazato, M. (1989). The rational litigant: Settlement amounts and verdict rates in Japan. *Journal of Legal Studies, 18,* 263–290.

Read, K. E. (1955). Morality and the concept of the person among the Gahuku-Gama. *Oceania, 25,* 233–282.

Regamy, C. (1968). The individual and the universal in East and West. In C. A. Moore (Ed.), *The status of the individual in East and West* (pp. 503–518). Honolulu: University of Hawaii Press.

Reiman, J. H. (1979). *The rich get richer and the poor get prison.* New York: Wiley.

Reynolds, D. K. (1980). *The quiet therapies: Japanese pathways to personal growth.* Honolulu: University of Hawaii Press.

Riskin, L. (1982). Mediation and lawyers. *Ohio State Law Journal, 43,* 29–60.

Roberts, J., & Doob, A. (1989). Sentencing public opinion: Taking false shadows for true substances. *Osgoode Hall Law Journal, 27,* 491–515.

Rohlen, T. P. (1974). *For harmony and strength.* Berkeley: University of California Press.

Rohlen, T. P. (1983). *Japan's high schools.* Berkeley: University of California Press.

Rohlen, T. P. (1989). Order in Japanese society: Attachment, authority and routine. *Journal of Japanese Studies, 15,* 5–40.

Rosch, J. (1987). Institutionalizing mediation: The evolution of the Civil Liberties Bureau in Japan. *Law and Society Review, 21,* 243–266.

Rosenberg, M. (1979). *Conceiving the self.* New York: Basic Books.

Ross, L. (1977). The intuitive psychologist and his shortcomings: Distortions in the attribution process. In L. Berkowitz (Ed.), *Advances in experimental social psychology* (Vol. 10, pp. 173–220). New York: Academic Press.

Rossi, P., & Anderson, A. (1982). The factorial survey approach: An introduction. In P. Rossi & S. Nock (Eds.), *Measuring social judgments: The factorial survey approach* (pp. 15–67). Beverly Hills, Calif.: Sage.

Rossi, P., & Nock, S. (Eds.) (1982). *Measuring social judgments: The factorial survey approach.* Beverly Hills, Calif.: Sage.

Rothman, D. (1971). *The discovery of the asylum.* Boston: Little, Brown.

Ryan, R. M., & Connell, J. P. (1989). Perceived locus of causality and internalization: Examining reasons for acting in two domains. *Journal of Personality and Social Psychology, 57,* 749–761.

Sampson, E. E. (1985). The decentralization of identity: Toward a revised concept of personal and social order. *American Psychologist, 40,* 1203–1211.

Sandel, M. (1982). *Liberalism and the limits of justice.* Cambridge: Cambridge University Press.

Sanders, J. (1987). Road signs and the goals of justice. *Michigan Law Review, 85,* 1297–1323.

Sanders, J. (1990). The interplay of micro and macro processes in the longitudinal study of courts: Beyond the Durkheimian tradition. *Law and Society Review, 24,* 241–256.

Sanders, J., & Hamilton, V. L. (1987). Is there a common law of responsibility? The effects of demographic variables on judgments of wrongdoing. *Law and Human Behavior, 11,* 277–297.

Sanders, J., & Joyce, C. (1990). "Off to the races": The 1980s tort crisis and the law reform process. *Houston Law Review, 27,* 207–295.

Sarat, A., & Grossman, J. (1975). Courts and conflict resolution: Problems in the mobilization of adjudication. *American Political Science Review, 69,* 1200–1216.

Sarbin, T. R., & Allen, V. L. (1968). Role theory. In G. Lindzey & E. Aronson (Eds.), *Handbook of social psychology* (Vol. 1, pp. 488–558). Reading, Mass.: Addison-Wesley.

Sasaki, N. (1981). *Management and industrial structure in Japan.* New York: Pergamon.

Sawyer, K. (1985, August 16). Lawyers compound disaster grief. *Washington Post,* p. A14.

Scholz, J. (1984). Cooperation, deterrence, and the ecology of regulatory enforcement. *Law and Society Review, 18,* 179–224.

Schonbach, P. (1980). A category system for account phrases. *European Journal of Social Psychology, 10,* 195–200.

Schonbach, P. (1985). *A taxonomy of account phrases: Revised, explained, and applied* (Report from the Working Unit). Bochum, West Germany: Ruhr-Universität.

Schuck, P. (1984). The transformation of immigration law. *Columbia Law Review, 84,* 1–90.

Scott, A. (1923). Small causes and poor litigants. *American Bar Association Journal, 9,* 457–459.

Scott, M. B., & Lyman, S. M. (1968). Accounts. *American Sociological Review, 23,* 46–62.

Selby, H. A. (1974). *Zapotec deviance.* Austin: University of Texas Press.

Semin, G. R., & Manstead, A. S. R. (1983). *The accountability of conduct.* London: Academic Press.

Shapiro, M. (1989a, May 8). School days, rigid rule days: Harsh discipline restricts Japanese student. *Washington Post,* pp. A1, A27.

Shapiro, M. (1989b, August 16). Japan seeks to accommodate record influx of "boat people". *Washington Post,* p. A14.

Shapiro, M., & Hiatt, F. (1989, February 22). Japan: From pauper to patron in 25 years. *Washington Post,* pp. A1, A24.

Shaver, K. G. (1970). Effects of severity and relevance on the responsibility assigned for an accident. *Journal of Personality and Social Psychology, 14,* 110–113.

Shaver, K. G. (1985). *The attribution of blame: Causality, responsibility and blameworthiness.* New York: Springer-Verlag.

Shaw, M. E., & Iwawaki, S. (1972). Attribution of responsibility of Japanese and Americans as a function of age. *Journal of Cross-Cultural Psychology, 3,* 71–81.

Shaw, M. E., & Reitan, H. T. (1969). Attribution of responsibility as a basis for sanctioning behavior. *British Journal of Social and Clinical Psychology, 8,* 217–226.

Shaw, M. E., & Schneider, F. W. (1969). Intellectual competence as a variable in attribution of responsibility and assignment of sanctions. *Journal of Social Psychology, 78,* 31–39.

Shaw, M. E., & Sulzer, J. L. (1964). An empirical test of Heider's levels in attribution of responsibility. *Journal of Abnormal and Social Psychology, 69,* 39–46.

Sherry, S. (1986). Civic virtue and the feminine voice in constitutional adjudication. *Virginia Law Review, 72,* 543–616.

Shultz, T. R., & Schleifer, M. (1983). Towards a refinement of attribution concepts. In J. M. Jaspars, F. D. Fincham, & M. Hewstone (Eds.), *Attribution theory and research* (pp. 37–62). New York: Academic Press.

Shultz, T. R., Wright, K., & Schleifer, M. (1986). Assignment of moral responsibility and punishment. *Child Development, 57,* 177–184.

Shweder, R., & Bourne, E. J. (1982). Does the concept of the person vary cross-culturally? In A. J. Marsella & G. M. White (Eds.), *Cultural conceptions of mental health and therapy* (pp. 97–137). Boston: Reidel.

Shweder, R., & Miller, J. G. (1985). The social construction of the person: How is it possible? In K. J. Gergen & K. Daviskoga (Eds.), *The social construction of the person* (pp. 41–69). New York: Springer-Verlag.

Silbey, S., & Sarat, A. (1989). Dispute processing in law and legal scholarship: From institutional critique to the reconstruction of the juridical subject. *Denver University Law Review, 66,* 437–498.

Skinner, B. F. (1971). *Beyond freedom and dignity.* New York: Knopf.

Smith, R. J. (1978). *Kurusu: The price of progress in a Japanese village, 1951–1975.* Stanford, Calif.: Stanford University Press.

Smith, R. J. (1983). *Japanese society: Tradition, self, and the social order.* Cambridge: Cambridge University Press.

Smith, R. J. (1985). A pattern of Japanese society: *Ie* society or acknowledgment of interdependence? *Journal of Japanese Studies, 11,* 29–45.

Smith, R. J. (1989). Culture as explanation: Neither all nor nothing. *Cornell International Law Journal, 22,* 425–434.

Smith, T. C. (1967). Merit as ideology in the Tokugawa period. In R. P. Dore (Ed.), *Aspects of social change in modern Japan* (pp. 71–90). Princeton, N.J.: Princeton University Press.

Steinhoff, P. G. (1984). Student conflict. In E. S. Krauss, T. P. Rohlen, & P. G. Steinhoff (Eds.), *Conflict in Japan* (pp. 174–213). Honolulu: University of Hawaii Press.

Stephan, W. (1985). Intergroup relations. In G. Lindzey & E. Aronson (Eds.), *Handbook of social psychology* (Vol. 2, pp. 599–658). New York: Random House.

Stern, G. (1976). *The Buffalo Creek disaster.* New York: Vintage.

Stevenson, H. W., Azuma, H., & Hakuta, K. (Eds.) (1986). *Child development and education in Japan.* New York: Freeman.

Stevenson, H. W., Lee, S. Y., & Stigler, J. W. (1986). Mathematics achievement of Chinese, Japanese, and American children. *Science, 231,* 693–699.

Strauss, A. (Ed.) (1956). *The social psychology of George Herbert Mead.* Chicago: University of Chicago Press.

Sulzer, J. L. (1971). *Heider's "Levels Model" of responsibility attribution.* Paper presented at the Symposium on Attribution of Responsibility Research, Williamsburg, Va., July.

Sutton, J. (1988). *Stubborn children: Controlling delinquency in the United States, 1640–1981.* Berkeley: University of California Press.

Suzuki, T. (1978). *Japanese and the Japanese: Words in culture.* Tokyo: Kodansha.

Sykes, G. M., & Matza, D. (1957). Techniques of neutralization: A theory of delinquency. *American Sociological Review, 22,* 664–670.

Tajfel, H. (1978). *Differentiation between social groups: Studies in the social psychology of intergroup relations.* London: Academic Press.

Tajfel, H. (1981). *Human groups and social categories.* Cambridge: Cambridge University Press.

Tajfel, H. (1982). The social psychology of intergroup relations. *Annual Review of Psychology, 33,* 1–39.

Tajfel, H., Flament, C., Billig, M. G., & Bundy, R. F. (1971). Social categorisation and intergroup behavior. *European Journal of Social Psychology, 1,* 149–177.

Tanase, T. (1990). The management of disputes: Automobile accident compensation in Japan. *Law and Society Review, 24,* 651–691.

Task Force, U.S. Department of Education. (1987). *Japanese education today.* Washington, D.C.: U.S. Government Printing Office.

Tawney, R. (1962). *Religion and the rise of capitalism.* Gloucester, Mass.: Peter Smith.

Tedeschi, J. T., & Reiss, M. (1981). Verbal strategies in impression management. In C. Antaki (Ed.), *The psychology of ordinary language explanations of social behaviour* (pp. 271–309). Orlando, Fla.: Academic Press.

Texas Family Code Sec. 33.01 (Vernon 1986).

Tonnies, F. (1957). *Community and society.* New York: Harper Torchbooks. (Original work published 1887.)

Tsurumi, K. (1979a). *Religious beliefs: State Shintoism vs. folk belief* (Research Papers Series A-37). Tokyo: Sophia University, Institute of International Relations.

Tsurumi, K. (1979b). *Social structure: A mesh of hierarchical and coequal relationships in villages and cities (Research Papers Series A-36).* Tokyo: Sophia University, Institute of International Relations.

Tuan, Y. (1982). *Segmented worlds and self: Group life and individual consciousness.* Minneapolis: University of Minnesota Press.

Turner, R. (1976). The real self: From institution to impulse. *American Journal of Sociology, 81,* 989–1016.

Upham, F. K. (1987). *Law and social change in postwar Japan.* Cambridge, Mass.: Harvard University Press.

Upham, F. K. (1989). What's happening in Japan, sociolegalwise. *Law and Society Review, 23,* 879–889.

Useem, B., & Zald, M. (1982). From pressure group to social movement: Organizational dilemmas of the effort to promote nuclear power. *Social Problems, 30,* 144–156.

Vidmar, N. (1977). *Effects of degree of harm and retribution motives on punishment reactions.* Paper presented at the meeting of the Canadian Psychological Association, Vancouver.

Vidmar, N. (1978, March). *Outcome, offense type, and retribution as factors in punishment reactions.* Paper presented at the Eastern Psychological Association Meeting, Washington, D.C.

Vidmar, N., & Crinklaw, L. (1974). Assignment of responsibility for an accident: A methodological and conceptual critique. *Canadian Journal of Behavioral Science, 6,* 112–130.

Vidmar, N., & Ellsworth, P. C. (1974). Public opinion and the death penalty. *Stanford Law Review, 26,* 1245–1270.

Vogel, E. F. (Ed.) (1975). *Modern Japanese organization and decision-making.* Berkeley: University of California Press.

Vogel, E. F. (1979). *Japan as number 1.* Cambridge, Mass.: Harvard University Press.

Vogel, E. F., & Vogel, S. H. (1961). Family security, personal immaturity and emotional health in a Japanese sample. *Marriage and Family Living, 23,* 161–166.

von Hirsch, A. J. (1976). *Doing justice.* New York: Hill and Wang.

Wagatsuma, H., & Rosett, A. (1986). The implications of apology: Law and culture in Japan and the United States. *Law and Society Review, 20,* 461–498.

Wahrhaftig, P. (1982). An overview of community-oriented citizen dispute resolution programs in the United States. In R. L. Abel (Ed.), *The politics of informal justice* (Vol. 1, pp. 75–97). New York: Academic Press.

Walster, E. (1966). Assignment of responsibility for an accident. *Journal of Personality and Social Psychology, 3,* 73–79.

Waterman, A. S. (1984). *The psychology of individualism.* New York: Praeger.

Weber, M. (1947). *The theory of social and economic organization* (T. Parsons, Ed.). New York: Free Press.

Weber, M. (1949). *The methodology of the social sciences* (E. Shils & H. Fitch, Eds. and Trans.). Glencoe, Ill.: Free Press.

Weber, M. (1958). *The Protestant ethic and the spirit of capitalism* (T. Parsons, Trans.). New York: Scribner.

Weisz, J. R., Rothbaum, F. M., & Blackburn, T. C. (1984). Standing out and standing in: The psychology of control in America and Japan. *American Psychologist, 39,* 955–969.

Whippler, R., & Lindenberg, S. (1987). Collective phenomena and rational choice. In J. C. Alexander, B. Giesen, R. Munch, & N. J. Smelser (Eds.), *The micro-macro link* (pp. 135–152). Berkeley: University of California Press.

White, M. (1987). *The Japanese educational challenge: A commitment to children.* New York: Free Press.

White, M. (1988). *Japanese overseas: Can they go home again?* New York: Free Press.

Wilder, D. A. (1986). Social categorization: Implications for creation and reduction of intergroup bias. In L. Berkowitz (Ed.), *Advances in experimental social psychology* (Vol. 19, pp. 291–355). Orlando, Fla.: Academic Press.

Wilson, J. Q. (1975). *Thinking about crime*. New York: Basic Books.

Wolf, E. R. (1966). *Peasants*. Englewood Cliffs, N.J.: Prentice-Hall.

Wolf, E. R. (1969). *Peasant wars of the twentieth century*. New York: Harper and Row.

Yamamura, K. (1974). *Study of samurai income and entrepreneurship*. Cambridge, Mass.: Harvard University Press.

Yeazell, S. (1977). Group litigation and social contract: Toward a history of class action. *Columbia Law Review, 77*, 866–896.

Yokoyama, M. (1980, March). *Juvenile delinquency and juvenile justice: Japan*. Presented at the annual meeting of the Academy of Criminal Justice Sciences, Oklahoma City.

Yoshino, I., & Murakoshi, S. (1977). *The invisible visible minority*. Osaka: Kaiho Shuppansha.

Young, M. (1984). Judicial review of administrative guidance: Governmentally encouraged consensual dispute resolution in Japan. *Columbia Law Review, 84*, 923–983.

Legal Cases

Brown v. Board of Education 347 U.S. 483 (1954)

In re Gault 387 U.S. 1 (1967)

Martinez v. Santa Clara Pueblo 402 F. Supp., 5, 15 (1975)

Santa Clara Pueblo v. Martinez 436 U.S. 49 (1977)

Sindell v. Abbott Laboratories 26 Cal.3d 588, 607 P.2d 924 (1980)

Valley Forge College v. Americans United 454 U.S. 464 (1982)

Yania v. Bigan, 397 Pa. 316, 155 A.2d 343 (1959)

Author Index

Subject Index

Actor
  individual, 19, 48–49, 58, 86–87, 119,
    122, 130, 133–34, 137–38, 140,
    142–43, 154, 171, 181–82
  contextual, 19, 48–49, 51, 56–58, 86–
    87, 119, 122, 130, 134, 137–38, 140,
    142–43, 145, 181, 183, 198
  responsible, 3, 5, 19, 48–49, 88, 119,
    122, 130, 134, 136–37, 142–43,
    181–83, 185, 195–96, 203–5, 218
  social, 48–49, 58–60
  See also Japan; Self; United States
Adult socialization. See Socialization
Ainu. See Discrimination (in Japan)
Alternative dispute resolution, 41, 199. See
  also Dispute resolution
Apology, 46–47, 137, 140, 149, 150, 169,
  170, 217–18
Attribution (of responsibility)
  Heider's levels, 76–78, 251n
  See also Responsibility
Authority. See Hierarchy

Buddhism. See Japan: religions
Buffalo Creek disaster, 38–39, 44–45
Burakumin (or eta). See Discrimination (in
  Japan)

Cases
  Brown v. Board of Education, 187, 213,
    216
  Chisso Corporation, 40, 45–46
  In re Gault, 205
  Pierce v. Society of Sisters, 44
  pollution cases in Japan, 39
  Showa Denko Corporation, 40
  Sindell v. Abbott Laboratories, 257n
  Valley Forge College v. Americans United,
    35
  Yania v. Bigan, 253n

Causation in law, 12, 14–15, 17, 248. See
  also Attribution (of responsibility)
Collectivism, 249n. See also Individualism
Communitarianism, 41, 198–200. See also
  Individualism
Conflict, 5–8, 247n
  avoidance of in Japan, 33–37, 212
  avoidance of in United States, 39, 42–
    43
  sensitivity to in Japan, 212–15
Conformity (vs. Autonomy), 25, 51, 60–
  62, 213–15
Confucian ethic, 33, 54
Confucianism. See Japan: religions
Consequences
  severity of, 75–78, 90–91, 97–99, 103–
    7, 110–12, 120, 136, 145, 152, 161–
    66, 168–73, 179–82, 184, 251n, 253n
Contextual factors in experiment. See Past
  pattern of behavior; Other's influence
Contextualism, 19, 51–53, 58, 60, 71,
  86–87, 198, 213. See also Individualism
Control
  internal vs. external, 61–62, 67, 250n
  crime, 174
  rates in U.S. versus Japan, 158–60
  sources of, 207–8
  See also Data analysis
Culture, 3–4, 8, 46–47, 60, 179
  contextual, 48, 51–60, 71
  cultural differences, 3, 12, 19, 44, 58–60,
    62, 83, 86–88, 181–85, 196, 249n
  empirical comparisons. See Data analysis
  individualistic, 48–51, 58–60
  Japanese individualism, 54–56
  vs. social structure, 3–4, 186–88, 202
  See also Legal culture; Legal systems

Data analysis
  auto accidents, 162, 164–65, 167, 169–
    73

crime, 162–63, 167–69, 172
everyday life incidents: effects of country on punishment, 141–52; effects of country on responsibility, 119–29; effects of deeds on punishment, 152–53; effects of roles and deeds on responsibility, 110–19
open-ended punishment items, 145–53, 167–73
techniques, 90–92, 142, 252n–55n
See also Punishment; Responsibility; Sanction
Deeds, 19, 75–78, 84–85, 87–88. *See also* Consequences; Mental state
Delta Air Lines crash, 5–6, 8. *See also* Japan Air Lines crash
Detroit, 91–96, 119–30, 140–42, 144, 147–54, 162–65, 168–73, 182, 184
Deviance, 70, 213–15
Discrimination (in Japan)
against *Ainu, Burakumin,* foreigners, and victim groups, 210–13
Dispute processing
adjudicative vs. non-adjudicative, 33, 36–39, 40–41, 44–45, 137, 197, 203
inquisitorial vs. adversarial, 33, 36–38, 137
Dispute resolution, 33–34, 37, 41–43, 46, 196–201. *See also* Apology
Japan and United States compared, 44–46
Due process, 205–8

Experimental design, 89–92
Latin square, 90
manipulation checks, 99–100, 103–9
manipulations, coding of, 233–35
See also Data analysis; Vignette method

Factorial survey, 88–90. *See also* Vignette method
Family in Japan
organization, 28–30
socialization, 62–65, 250n
See also Japan

Generalizability. *See* Validity: external

Harmony, 5–8, 39, 193, 213–16. *See also* Japanese language, key words: *wa*

Hierarchy, 8–12, 15, 19–20, 21–25, 58–60, 80–81, 204, 208, 247n–48n, 251n–54n
effects on responsibility, 112–18, 122–29, 164–67, 179–81
in experimental design, 91, 97–100
Holism. *See* Contextualism

Individualism, 49–51, 55, 249n
in Japan, 54–56
See also Actor: individual
Inequality
civil cases, 206–7
criminal cases, 207–8
Intent. *See* Mental state

Japan
crime rate, 158–59
discrimination: against *Ainu, Burakumin,* foreigners, and victim groups, 210–13
legal system: alternative procedures, 40–41; automobile accident law, 37; barriers to litigation, 35–36; dispute processing, 33–35; general, 22–23; legal structure vs. legal culture, 186–96
pollution cases, 39–40, 44–46
religions: Buddhism, 175, 211, 217; Confucianism, 33, 54; Shinto, 24
self, 19, 28, 49, 54–58, 60. *See also* Actor
social relationships, 12, 21, 23–31, 58–60, 204, 207, 213–16. *See also* Social relationships, types of
socialization: adult, 27, 67–70, 250n–51n; in family, 62–65, 250n; in school, 65–67, 250n; resocialization (*see* Naikan therapy)
work environment, 25, 27–31
See also Conflict; Culture; Data analysis; Dispute resolution
Japan Air Lines crash, 6–7. *See also* Delta Air Lines crash
Japanese Civil Liberties Bureau, 33, 47
Japanese language: key words
amae, 64
chokai, 200–201
dozoku, 29–30
giri, 248n
ie, 28–30, 200. *See also* Family in Japan
iemoto, 29